HISTORY OF ENVIRONMENTAL ECONOMIC THOUGHT

This volume presents the ideas of major figures in economics throughout history on key environmental issues such as population growth, resource scarcity and environmental contamination. Discussion begins with the early days, the Roman Empire, mercantilists, physiocrats, liberals and Adam Smith and progresses to explore the views of Malthus, Ricardo, socialism, market environmentalism and the Interventionist School. Throughout, the historical roots of current debates are explored, with empirical case studies illustrating the link between theory and practice. The final chapters look at current ideas on sustainability, and ethical and spiritual dimensions of humanity's relationship with the environment.

Providing fascinating insight into the development of environmental economic thought throughout history, this volume will be of great interest to students and researchers in general economics, the history of economic thought and environmental economics.

E. Kula is Senior Lecturer in Economics at the University of Ulster.

ROUTLEDGE STUDIES IN THE HISTORY OF ECONOMICS

1 **ECONOMICS AS LITERATURE**
Willie Henderson

2 **SOCIALISM AN D MARGINALISM IN ECONOMICS 1870–1930**
Edited by Ian Steedman

3 **HAYEK'S POLITICAL ECONOMY**
The Socio-economics of Order
Steve Fleetwood

4 **ON THE ORIGINS OF CLASSICAL ECONOMICS**
Distribution and Value from William Petty to Adam Smith
Tony Aspromourgos

5 **THE ECONOMICS OF JOAN ROBINSON**
Edited by Maria Cristina Marcuzzo, Luigi Pasinetti and Alesandro Roncaglia

6 **THE EVOLUTIONIST ECONOMICS OF LÉON WALRAS**
Albert Jolink

7 **KEYNES AND THE 'CLASSICS'**
A Study in Language, Epistemology and Mistaken Identities
Michel Verdon

8 **THE HISTORY OF GAME THEORY, VOLUME 1**
From the Beginnings to 1945
Mary Ann Dimand and Robert W. Dimand

9 **THE ECONOMICS OF W.S. JEVONS**
Sandra Peart

10 **GANDHI'S ECONOMIC THOUGHT**
Ajit K. Dasgupta

11 **EQUILIBRIUM AND ECONOMIC THEORY**
Edited by Giovanni Caravale

12 **AUSTRIAN ECONOMICS IN DEBATE**
Edited by Willem Keizer, Bert Tieben and Rudy van Zijp

13 **ANCIENT ECONOMIC THOUGHT**
B.B. Price

14 **THE POLITICAL ECONOMY OF SOCIAL CREDIT AND GUILD SOCIALISM**
Frances Hutchinson and Brian Burkitt

15 **ECONOMIC CAREERS**
Economics and Economists in Britain 1930–1970
Edited by Keith Tribe

16 **UNDERSTANDING 'CLASSICAL ECONOMICS'**
Studies in the Long-period Theory
Heinz Kurz and Neri Salvadori

17 **HISTORY OF ENVIRONMENTAL ECONOMIC THOUGHT**
E. Kula

HISTORY OF ENVIRONMENTAL ECONOMIC THOUGHT

E. Kula

ROUTLEDGE

London and New York

First published 1998
by Routledge
11 New Fetter Lane, London EC4P 4EE

Simultaneously published in the USA and Canada
by Routledge
29 West 35th Street, New York, NY 10001

Typeset in Garamond by Routledge
Printed and bound in Great Britain by T.J. International Ltd,
Padstow, Cornwall

British Library Cataloguing in Publication Data
A catalogue record for this book is available from the British Library

Library of Congress Cataloguing in Publication Data
A catalogue record for this book has been requested

ISBN 0–415–13389–0

IN MEMORY OF MY FATHER

CONTENTS

ILLUSTRATIONS

FIGURES

TABLES

PREFACE AND ACKNOWLEDGEMENTS

This book arose out of the need to bring together in a historical context the major ideas on population growth, resource scarcity and environmental contamination. In the economics profession, there has been concern about these problems for more than 200 years, and indeed a good deal of modern discourse rests on the works of classical economists such as Malthus, Ricardo and Mill. For example, Boulding's 'Spaceship Earth' concept has some parallel with Ricardo's analysis, which treated the world as a giant farm of a fixed acreage; the Malthusian theory is still going strong and will no doubt be prominent in debates into the twenty-first century, and perhaps even beyond.

Up until the mid-eighteenth century, when Quesnay published his famous *Tableau*, there had been no analytical economic thinking to speak of. Nevertheless, when planning this book, I decided to start from a much earlier period – the time of the Roman Empire – for two reasons. First, despite the abundance of natural resources that the Roman administration commanded, its empire failed to establish a viable economic system and, in the end, this led to its demise. Perhaps the lesson to learn from this is that an abundance of resources does not guarantee the survival of communities. Second, it was during this period that for the first time, due to the reckless use of resources, serious environmental problems in the form of over-salinisation, deforestation, desertification, and water and land pollution became widespread in various regions in and around Europe.

I felt a suitable volume should aim to be reasonably comprehensible to a wide range of readers and so I have tried to avoid equations, excessive jargon and other technicalities as far as possible. Furthermore, although following a tight chronological order might have beeen desirable from the viewpoint of tidiness, I decided during the course of my research for the book that this could create a major problem in that by restricting a particular theory to the time of its construction – say, the end of the eighteenth century – we would fail to see its wider implications. In this respect, I have made four leaps in time: two relating to the Malthusian theory, one to Marxism and the last to Arthur Pigou. I hope therefore that this use of hindsight not available to the creators of these ideas will tell us more about such theories and their development in time.

I am indebted to a number of individuals and institutes for their help in writing this book. I decided to go ahead with it a couple of years before the 1996 Research Assessment Exercise, although I had been toying with the idea for a much longer period of time. In the run up to the Research Assessment Exercise, a feeling had developed among the academic community that the time and effort involved in book-writing was not cost-effective by comparison to that needed for the production of journal articles, and a number of university administrators were arguing that perhaps book-writing should be discouraged in favour of a few pages of journal articles. Against this background, I feared that my proposed work might not be encouraged. I was pleasantly surprised to find, therefore, that not only did this not happen, but that in fact my university created some space for me to produce this book.

A part of the book was written during my study leave at the University of Bosphorus, which has a good library for historical research, and where I was able to benefit from the help of the late Professor Kriton Curi, former Head of the Institute for Environmental Sciences, who had endless enthusiasm for all kinds of environmental research. Dr. Andrzej Furman, with whom I shared an office, provided me with a large number of research articles and books and broadened my thinking with enthusiastic debates.

I am also grateful to Professor R. D. C. Black of Queen's University, Belfast, who made valuable comments on the early parts of the book, and to Mr Stig Wanden of the Swedish Environmental Protection Agency, who provided comments on the later chapters. Finally, I would like to thank Mr Ryan Mclauglin for assistance with the glossary and indexes, my wife Karen for her help with the typing of the text and my son Adam (13 years old) for suggesting and drawing the figure for the spaceship economy on p. 132.

Erhun Kula
University of Ulster, Belfast
University of Bosphorus, Istanbul

INTRODUCTION

In Adam Smith's early and rudimentary stage of society, which precedes both the accumulation of capital stock and appropriation of land, nature, left to its own devices, provided a certain quality and quantity of items that man used for his activities. At that stage, human numbers were small, their needs were basic and nature abounded with natural resources. There were vast forests in which to live and hunt, extract wood and gather fruits and nuts; fish was plentiful in the seas, lakes and rivers, and water and air was unpolluted. Man, as a hunter, was merely nibbling around the edges of a seemingly inexhaustible supply of natural resources.

The next stage, which may be termed as preliterate settlement civilisation, was the adoption of a more settled lifestyle in which suitable animals were domesticated and the cultivation of land was begun. At first, the change in lifestyle did not have too much impact on the landscape as it was still shaped by the elements of nature. However, as human numbers increased, so did the pressure for land on which to grow more food to sustain the expanding communities. Forest clearance began to intensify as new territories were opened up for agriculture and the extraction of wood for construction and energy purposes.

Deforestation, land erosion and over-salinisation were the earliest environmental problems created by man, and these were most extensive in the Middle East, North Africa, southern Europe and China. In the course of history, the reckless use of resources and lack of foresight have repeatedly led to environmental degradation which, in turn, has contributed to the downfall of many civilisations.

In the eighteenth and nineteenth centuries, rapid urbanisation and industrialisation in northern Europe created mainly localised pollution and health problems. In most European cities, hygiene was very poor well into the nineteenth century as human and animal wastes were thrown into the streets. In England, especially, the concentration of the working population in sub-standard accommodation with insufficient sanitation, poor air and contaminated water made life a misery for the masses. Many industrial districts were blackened with soot. Diggle (1961) reports that the air and water in the industrial parts of Liverpool were extremely dirty due to the effluent and fumes created by the chemical industry, which also affected the surrounding countryside. The Alkali Act of 1863 brought these industries under public control, but the already created environmental problems persisted for a long time. According to Respail (1857), the ill-effects of pollution created by certain factories in France was far more serious for the health of infants than for crops and trees.

Fuelled by the industrial revolution, and alongside rapidly increasing human numbers, growth and diversification in economic activity were not only increasing the pressure on the extractive sector, but, on a wider scale, also changing the landscape and the quality of air and water. During the eighteenth century, economists and others were beginning to write about matters concerning natural resources and the environment. The seeds of optimism and pessimism, which now overwhelm the current debates on future prospects, were planted at that time. In *The Wealth of Nations* (1776), Adam Smith gave a comprehensive discussion of the mineral industries – including coal, tin mining and quarrying in Britain, and the extraction of precious metals and stones elsewhere – which stemmed from the empirical evidence existing at that time. In anticipation of new discoveries, Smith took an optimistic view, by and large, of the availability and extraction costs of mineral deposits.

Twenty-two years after the publication of *The Wealth of Nations*, Malthus expressed great concern about the availability of arable land and the adequacy of food supplies in the face of rapidly growing populations in *An Essay on the Principle of Population as it Affects the Future Improvement of Society* (1798). Later, Ricardo, in his *Principles of Political Economy and Taxation* (1817), contended that economic growth would eventually peter out due to scarcity of land and its falling food production capacity, and this would stabilise the population at a subsistence level. Marsh (1865), in a somewhat less pessimistic tone, pointed out that the growth of economic activity actually improved the agricultural capacity, and that the value of land in many places appreciated due to drainage, irrigation, and the clearing of stones and scrub. On the other hand, as a result of misuse, some lands suffered soil erosion, silting, over-salinisation and overgrazing. Marsh warned that the earth was given to man for usufruct alone, not for consumption, still less for profligate waste.

Resource depletion and environmental degradation gathered pace during the rapid industrialisation that took place in the nineteenth and twentieth centuries in western Europe and North America, and this created concern among many thinkers, including economists. The American Conservation Movement of 1890–1920, which popularised Ricardo–Malthusian scarcity, was the first political initiative and paved the way for the formation of many environmental pressure groups in later years. Unfortunately, economic principles, which could have been useful tools in implementing policy measures to protect natural resources and the environment, were not given importance at all in the movement. The economic analysis of resource and environmental problems that became vigorous towards the end of the neo-classical age now fills most textbooks in the field.

In the the course of the twelve chapters of this book, I describe the progress of environmental economic thinking over more than two thousand years, beginning, in Chapter 1, with the early days of the Roman Empire and the Middle Ages, through to the mercantilists, physiocrats, liberals and Adam Smith, the founder of modern economics. According to Smith, the crucial factor in the progress of society was the creation of an economic structure which would allow individuals maximum freedom to pursue their self-interest; this alone would create prosperity. As he lived during a period when the natural resources of England and other countries looked inexhaustible, arguments regarding resource scarcity or stagnation did not appear important to him. Smith was largely optimistic about future prospects, provided that governments did not become a burden on individual freedom.

In contrast, Robert Thomas Malthus, whose works are discussed in Chapter 2, adopted a dramatically different position by taking an ominous view of population growth, which he believed would have disastrous consequences. This chapter also includes the arguments of the post-Malthusians, such as Huxley, who predicted that due to worldwide over-population, future generations would not only live in poverty, but under unrelenting dictatorships.

The issue of Ricardian stagnation, which has attracted a number of opponents as well as followers, is considered in Chapter 3. Among its opponents, Carey and Cannan point out a number of flaws in Ricardo's analysis and predict a largely optimistic future for mankind. In support of Ricardian scarcity, John Stuart Mill and William Stanley Jevons put forward some of their own cases. The former differentiated, for the first time, between the agricultural and mining sectors by pointing out that mine deposits are exhaustible and therefore current and future profits are antagonistic. Jevons, on the other hand, focused on coal, the main source of energy at the time, and predicted that Britain would experience serious difficulties during the course of her economic development due to the rapidly rising price of this commodity as a result of inevitable exhaustion of productive mines.

Chapter 4 looks at environmental and resource problems in terms of the Marxist theory, in which the important issue is the overthrow of capitalism to create a socialist system that eventually leads to communism and the salvation of the working classes. Under capitalism, no matter how fast the economy grows, workers are deprived of their fair share of production and thus condemned to poverty by the ruling classes. The Marxist theory contains a long and intricate analysis of capitalism which has implications for resource use and environmental quality whereby these issues are seen from the viewpoint of class struggle. Some of Karl Marx's publications – in particular, his *Theories of Surplus Value* (1951, 1969) – give a notable treatment of the mining and fishing sectors, which are critically analysed in this section. The second part of this chapter turns to some of the appalling environmental problems created by Marxist governments in the former Soviet Union and East European countries.

Chapter 5 deals with the treatment of natural resources and the environment in the neo-classical school. In particular, the views of Sorley, Marshall, Gray, Cassel and Hotelling are analysed alongside those of other contributors to this era. Among the most salient features of this chapter are Marshall's synthesis of marginal benefits and costs, which forms the foundation of modern analysis of external effects and advances in the theories of exhaustible resources.

In Chapter 6, we look at the views of members of the interventionist school, such as Pigou, Keynes, Galbraith and Mishan, who largely rejected the market-based policies that rely upon marginalist principles. It has become rather fashionable nowadays to treat Pigovian taxes in a marginalist spirit – and this is explained at some length – but the main thrust of the interventionist school has been one of preventive legislation to protect the environment.

Chapter 7 covers the subjects of property rights and market environmentalism, which draw on the work of Ronald Coase who rejects regulatory legislation as well as fiscal measures to manage the environment. According to this school of thought, assignment of property rights to previously common property resources will help to create a situation in which environmental resources can be managed successfully. The chapter points out that the property rights approach in some instances, such as the greenhouse effect of atmospheric pollution and ozone depletion, has been overtaken by events. However, there is evidence that Coase's theorem can be extremely useful in the management of some environmental assets such as open-sea fisheries.

Reports on the post-war empirical studies on scarcity of natural resource-based commodities are reviewed in Chapter 8. In particular, research studies by the US President's Material Commission (1952), Potter and Christy (1962), Barnett and Morse (1963), US Bureau of Mines (1970), Nordhaus (1973) and Rajaraman (1976) are critically analysed.

Chapter 9 takes the concept of Boulding's Spaceship Earth through to the present time by pointing out its strengths as well as its weaknesses. In this connection, studies by Forrester and the Club of Rome are given critical treatment and the most recent contributions on the subject analysed. Boulding's article must be one of the most thought-provoking pieces written on the environment this century, but unfortunately Forrester's systems dynamics and the Club of Rome's world models, which build upon Boulding's work, both prove to be disappointing.

After considering the roots of the sustainable development concept,

Chapter 10 analyses recent debates on it. Although it has become a buzzword in recent years, 'sustainable development' has been defined and interpreted in many different ways by different groups of academics. Unfortunately, what have been produced so far in the name of sustainable development are hazy concepts, confusions and contradictions.

A number of writers who have contributed to the sustainable development debate feel that the concept should have an ethical dimension. In this respect, Chapter 11 discusses the moral, ethical and spiritual dimensions of scarcity and the environment. Religious as well as secular views are considered, including those of both the Western (i.e. Judaeo–Christian–Muslim) and Eastern faiths, together with ideas such as the Gaia hypothesis, deep ecology, land ethics, feminism and Dawkins's 'selfish gene'.

Chapter 12 provides a summary and conclusion, including a look at the past experience of economic development in small islands where issues such as resource limitation and fragility of the ecological balance are inescapable. Finally, projections by the Worldwatch Institute, based upon recent trends in population growth and food availability, are outlined.

1

THE EARLY DAYS

THE ROMAN EMPIRE AND MIDDLE AGES

The Roman Empire had its roots in small, self-sufficient agricultural communities with impoverished farmers. At first there was little trade, but this changed with the conquest of colonies that had an abundance of natural resources and a favourable climate for farming. For a time, the Empire transformed the conditions of small farmers, until a more complex social structure was established. Slavery, which had existed in earlier Greek times, continued to be an institution and slaves were used in agriculture, the construction of public works and the domestic needs of the larger households. For a while, economic activity developed as the conquest of new territories made more and more slaves available.

In later years, however, as supplies of slaves diminished, the basis of the slave-dependent agriculture began to suffer. The administration of large estates became unmanageable and landlords began to rent out the larger part of their holdings to free tenants or slaves, retaining only a small part for themselves, which they kept under cultivation. In order to defend the outer parts of the Empire, the Romans settled people who were loyal to them in the sensitive regions and who had the military capacity to defend the frontiers. These tenants were given certain privileges, but they were also under considerable obligations.

Eventually, military threats from outside and within the Empire, together with the huge encumbrances of administration and the extravagant living of the ruling class, began to bear down heavily on the people. Widespread discontent created by the burden of taxation and the mass of despairing slaves began to chip away the power of the Empire and undermine its largely land-based economy.

Surprisingly, Roman intellectuals produced no alternative economic theories. Roman law was created and developed by the necessities of the times; it maintained the right to own land without limit and guaranteed freedom of contract. In ancient Greece, land ownership had been limited by a strong ethical concern, but in the Roman Empire the individualism of the owner was prominent.

Reckless usage of natural resources became a widespread practice. For example, aqueducts constructed to provide Rome with an ample supply of water resulted in too much water being drawn from the surrounding countryside. Furthermore, the used water was discharged without treatment into the Tiber, leading to land contamination. Before its conquest by the Romans, the Libyan coast had been covered with vineyards and the hinterland with dense forests (Dobben 1966). Today, in Libya and other parts of North Africa, the remains of sizeable ancient settlements in what is now desert are testimony to the land's environmental impoverishment during, and after, Roman times. Similarly, deforestation, over-salinisation and land erosion were widespread in other parts of the Empire. The Old Testament mentions large-scale commercial transactions for timber and agricultural produce in biblical lands (see Kings 5: 6–17; II Chronicles 2: 8–13), but under Roman administration the timber supplies of these regions rapidly declined, while intensive agriculture in Palestine and Mesopotamia turned large areas into desert.

Despite the abundance of natural resources, the Roman Empire failed to establish a viable economic structure. Its dependence on slave labour neither allowed efficient production, nor established loyalty to a state which tried to survive by way of militarism, oppression and harsh punishment of dissidents. Unlike the Greeks, the Romans did not produce great philosophers and thinkers, although Pliny the Elder, one of the few Roman thinkers, expressed concern about the use of slave labour, which he considered was inefficient. In large land holdings, supervision of slave labour was costly. Furthermore, slaves had no incentive to become productive or use natural resources wisely. Even tenant farmers did not strive to increase production, since they knew that whatever they achieved would be taken, one way or another, by the state, which was chronically short of money.

Trade and expansion of the urban industries could not be carried out with the existing economic structures; they was also hampered by a shortage of manpower. Although the requirements for slave labour gradually disappeared from agriculture, making manpower available for other sectors, trade and industry were looked upon as unworthy occupations. During the height of the Empire, landowners had lived in relative harmony with the commercial classes, but this did not last. The seeds of dissent had been planted right at the start of the Empire and, as the difficult times arrived, the struggle between the landowners and the industrial and trading classes not only failed to create a new ruling class, but contributed to the decay of Roman society. Moreover, as slaves and the proletariat embraced Christianity further divisions were created and, eventually, invading barbarians put the final nail in the coffin of the Empire.

The Middle Ages cover a period of roughly a thousand years, between the fifth century AD and the fall of Constantinople to the Ottomans in 1453. The essential characteristics of this period are stagnation or very slow economic progress, unquestioned acceptance of rigid social divisions and domination by the Church. The medieval times were not a complete break with the earlier period since its class structure and the distribution of land and its regulation had had their origins in the later period of the Roman administration. Economic activities were overwhelmingly land-based and the land was acquired by the conquerors who then divided it up between their past and future supporters. A manorial system was first established in northern Europe, particularly among German-speaking communities, which then spread to other parts.

The division of the social classes was rigid with different and carefully defined rights and obligations, and everyone knowing their place in society. The decline of the Roman Empire had given more and more administrative power to the landowners and eventually the estate became the new economic unit. Trade that had existed in Roman times was continued by northerners and southerners. Industry was confined to the needs of this trade and the demands of the small local markets. Various restricting forces developed in the form of guilds, friendly societies and monopolies.

After the fall of Rome, the power of the Church grew steadily both in its institutional sophistication as well as in its acquisition of land and privileges. There was a good deal of rivalry between the feudal landlords, who were scattered and lacked links of national union, and the Church was a unifying power for all. Ownership of private property by the Church, once the sole privilege of the nobility, was in contrast with the early teachings of Christianity in which the search for earthly wealth was not encouraged. However, there was an insatiable desire by all powers to acquire more and more land – the foundation of wealth, power and influence – and the Church's growing land ownership eventually made it the greatest landowner in the Middle Ages.

MERCANTILISM

During the sixteenth and seventeenth centuries, the economic and social structures established in the Middle Ages began to crumble, largely due to growing economic activities. The medieval economic structure had a strong regional focus in which the nobility was at the centre of economic and political power. The monarchy had the strongest interest in the decline of the power of the landlords as this would lead to an increase in its own influence. It wanted change, but could not bring this about on its own; it needed alliances with other dissatisfied groups.

One such group was that of the smaller landowners, the gentry, who looked upon the state as a counterweight to the powers of the great landowners. Their interests were quite different from those of the barons, who were preoccupied with family power, wars and jousts. The smaller landholders were interested in commerce and agriculture and thus desired a strong central authority to maintain order, reduce restrictions, and promote the already growing markets. They realised that a decrease in the power and influence of landlords and an increase in the authority of central government would lead to a rise in their wealth.

Another dissatisfied group was that of the professional classes such as the lawyers and public administrators who lived in the developing cities. The legal profession wanted a greater role in society in the interpretation and definition of the complicated economic relationships that were developing from free association and private contract in the growing market economy. As the markets opened up, old and familiar legal relationships were becoming obsolete. On the other hand, public administrators had a vested interest in the growth of the power of the monarchy.

The third and most important group who desired a rise in the power of the Crown were the merchants who were beginning to benefit from the expanding trade. This group was already engaged in transactions with the New World and Asia and wanted to increase trade with the other countries of Europe as well. But for international trade to develop there was a need to eliminate tolls on roads and waterways, to have national monetary systems and regulatory fiscal measures such as taxes and tariffs. Fusfeld (1977) contends that these structures, which we take for granted today, were gradually formed by the forces of the Crown acting against the interests of the feudal landlords in the fifteenth and sixteenth centuries. Merchants began to argue that the widening international trade, in addition to increasing their own profits, would benefit national interests through such diverse groups as industrialists, workers and farmers.

Mercantilism was the first systematic body of economic thought that relied upon the power of the central authority (the Crown), national interest, self-sufficiency, exports (in particular, finished goods), the desire to accumulate treasure (in particular, bullion), opposition to usury and last, but not least, extensive regulatory and protectionist measures implemented by the Crown. Exports were stimulated by the acquisition of colonies, agriculture was encouraged by import restrictions as well as the taxation of food coming from outside, industry – including the supply of military hardware – was protected by various measures, wages were kept down and money supply was increased to keep economic activity buoyant. Many in the mercantilist school of thought believed that a favourable balance of trade was absolutely essential in order to bring gold, silver or other treasures into the country. With the accumulation of such treasures a country would increase its wealth. For example, Sir Francis Bacon argued in 1616 that care ought to be taken that exportation exceeded the value of importation and that the balance of trade be returned to the country in bullion. Likewise, Miselden, in 1623, wrote that in order to create a balance of trade surplus importation of foodstuffs and luxury goods should be discouraged and exports should be encouraged, creating employment opportunities for the poor at home. With a trade surplus England should be able to import bullion from other countries in order to enhance her natural wealth. (For further discussion of these views, see Roll 1953.)

The issues of population and natural resources featured in the mercantilist economic thought. An Austrian mercantilist, Phillip Von Hornick, wrote in 1684 that it was a good mercantilist principle to encourage the maximum growth of population that a country could support as this would strengthen the nation. Another writer, Antonio Serra, an Italian mercantilist, suggested that by favouring industry over agriculture a growing and healthy population would provide the industry with a diligent workforce which would enhance the nation's balance of trade. Improved methods of farming were already making a large number of farmers redundant in the countryside and an urban drift was beginning to be seen. However, growing trade and industry were already absorbing a good proportion of migrant workers coming to the cities.

Early mercantilists were obsessed with the accumulation of gold and silver, a practice which had been common in the ancient world. The Greeks and Romans had had a policy of storing precious metals which would serve in case of need. In a letter from Jamaica in 1503, Christopher Columbus said that gold was a wonderful commodity. Whoever acquired it became the master of everything he desired; with gold one could even get souls into paradise. The more gold there was in a country's coffers, the wealthier she became.

In Germany, Martin Luther abhorred the stupidity of his people by stating that Germans were making the whole world rich at the expense of their own country by sending their gold and silver to foreigners. Frankfurt was a hole through which Germany was losing her wealth. Mercantilist John Hales was especially concerned about the loss of precious metals in trade with other nations in order to import useless trifles.

It was a strong feature of the mercantilist doctrine to achieve its objective of hoarding precious metals by strict regulation. Since precious metals were the most highly prized representations of the wealth of a nation, it was a necessary policy to regulate their movements across national frontiers. Export of gold and silver was prohibited and their import was encouraged. In effect, prohibition of exports dates back to the medieval times. As trade with other nations increased, merchants were required to acquire a certain amount of treasure. For example, in England, an Act of 1339 required wool merchants to bring in a certain amount of plate for each sack of wool exported. The Navigation Act of 1381 also prohibited the export of gold and silver. The office of the Royal Exchequer was created to register all exchange transactions.

Mercantilist regulation was not confined to foreign trade, but extended to other parts of the economy, in particular, to manufacturing. Such regulation was tighter in some countries than others. In France, government regulation of industry was so detailed as to specify the required number of threads per inch in the manufacture of cloth. In England, however, although regulation was also tight, its implementation was not successful because the government was not able to administer regulations effectively, largely because of shortage of money.

Gradually, the basis of regulation began to change. Instead of acquiring bullion to increase the wealth of the nation, many recognised that wealth was created by trade, but that internal as well as external restrictions, aimed ultimately at hoarded bullion, were hindering rather than encouraging it. In the late mercantilist era, a different protectionist policy emerged to nurse industries and encourage work and employment within a country. Exports stimulated domestic employment and therefore they were encouraged; imports undermined it and thus they were restricted. The late mercantilist answer to 'What is the source of the wealth of the nations?' differed from the early one. It was the growth of trade and commerce rather than stock of precious metals.

According to Roll (1953), mercantilist doctrine and policy had a commonsensical validity in its time and was, by and large, successful in achieving its goals. Its main achievement was the abolition of medieval restrictions and the creation of unified and strong states that were powerful instruments in fostering trade. This prepared the ground for the development of industrial and commercial capitalism in later years. Mercantilists also turned out to be right about trade and national power, since the most powerful nations in Europe in the sixteenth and seventeenth centuries were those which had developed their international trade. However, as a criticism of the mercantilist doctrine, one could argue that the whole movement was, essentially, a means of justifying all sorts of interventionist policy by the state.

With regard to the natural resource scarcity, apart from precious metals, mercantilists had little to say. The population issue was not regarded as ominous. As previously mentioned, some mercantilists actually encouraged the growth of population with the understanding that a large supportable population would increase the strength of a nation. As new territories were opened up, land and natural resource-based commodities appeared to be endless, and there were no overwhelming pollution problems.

THE PHYSIOCRATS

Physiocrats was the name given to a number of French economists in the eighteenth century who were identified as anti-mercantilists. The most famous of these were Quesnay and Turgot. They disagreed with the doctrine of the mercantilist school and held that it was not the trade or volume of precious metals which created the wealth of nations but its land. Quesnay, in his famous economic *Tableau économique*, first published in 1758, tried to prove that surplus was first created by agriculture, which was then made available to other sectors and social classes. Although the land was owned by landlords, it was cultivated by tenant farmers, who were the real productive class. In addition to satisfying their own needs, farmers also provided for the needs of the landowners, public servants, artisans, merchants, the Church, and the monarchy.

The tableau attempts to show how agricultural output is shared between different classes in society, which is then repeated each year. Artisans, merchants and others cannot create any value themselves; they can only transform the value created by agriculture into manufactured goods which are consumed. Thus, it is agriculture alone which creates a surplus. The tableau ignores the exchange value of the product. It only differentiates between the use value, which is consumed, and that which is produced.

Turgot, like Quesnay, believed that only agricultural workers could create a surplus. Unlike Quesnay, however, Turgot contended that exchange value for goods existed, which he called *valeur appréciative*. When he became a minister, he introduced anti-mercantilist and anti-feudal reforms, which were supported by the king but opposed by the nobility. Eventually he was forced out of office. Turgot was essentially a non-interventionist with a capitalist flavour. In a way, he regarded landowners as capitalists who employed the farm labourers.

The physiocrats believed in the natural order which ruled human society. This order could not be changed by the state. The natural order was established by the benevolent providence for the good of humanity, which was so clearly in evidence that it should require only a little reflection to recognise it. Some important aspects of this order were the right to enjoy property, to exercise labour and pursue self-interest. The physiocrats' view of wealth and the economic system in general was entirely based upon the ultimate natural resource – land.

Another name often associated with these ideas is that of Richard Cantillon, who has been regarded by economic historians as an independent thinker rather than as a physiocrat, despite the fact that some of his views share the same ground as those of Quesnay and Turgot. In his book *Essai sur la nature du commerce en général*, published in 1755, Cantillon (1931) defined land as the source of all wealth and labour as the power which produced it. All material goods and their value essentially stemmed from land and labour.

Cantillon pointed out that as a nation developed a trade surplus, spices, and other commodities, would eventually be drawn into increasing the purchasing power and availability of money at home, but scarce national resources such as land, domestic mines and labour would slowly become dearer. With regard to mines, their output at home would increase and the miners who worked them out would demand more food, clothes and manufactured goods. With this process, the share of commodities going to miners would increase, but to others, who did not participate in the mining operations, their share would decrease. The same would happen to the other products of land. Since land and labour were the only source of wealth, the intrinsic value of commodities would depend on the content of the two primary factors of production.

However, Cantillon realised that excess supply would depress the price of commodities below the intrinsic value. The output of metal deposits would be particularly vulnerable to the forces of supply and demand as excess supply would depress the intrinsic value of metals. This dual source of value, market price and the intrinsic element relating to land and labour content of commodities did trouble Cantillon. On the population issue, Cantillon was the first writer to anticipate the Malthusian effect. He forecast that as economic activity increased, this would push up the subsistence wage and hence the birth rate. James Stewart, a contemporary of Cantillon, was also able to see the coming of the Malthusian theory in his analysis of the origins of society and its class structure. In this, Stewart starts from the concept of agricultural surplus which then gives rise to industry; but the agricultural surplus then permits workers to have more children.

THE LIBERALS

The seventeenth and first part of the eighteenth centuries also produced a number of economists who can best be described as liberals. This group argued vigorously against the restrictions on international trade, monopolies and state regulations on industry. One notable writer was English economist William Petty who had similar views to Cantillon with regard to the source of wealth. In his *Treatise on Taxes and Contributions* (see Hull 1954), Petty wrote that labour was the father and active principle of wealth as lands were the mother. The wealth of a nation was the effect of the farmer and his past labour. With regard to rent, at any particular year it was the difference between the proceeds of the harvest minus seeds and the keep of the peasants. Petty was categorical that rent was determined by price and not vice versa. The value of land, in turn, was determined by the capitalisation of rent.

Dudley North, another liberal who served as a treasury officer was bitterly opposed to the restrictive and nationalistic policies of mercantilism. Instead, he promoted free trade and division of labour to increase the wealth of the nations. In his view, all trade was profitable because nobody would continue with an unprofitable activity and thus there was no need to restrict a beneficial occupation. His book *Discourses upon Trade* was published anonymously immediately after his death in 1697.

North also emphasised the similarity between land and capital. The interest received on borrowed capital is akin to the rent of land received by the landlord, just as the unused land surplus capital that an owner may not be able to use himself can be borrowed by an entrepreneur to be used productively. In North's analysis, capital, and hence interest, is derived from the land, the source of all wealth. With regard to the early mercantilist belief of hoarding precious metals to enhance national wealth, North did not accept this.

Other liberals such as David Hume, John Locke and John Law all disliked the restrictive policies of the mercantilist era. Furthermore, they were, by and large, in agreement that it was human labour, not precious metals or trade, that created wealth. Land provided the basis for wealth, but without human effort what nature provided in crude form would be of little use. Since labour is the wealth creating power then there ought to be incentives for all people, not only for merchants. Locke argued that by adding their labour to natural resources, individuals add part of themselves to the final product. Hume, on the other hand, showed that the mercantilist idea of a constantly favourable balance of trade is not workable in a free market economy. A surplus of exports will bring in gold and silver which means an increase in the money supply. This will cause prices to rise which in turn reduces exports until the country achieves a balance in foreign trade.

All these writers prepared the ground for Smith's ideas of free market economy based upon self-interest. In effect, it was Vincent de Gourney who, well before the publication of *Wealth of Nations*, originated the famous phrase, 'laissez faire, laissez passer'. The importance of land as the wealth creating power is prominent in the writings of physiocrats as well as liberals.

ADAM SMITH

In *The Wealth of Nations*, Smith argued, amongst other things, that the pursuit of self-interest, together with rationalisation of labour and a steady expansion of the market place are the keys to economic growth and improvement in human well-being. He contended that expansion and improvement in the agricultural sector would lead the way to greater prosperity:

> the towns could nowhere have increased beyond that the improvement and cultivation of the territory in which they were situated could support: till such time, at least, as the whole of that territory was completely cultivated and improved. In ordinary circumstances there would be no attempt made by capitalists to invest in manufacturers designed for distant sale as long as agricultural resources remained unused.
>
> (Smith 1776)

It was emphasised in the book that much good land still remained uncultivated and the greater part of cultivated land was not improved to realise its full potential. Agriculture, therefore, was almost everywhere in a position to absorb a greater capital than what was used. According to Hollander (1973), by arguing in this way, Smith had in mind the issue of relative profitability determined by factor endowments.

Furthermore, the profits in agriculture would be less risky than those of manufacturing. This was because man had far more experience and familiarity with agriculture than with industry. 'As to cultivate the ground was the original destination of man, so in every stage of his existence he seems to retain a predilection for his primitive employment' (Smith 1776). Market processes would assure that while land remained cheap, risk adjusted profits in agriculture would exceed those in industry so that investors would prefer the former. However, the rate of profit in the agricultural sector would fall relative to manufacturing as population expanded making land scarce and this would push up rents.

In the Smithian scheme of things the relative importance of rent in manufacturing will tend to decline for each stage of development. As manufacturing expands, price related to wages and profits will grow in proportion to rent. The more refined the commodity, the greater is the importance of the labour and capital compared with the land content. The development of manufacturing and refinement of products initially depends upon the development of the agricultural sector. When improvements take place in agriculture, more and more labour will be released for industry without any decline in food output – whereas man's capacity to consume food is limited by the capacity of his stomach, his desire to have other things seems to have no bounds.

Smith lived during a time when agriculture and industry were developing rapidly, but according to him, there was still plenty of land available for agricultural expansion in Britain and elsewhere. Also, improvement in cultivated land was possible. British agriculture was advanced in its day as it was one of the most intensive capital-using sectors, but still improvements were possible, or even needed. However, Smith realised that structural changes in the manufacturing sector were transforming the economy and expanding trade, which would reduce the relative weight of agriculture in overall economic activity. The surplus created in agriculture would feed the progress in other sectors. Thus, he was quite optimistic about the future prospects provided that man was allowed to pursue his own interests in a market structure that was free.

Smith did not express a great deal of concern about the cost and availability of mineral deposits which were necessary for the development of industry. Despite the fact that the relative importance of mining, metallurgy and hardware industries were small in Britain at the time when Smith was writing *Wealth of Nations*, he gave the extractive sector a substantial treatment, possibly because he realised its potential importance. Young (1928) notes that mining, metallurgy, building and hardware sectors constituted only about 11 per cent of the British national income in 1770, but they were growing in independence.

Smith draws a distinction between rent from land which produces food, and rent from land which yields mineral deposits and other items for clothing and housing. The former, according to Smith, always captures a rent, whereas the latter may not. However, this situation may change as population expands and industrial activities intensify, pushing up the rent connected to the non-food part of the land. New discoveries and technological improvements in the extractive sector and improvements in manufacturing could make more efficient use of land-based inputs and this would slow down the rate of increase in non-food rent.

Some mines, due to their poor quality, might afford no rent at all to the owner of the land, yielding only the essential profit to the entrepreneur who operated them. In such cases only the landowner would be able to work them. Smith gives examples of marginal coal mines in Scotland to prove this case. On the other hand, in remote areas some deposits might be rich but, due to lack of transport infrastructure and availability of manpower in their vicinity to work them, they could not be operated even by the landlords themselves. Smith, by noting that the cost of extraction from each seam is an important part of the price component, lays emphasis on the role of the richest seams in determining the market price. With reference to the coal sector, he points out that the most fertile mine regulates the price of produce in all other mines in the area. For natural resource deposits such as coal, for which substitutes such as wood exist, there will always be a limit on price level imposed by the substitutability. In the case of precious metals such as gold, silver and diamonds, the lack of good substitutes means that there is no effective limit on their price.

As long as rich deposits are in operation, poor ones and fertile deposits in remote or inaccessible areas will be left untouched. Even rich deposits could be put out of action by far richer new discoveries. Smith cites as an example the discovery of rich silver mines in Peru, which made a large number of productive silver mines in Europe idle. As for the general trend in mining, he points out three distinct stages. First, growing demand outstrips supply confined to old deposits and, as a result, the price goes up. In the second stage, high prices lead to more output by way of new discoveries as well as improvement in the efficiency of the existing ones, then prices begin to fall. In the third stage, supply and demand go up at more or less the same pace, which results in stable prices. This summary of Smith's analysis, which is very much like a converging cobweb model, was formalised by Ezekiel (1938), and is now standard textbook material in introductory microeconomics. But this process can only happen in the extractive sector if the deposits are abundant. The world that Smith envisaged was one of abundance; this led him to an essentially optimistic view regarding the availability of mineral deposits at the threshold of most intense industrial development, which he did not witness.

As we shall see later, in Malthus, Ricardo, Jevons and Mill, the optimism of Adam Smith regarding future prospects was to be challenged. At this stage, it is worth mentioning the ideas of Joseph Townshend (1786) who, ten years after the publication of *Wealth of Nations*, gave a lucid example for natural equilibrium which underpins some economic theories of stagnation. Townshend's preoccupation was the undesirability of the Poor Laws which would encourage too many families to have too many children. In his example, some Spanish sailors leave goats on a fertile island. Due to the abundance of vegetation the goat population grows rapidly, ultimately putting pressure on food resources. As this point is reached, the once idyllic existence of the goats becomes one of hardship and the weakest fail, leaving only the strongest to sustain life with just adequate resources. In the process, the goat population, consisting of only the toughest, is stabilised in harsh conditions. After a while, English pirates begin to use the island as a base from which to attack Spanish shipping and while there sustain themselves by hunting goats. In order to undermine the English pirates, the Spanish introduce dogs to eat the goats. Initially, the dog population grows rapidly due to the abundance of meat, depleting the goat population. Eventually, some goats escape to the rocky hills to survive and only the weaker and less careful goats get caught by the dogs, whose population has now become stabilised. In this example, only the strongest animals remain in existence on the island, which is no longer a place of abundance for either goats or dogs.

According to Edel (1973), the ecological model described by Townshend, together with an expanding economic system described by Smith, were used by Malthus to construct a new description of a system in which the human population, economy and nature interact. One point which must be emphasised here is that Townshend's model is very much in line with the Darwinian theory that only the fittest survive. As we shall see later, the view among the post-Malthusian thinkers, such as Huxley, was that the weak – genetically as well as intellectually – would eventually dominate the human species which would be forced to live under unrelenting dictatorships. Resource scarcity, together with a compassionate social attitude that allowed genetically weak human beings to expand beyond what the earth could reasonably sustain, would be responsible for the ultimate destiny of mankind – misery.

Another contrasting point between Smith's views and those of other classic thinkers such as Ricardo, whose ideas will be discussed in Chapter 3, is that the former considered that the most productive and lowest cost resource operation would regulate price, while the latter considered the highest cost operation would do so. Schumpeter (1954) contends that, in fact, there is no contradiction between the two. As emphasised in Hollander

(1973) and Robinson (1989), Smith talked of a process in which more productive operations crowd out less efficient firms and, for a time, force them to sell at a loss. In the Smithian scheme of things this is a temporary or transitional stage. Ricardo, on the other hand, describes an equilibrium state.

Schumpeter believes that Smith's analysis is dynamic in the sense that it is a route to an equilibrium. As high cost mines are replaced by low cost ones in the extractive industries, a similar process is likely to take place in agriculture, the sector which is prerequisite for industrial development. Improvements in transport infrastructure will open up more and more territories, some highly fertile, for agriculture. This will affect the prices of land around urban settlements.

Smith's essentially optimistic writings regarding the adequacy of natural resources were influenced by his world which, by and large, was one of abundance with steady technological progress taking place in manufacturing, agriculture and extractive industries. For instance, the cotton textile industry was transformed by a series of innovations which created the modern form of cloth manufacture. Many of the inventors were of humble origin, who, by imagination and persistence, made a great impact on the industry. Cotton production to supply the fast growing textile industry began to expand throughout the world and thus there was no shortage of raw material.

Activities in fine art were growing in all directions, from furniture making to painting, from literature to music. Names such as Chippendale, Gainsborough, Defoe and Handel were asserting their influence on the cultural life of eighteenth-century England. The British Empire was expanding with the inclusion of Canada, Ceylon and India. Captain Cook's explorations in the Pacific and George Vancouver's adventures along the north-west coast of America were creating great excitement.

Developments in agriculture were also noteworthy. An inventor farmer, Jethro Tull, developed a drill for planting seeds and devised a method of planting in rows. Charles Townshend, after his retirement, devoted his time to the development of new crops, especially the fodder variety. At the time, the established farming tradition was to leave land fallow to recoup its fertility. The development and plantation of new feed crops in turn with established varieties still allowed the land to rest and this increased agricultural output greatly. Stock breeding and management techniques were also developing.

During his lifetime, Smith witnessed many individuals taking advantage of opportunities in industry, agriculture, science, technology and the fine arts with their initiative and imagination. But there was no economic development plan by the government; all around him Smith could see an economy in ferment, with progress being made by individual efforts and entrepreneurs acting alone with the help of an invisible hand.

Political thinking, up until Adam Smith, had been dominated by the philosophers Hobbes and Locke, who contended that individuals were essentially self-centred and thus they would be inclined to institute a government to protect their natural rights, including property rights, from damaging selfishness. Hobbes was an advocate of strong authority in the form of monarchy to restrain selfish behaviour. Locke, on the other hand, took a more moderate position by saying that a government was needed in order to create order and curb reckless, selfish behaviour, but absolute power should be granted to no one. Spinose also conceded that a government was a necessity, but that checks and balances must be put into the structure of this authority to prevent abuse of power.

Smith, viewing what was happening in society, took a dramatically opposing stance to these philosophers. According to him, the greatest hindrance to economic progress was government. Thus, his main concern in *Wealth of Nations* was the development of an economic structure that would allow man to enhance himself as a free and rational being in pursuit of his self-interest; this, in turn, would also serve the interests of society as a whole since, provided the individual was allowed this freedom, economic progress would be sustained and even remarkable. He did mention a few problems such as the tendency of entrepreneurs to conspire to their own advantage against the public. According to him, when people of the same trade socialise the conversation tends to end in conspiracy against consumers to raise prices; however, he was not over-concerned about that as, in his opinion, competition would in the end sort things out.

Smith did not deny a role for the government, but he believed that the state should never become a burden on individuals when they work towards furthering their own interests. There were only three legitimate roles for the government: judiciary, national defence and construction of certain public works which, due to their nature – such as high capital cost requirement and long gestation periods in returning net benefits – can never be for the interest of any individual or small number of individuals. He did not admit too many projects into this category (Fusfeld 1977) and, once these works were erected, the public should be charged an appropriate sum to cover their cost.

Smith's ideas became popular partly due to his analytical powers –which ultimately made economics a respectable social science – and partly because he put forward a solution to the problem which had puzzled earlier writers: namely, the conflict between self-interest and social well-being. By arguing that self-interest would result in order, not chaos, Smith provided social philosophers and moralists with an answer to the problem which had gone unresolved for centuries.

Problems such as population growth, rapid urbanisation, poverty and urban squalor were becoming noticeable in Smith's time, but were not yet the serious cause for concern that they were to become in later years. To him, agriculture posed no problem, thanks to the abundance of land and improving farming methods. As for the 'rude produce of land', such as metal deposits, precious stones, energy resources, timber, cotton, flax and so forth, available facts at the time did not undermine his optimism about future prospects. According to Smith, rent related to the 'rude produce' would be lower than rent related to food (or, in some instances, zero), although he conceded this might change with the advent of industrialisation.

Today, our world is very different from the one in which Smith lived and many are becoming increasingly concerned that the laissez-faire doctrine could lead us to an environmental catastrophe. There is ample evidence in the form of acid rain, the greenhouse effect of atmospheric pollution, ozone depletion, deforestation, land and water contamination, soil erosion and accumulation of vast quantities of highly toxic nuclear or other wastes, all of which are created and aggravated by the pursuit of narrow interests. For example, a businessman driven by self-interest is more concerned with the profit levels of his manufacturing enterprise than its effect on global warming. This is not to say that the businessman has a reckless tendency towards the environment, but that he realises his own contribution to the problem is relatively small and he will thus weigh this against his own benefits. Since every businessman may be driven by this thought, the combined effect of the damage on the environment can be substantial. In isolation, no businessman is likely to go out of his way to take steps to minimise or eliminate environmental damage at the expense of profits. Furthermore, his good deed in isolation could even threaten the very survival of his business. As far as the environment is concerned, many now accept that laissez-faire is an unconvincing theory. Even Smith's disciples now concede that environmental protection should be taken to be the fourth legitimate function of the government in addition to justice, national defence and public works.

Long before the environment became a cause for concern, Smith's free market ideals became a target for the socialists of the nineteenth century as they discovered a number of flaws in the free market philosophy. First, there was a widespread belief among the socialist school that Adam Smith's ideals would lead owners of private property to effect results that would impoverish the masses. They considered that if the distribution of income became highly unequal, to the point of becoming socially undesirable – which would be inevitable with the laissez-faire approach – then the matching production patterns would also become socially undesirable. In such a world, where income distribution is undesirable, the pattern of production will also be undesirable no matter how efficiently the market works. Second, to a large extent, the roots of property ownership lie not in innovation and hard work rewarded by the free market mechanism, but in wars, invasions, occupations and confiscation. Third, in early societies, labour was the only cost of production that needed to be rewarded. In the more advanced stages of production of the eighteenth century, in addition to wages, rents and profits became a substantial part of production costs in spite of the fact that these two factors, and in particular the profit, were the products of social organisation. As production was becoming more and more collective, profits and property ownership became more and more privately concentrated in the hands of the few.

The socialist school's dream of a command market structure, as opposed to Smith's free market, became a reality with the Russian Revolution. Then, after almost seventy years of experiment, communism in the Soviet Union collapsed leaving behind appalling environmental problems, which will be touched upon in Chapter 4. If Smith's laissez-faire approach was to become viewed as potentially environmentally unfriendly, the command market structure produced results which were far worse than anybody had anticipated.

However, it would be unfair to limit Smith's thinking to the ideas expressed in *Wealth of Nations*. Seventeen years before the publication of this book, Smith had published another text, *A Theory of Moral Sentiments*, which is crucial to an understanding of his broader social theory. In this earlier publication, the emphasis was on the moral qualities of man whereas in *Wealth of Nations* it is on economic self-centredness. In this respect, some of Smith's followers argue that present environmental problems can be analysed within the framework of Smith's broader social theory and its institutional structures.

2
THE MALTHUSIAN PROBLEM

ESSAYS ON POPULATION

Adam Smith's death in 1790 passed almost unnoticed by his contemporaries. However, soon afterwards, his ideas on free enterprise and the pursuit of self-interest began to take root. In 1804, Arthur Young published a book entitled *General View of Agriculture of Hertfordshire* in which he made a case for a crusade in favour of private property ownership in agriculture, as opposed to communal ownership. In his travels throughout the British Isles, Young observed the benefits of the change from communal to private farming. Under the old system, large open fields had been farmed in common by local groups. Private farming not only allowed each farmer to reap all the benefits of his hard work, but also the freedom to try out new methods, whereas before he had been compelled to use traditional communal methods. The result was a great improvement in productivity and led to intensification of the so-called enclosure movement in which open lands were converted into hedged or fenced private farms. Young (1804) emphasised that the magic of private property ownership turns sand into gold; with this already happening, opportunities to improve agricultural productivity looked boundless.

As Smith predicted, intensifying industrialisation began rapidly to change the structure of the economy, which was already supporting an increasing proportion of the population earning its living from non-agricultural pursuits. Although the population was expanding, agricultural output and productivity were increasing even faster. England's achievements in fighting its long wars with the French at the end of the eighteenth century while, at the same time, feeding its growing population were particularly impressive. Many branches of science, such as physics, chemistry, astronomy and zoology, were making rapid progress and the banking system was improving alongside developing trade. Advances in medicine and improvements in sanitation were achieving a remarkable reduction in death rates, and conditions in cities were gradually beginning to improve with the construction of sewers.

One of the events which impressed many influential writers towards the end of the eighteenth century was the French Revolution. Compared with England, France was a backward country lagging behind in agricultural development, industrialisation and the establishment of democratic institutions. The French Revolution was greeted with enthusiasm in England in the belief that it would bring democracy to France, developing a country similar to England, and thereby establishing peace between the two nations which had been at each other's throats for more than a century. After the French Revolution, the English prime minister, William Pitt, predicted at least fifteen years of peace between the two countries.

Some leading philosophers of the time, such as Goodwin and Condercet, were deeply inspired by developments in art, science and technology, but particularly by the French Revolution; they had a view of a future society largely free from war, disease, crime and resentments, where every man sought the good of all. Unimpressed by the developments and positive views of Goodwin and Condercet, Thomas Malthus, then an obscure young English clergyman, published his book *An Essay on the Principle of Population as it Affects the Future Improvement of Society* (1798), which came as a shock to those who were optimistic about future prospects. In this Malthus wrote that he had heard the optimistic views about the future of mankind with great pleasure. Such theories warmed and delighted him that powerful minds were painting an enchanting picture and indeed he himself wished for such improvements. He did not express any doubts about the talents of writers such as Goodwin and Condercet, but he was not certain about their frankness.

In his estimation, in general, advocates of the existing order of things regarded the sect of speculative philosophers either as skilful manipulators whose aim was to destroy the existing structures to forward their own ambitions, or as wild enthusiasts and silly wishful thinkers who were not worthy of attention. Speculative philosophers either prostituted their understanding to their interests; or blinded by wild enthusiasm were unable to see a few yards before them:

> The speculative philosopher equally offends against the cause of truth. With eyes fixed on a happier state of society, the blessing of which he paints in the most captivating colours, he allows himself to indulge in the most bitter invectives against every present establishment, without applying his talents to consider the best and safest means of removing abuses, and without seemingly to be aware of the tremendous obstacles that threaten, even in theory, to oppose the progress of man towards perfection.
>
> (Malthus 1798)

As the population of England grew, Malthus noticed that in some areas poverty increased. Before the industrial revolution each parish had cared for its own poor, but the enclosure movement displaced many farmers from their previous activities. Cottage industries, which were largely a rural phenomenon, were also beginning to dwindle due to the establishment of large new mills in cities. The increasing numbers of poor in each parish put a great financial burden on wealthy landlords who became unable to cope, and people began to drift into the towns in search of work.

As stated in Chapter 1, at the end of the eighteenth century there was a strong opinion against poor relief, as there is today, on the grounds that relief would encourage idleness as well as population growth (Townshend 1786). Malthus was taken by this argument and with Townshend's example of a natural equilibrium model on an island with goats and dogs. These were in conflict with Adam Smith's theories of continuous progress and abundance, and convinced Malthus that the future of mankind was very bleak indeed.

After observing the growth of population in some northern states of America where food was plentiful, Malthus came to the conclusion that, if unchecked, population had a tendency to double itself in every twenty-five-year period:

> In the United States of America, where the means of subsistence have been more ample, the manners of people more pure, and consequently the checks to early marriages fewer, than in any modern states of Europe, the population has been found to double itself in twenty-five years.
>
> (Malthus 1788)

He implied that this was neither the maximum nor the actual growth rate as the available statistics at the time were unreliable, but he suggested that if unchecked the population would increase in a geometrical fashion, thus:

1, 2, 4, 8, 16, 32, 64, . . .

On the other hand, the food supply could only be increased in an arithmetical progression:

1, 2, 3, 4, 5, 6, 7, . . .

The main reason for this was that since the supply of land is fixed, in accordance with the law of diminishing returns, increasing other inputs on it will increase the food supply at a diminishing rate. Malthus recognised the possibility of opening up new territories, but argued that this would be a very slow process and furthermore the quality of land in new territories would be inferior to that in existing ones. The law of diminishing returns was, after all, only common sense and thus did not require much empirical proof.

Even if more territories were discovered and more land on existing territories brought into agriculture this would quickly exhaust the whole world:

> Let us take any spot of earth, this Island for instance, and see in what ratio the subsistence it affords can be supposed to increase. We will begin with it under its present state of cultivation. If I allow that by the best possible policy, by breaking up more land, and by great encouragements to agriculture, the produce of this Island may be doubled in the first twenty-five years, I think it will be allowing as much as any person can well demand. In the next twenty-five years, it is impossible to suppose that the produce could be quadrupled. It would be contrary to all our knowledge of the qualities of land. The very utmost that we can conceive is that increases in the second twenty-five years might equal present produce. Let us take this as our rule, though certainly beyond the truth; and allow that by great exertion, the whole population of this Island might be increased every twenty-five years, by a quantity of subsistence equal to what it at present produces. The most enthusiastic speculator can not suppose a greater increase than this. In a few centuries it would make every acre of land in the Island like a garden. Yet this ratio of increase is evidently arithmetical.
>
> (ibid.)

Two conflicting powers are in operation in Malthusian theory: the power of the earth to produce food and the power of population growth fuelled by the passion between the sexes. As the productive land and its food growing capacity are limited, the passion between males and females is undiminishing and eternal. These two factors led Malthus to believe that the power of population is infinitely greater than the power of the earth to produce subsistence. The effect of these two unequal powers will, somehow, be brought in line by strong and constantly operating checks on population. The ultimate check on population is food shortage. If the supply of food increased there would be a corresponding increase in population until the level of food per capita had fallen back to the subsistence level, at which point population growth would stop.

Malthus placed other checks in two groups: positive and preventive. The former included wars, famine and pestilence; the latter, abortion, contraception and moral restraint. He saw neither contraception nor abortion as practical means of curtailing the population growth. The poor were responsible for their own predicament and the only way out was to have fewer children. But Malthus was convinced that they were not able to do so.

In the Malthusian scheme of things, improvements in medical treatment and sanitary conditions will only add to the problem. This is because the size of human population, just like any other population, is determined by the relationship between natality and mortality. Improvements in hygiene and medical conditions would only widen the gap between birth and death rates, fuelling the population fire. In a more formal expression, the size of a population at any time will be determined by:

$$N_t = N_0 e^{rt}$$

where

N_t = size of population at time t

N_0 = size of population at time zero

e = base of natural logarithms

r = rate of population growth

t = time elapsed

If the mortality rate falls, natality rate being unchanged, this would increase r, the rate of population growth. For example, if the growth rate is 3 per cent, it will take only twenty-three years to double the population. The doubling time is, approximately, 70 divided by growth rate (not expressed as a percentage). That is:

Rate of increase	*Doubling time*
5	14
4	18
3	23
2	35
1	70

In this respect, Malthus realised that the size of the human population, if unchecked, would in the not so distant future become very large indeed – a prediction which has already become a reality. For example, towards the end of the eighteenth century the total world population was about 900 million. Today it is about 6,000 million, a nearly seven-fold increase in less than 200 years (Davey 1960; Durand 1967).

Figure 2.1 shows the behaviour of growth function at two different rates. The curve on the right implies a lower growth, the one on the left is higher after, say, improvements in medicine. Of course, no species can grow in this fashion indefinitely due to environmental resistance, which puts a break on the growth pattern and eventually halts it at a carrying capacity, as seen in Figure 2.2. The logistic growth schedule flattens out when the carrying capacity is reached. If the environmental resistance is tougher, the logistic curve will move further to the right and flatten out at a much later time.

Malthus was one of the earliest writers to realise the world's natural limitations, which at that time were land and its food growing capacity in the

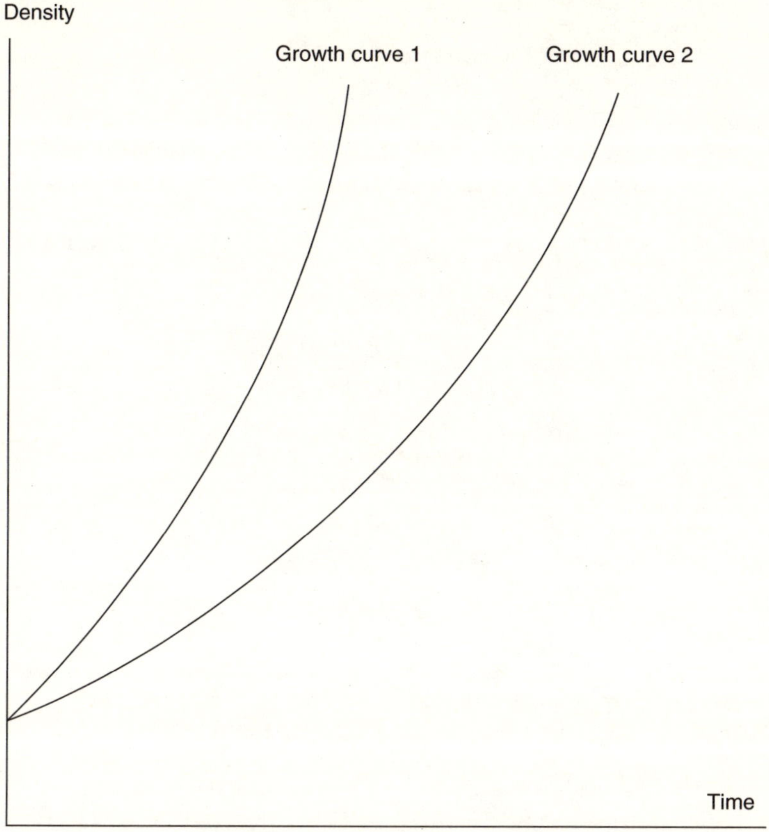

Figure 2.1 Population curves, biotic potential (curve on left implies faster growth)

face of a constantly growing population. He sincerely believed that, sooner rather than later, humanity would be trapped in a dismal state of existence from which it would not be able to escape as the carrying capacity would be very quickly reached.

Another implication of the Malthusian theory is that poor relief will not solve the problem of poverty, but will only aggravate the situation in that the predicament of the poor is created by themselves; welfare systems will only generate more poverty until the crisis reaches greater proportions, which will then make the relief system unable to cope. Furthermore, the welfare system will shift income from those who use it productively to an essentially unproductive population. Malthus's theory not only inspired the doom and gloom theories which became fashionable in the second half of this century, and which will be discussed later in the book, but it also gave ultra-conservatives the best reason for doing nothing about poverty. 'Do not help the poor by way of relief which will be counter-productive' is an expression which we sometimes hear today, as many had heard it in the eighteenth

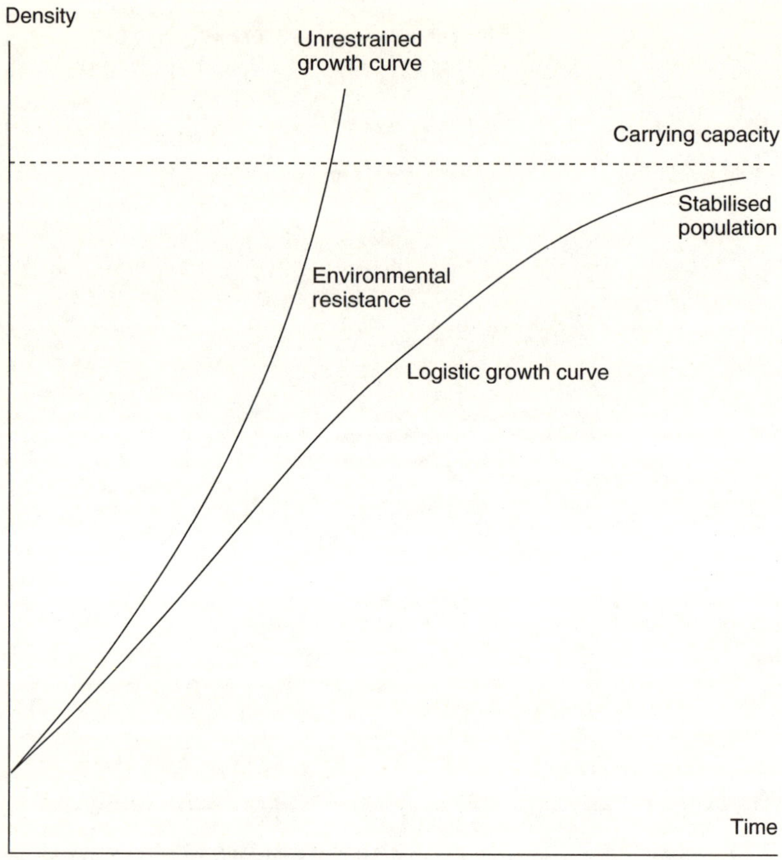

Figure 2.2 Unrestricted and restricted population growth schedules

century. Today, some Conservatives believe that single-parent families and, in particular, teenage mothers (who are on the increase in countries such as Britain and the United States) are a product of the welfare state and that their increase will create even greater social, economic and environmental problems for future generations. Malthus was not a hard person, or a redneck of his time, but a well-educated man of the cloth. He cared for the poor and felt great compassion for them, which he expressed to his friends on many occasions. His analysis of human society at that time, however, led him to believe that poor relief would only make things much worse.

Many years after Malthus's publication, anthropologists discovered that positive population checks had been in operation in primitive tribes in many parts of the world, and even, possibly, throughout history. Rappaport (1967), by studying the Tsemboga tribe of New Guinea, describes a mechanism that keeps the population there in check. The Tsemboga live in an isolated jungle and operate slush-and-burn agriculture to grow root vegetables and raise pigs.

The latter serve as an emergency store of food because the root vegetables, such as yams and tara, cannot be stored for long periods of time. Pigs also ensure that a local crop failure will not wipe out the tribe. As the tribe moves about the jungle they take their pigs with them; when the animal population rises, the tribe engages in great ritual pig feasts to reduce the numbers.

The human numbers in the community are also kept in check by the conditions of the territory, tribal wars and their refrainment from sexual activity during such wars. The Tsemboga, unlike some other tribes in New Guinea, have learned not to overcultivate their land. Relationships with neighbouring tribes are volatile, and there are periods of hostility as well as peace; the start of a war depends upon the level of grievances that have accumulated between the tribes over a period of time. These wars ensure that the tribal population does not grow too much and, since the Tsemboga religion imposes a taboo on sexual activity during hostilities, this reduces the birth rate. During peacetime, tribes get together for feasting, especially when there are surplus animals; this encourages intermarriage between communities, reducing inbreeding and all the genetic problems associated with it (Edel 1973).

The Malthusian theory also inspired Charles Darwin in his quest for an answer as to the reason why there is such a large number of species on earth:

> [A]fter I had begun my systematic inquiry, I happened to read for amusement Malthus on population and being well prepared to appreciate the struggle for existence which everywhere goes on from long-continued observations of the habits of animals and plants, it at once struck me that under these circumstances favourable variations would tend to be preserved, and unfavourable ones to be destroyed. The result of this would be the formation of new species. Here, then, I had at least got a theory by which to work.
>
> (Darwin 1859)

According to Edel (1973), Darwin elaborated on the Malthusian theory by showing that failing populations consist of the unfit, whereas social groups who take a responsible attitude by marrying at a later age when they can afford to have children will survive in largest numbers. Groups who tend to breed at an early age, even though they are unable to support their offspring, or those with unthrifty habits and a reckless outlook on life, will progressively be thinned out in the fight for survival. Barnett and Morse (1963) imply that in spite of using the well-established Malthusian theory, Darwin rose to greater prominence than Malthus mainly because, being a practising scientist, he commanded greater respect in the scientific and intellectual community.

A LEAP IN TIME – MALTHUS AND CONTEMPORARY CHINA

Almost 200 years after its publication, the Malthusian theory is still a popular subject for debate among economists as well as other social scientists. In some parts of the world the theory even dominates government policies; it may go out of fashion for a while, only to come back again with vigour. The events which took place in China during the Great Leap Forward are an interesting example of this.

The first Five Year Plan of 1953–7 turned out to be a very successful experiment in China: the average annual growth rate of the gross domestic product has been estimated to have been at least 12 per cent in real terms (Deleyne 1973). This was followed by a bumper harvest in 1958, which increased the conviction of the communist rulers that China was ripe for a great leap forward to emancipate her from reliance on the Soviet Union and to break out of the vicious circle of backwardness. In the autumn of 1958, the New China News Agency reported that incredibly high yields in grain output had smashed the defective law of diminishing returns and finally disproved the Malthusian theory. In line with this belief, the press campaign promoting family planning was reduced substantially and posters, lectures and films promoting birth control began to disappear. The manufacture of contraceptive medicines and devices was also cut back and they were no longer displayed in pharmacies.

In 1958 the Communist Party of China declared that the Great Leap Forward had completely destroyed the pessimistic view that agricultural development could not keep pace with population growth and had 'blown sky high' the notion of Malthus and his followers that a large population impedes economic development. Economists were ridiculed for underestimating the revolutionary peasants of China and for failing to see that human beings are producers as well as consumers. At the same time, some statisticians were trying to make accurate forecasts for the country's agricultural potential, but they were attacked for undermining the enthusiasm of the peasants and were told that the main function of statistics was to arouse revolutionary fervour; everything else was secondary. The result was the beginning of a process of mutual deception between the top and bottom levels of society.

In 1958 Mao himself stated that the decisive factors for the success of the revolution were the leadership of the Communist Party and the growing population (New China News Agency 1958). Malthus was wrong: the more people there were, the more available were views and suggestions, fervour and energy. Though China's millions were poor, this was not a bad thing because poor people would want change – above all, they would want revolution.

Intoxicated by wildly false statistics and the propaganda that politically inspired peasants were transforming the countryside overnight, Mao abandoned Malthusianism, convinced that China's food problems were completely resolved. He instructed party workers to redirect their efforts towards industry. Early harvest reports indicated that a total grain output of 450 million tons would be achieved in 1959, leading Mao to express concern over what to do with the surplus grain.

In the spring of 1959 the truth began to dawn on some party members that agriculture was failing badly, while party leaders, on the other hand, were trying desperately to protect the illusion created by the Great Leap Forward. By August of that year, despite renewed attacks against counter-revolutionaries who were trying to deny the achievements of the Great Leap, the rising tide of disillusionment had dampened enthusiasm in the Central Committee of the Party.

The extent of agricultural failure during the 'Leap' years was very substantial. Table 2.1 shows grain output figures reported by seven different agencies, including Chinese officials. On the basis of the average figures, given in the last row of the table, the decline in grain output was 23 per cent between 1958 and 1961, during which time there were no imports. In 1961 the harvest improved marginally, but it was still well below the 1957 level.

There were numerous reasons for the failure of agriculture: close planting, recommended by the revolutionary cadres against the advice of agriculturists, which resulted in contraction of output; adoption of untested farming methods, irrespective of local conditions; over-ambitious irrigation schemes without proper consideration of water, manpower and other resources; widespread shortages of agricultural labour created by drafting millions to work in industry, in particular to produce steel in backyard furnaces; failure of rural industries to provide machinery, tools, fertiliser, and other materials for agriculture; destruction of productivity incentives for farm labourers, which were condemned as capitalist practices; and unfavourable weather conditions. Food shortages lowered peasants' incentives as well as their

Table 2.1 Grain output estimates for China

	Grain output (million tons)				
Reporting body	*1957*	*1958*	*1959*	*1960*	*1961*
Chinese officials	185	250	270	150	161
US Consulate in Hong Kong	-	194	168	160	167
Taiwanese sources	-	185	160	120	130
Japanese sources	185	200	185	150	160
W. Hober and Rockwell	185	175	154	130	140
Dawson	185	204	160	170	-
Janes and Poleman	185	210	192	185	-
Average	185	204	184	152	157

Source: Kula (1989)

physical capabilities. A large number of animals died due to lack of feed and care, and weeds overran fields due to diminished human effort.

In 1962 the weather improved and the outlook for agriculture looked better. Some policy-makers were able to talk, mostly in private, about the dark years of the Great Leap Forward and admit failure. By the end of 1962 the family planning campaign was reinstated, signifying the renaissance of Malthusianism.

During the 'Leap' years, the Malthusian ultimate check on population was ruthlessly efficient. For obvious reasons, information about the famine and its casualties was suppressed by the communist rulers, but in 1962 Liu Shao-chi, a Communist Party spokesman, admitted that there were more deaths in 1961 than births (Wan 1962). Between 1953 and 1959 annual death rates were hovering around the 1.2 per cent mark in China. Despite efforts to control population the average annual birth rate remained high, at about 3.4 per cent. In 1958 the Chinese population was about 650 million and, with a 2.2 per cent growth rate, the annual increase in population in 1961 would have been about 15 million had there been no Great Leap Forward. Since deaths were greater than births in 1961, this would make the famine casualty figure at least 15 million in one year alone. As for the famine related deaths in 1959, 1960 and 1962, here we are talking about an overall casualty figure of about 40 million, which makes the Chinese famine the most effective Malthusian check in recorded human history.

Today, Malthusianism is back in China with vigour as the country implements a minimum age for marriage and a single child policy, which started in earnest in the 1980s. Couples who produce more than one child are fined and on occasions sacked from their jobs. Exceptions are granted to couples who have a disabled first child.

A FURTHER LEAP – THE NEXT STAGE

In a number of parts of the world, such as the Indian sub-continent, south-east Asia and parts of Africa, the pressure of population on land has been growing relentlessly. Many forecast that with current trends the combined population of the Indian sub-continent and China alone will be approaching four billion in the second half of the next century, which is likely to keep the Malthusian theory alive throughout the twenty-first century and beyond. In this respect, Huxley (1959) argues that the coming age will not be the space age or the age of enlightenment or prosperity, but will be the age of over-population with all of its frightening consequences such as poverty, environmental degradation, wars, falling average intelligence and erosion of civil liberties, not only in the developing countries but throughout the world. The fantastically increasing human numbers are taking place not in desirable and productive areas, which are already densely populated, but in inhospitable regions whose soils are being eroded by the frantic efforts of bad farmers to raise more food and where easily available mineral and other deposits are being squandered with reckless extravagance. This biological background will advance, ever more insistently and menacingly, towards the front of the historic stage and will remain the central problem for centuries to come throughout the globe.

Clean water, penicillin and various preventive medicines are relatively cheap commodities which help to reduce death rates; even the poorest governments are rich enough to provide their subjects with a substantial measure of *death control* by making these commodities easily available. *Birth control*, on the other hand, is a different matter which depends upon the co-operation of an entire population. It must be practised daily by countless individuals from whom it demands more will-power and intelligence than most of the world's illiterates possess. Whereas death control is achieved easily, birth control is achieved with great difficulty. In this century when death rates have fallen with startling suddenness, birth rates have either remained at their previous levels or if they have fallen, have fallen by very little.

In addition to deteriorating environmental quality and dwindling natural deposits, Huxley emphasises two more problems: creeping dictatorship and falling average intelligence. In unbearably overcrowded regions, conditions for freedom and democracy will become impossible, almost unthinkable, as the primary needs of the overwhelming majority will never be fully satisfied. History has amply demonstrated that when the economic life of a nation becomes precarious, the central government assumes additional responsibilities. In similar circumstances in the future, the central authority will be required to work out elaborate plans for dealing with critical conditions created by overpopulation and impose many restrictions upon the daily activities of individuals. When the crisis deepens, the central government will be compelled to tighten its authoritarian grip to preserve public order and its own authority. More and more power will be concentrated in the hands of governments.

The nature of power is such that even those who have not sought it, but have had it forced upon them, tend to acquire a taste for more. In countries where human numbers reach a crisis point, increasing economic insecurity and social unrest will lead to more control by authoritarian governments which will give way to oppression and corruption: 'Given this fact, the probability of over-population leading through unrest to dictatorship becomes a virtual certainty' (Huxley 1959).

This situation in hard-pressed regions will affect the established democracies of Europe, Japan, Australia, New Zealand and North America – the West. It is more than likely that the dictatorial governments in the impoverished world will be hostile to the West and could reduce, or even stop, the flow of raw materials that the West needs for its survival. Due to lack of critical materials, industrialised systems established in the West will break down and their highly developed technology, which until now has allowed them to sustain a high population in a small territory, will no longer be effective. When this happens, the powers forced by unfavourable conditions upon Western governments may come to be used in the spirit of dictatorship.

Huxley asserts that in free and tolerant societies most of us know that pursuit of good ends does not justify the employment of bad means. But what about those situations in which good means have end results which turn out to be bad? In particular, advances in modern medicine, improved sanitation and compassionate social attitudes are making most children born with hereditary defects reach maturity and multiply their kind. In the past, children with even slight hereditary defects rarely survived. Today, thanks to modern medicine, the lives of illness-prone individuals with terminal diseases are prolonged. In spite of 'improved' treatment, the physical health of the general population will show no improvement and may even deteriorate along with the fall in the average level of intelligence.

Huxley draws attention to research which suggests that such a decline has already taken place and that it is continuing along its downward trend as our best stock is outbred by stock that is inferior to it in every respect. With declining physical health and IQ levels, how long can we maintain our traditions of liberty, tolerance and a sense of justice? 'To help the unfortunate is obviously good. But wholesale transmission to our descendants of the results of unfavourable mutations and progressive contamination of the genetic pool from which the members of our species will have to draw are no less bad' (Huxley 1959).

Years before Huxley, Pigou (1920) expressed concern about the survival of weak children setting up a cumulative effect which could weaken a nation. He posed the question of whether in the course of economic and social progress the seeds of disaster had been planted which could contaminate our genetic pool:

> The danger to national strength that results from a growth of wealth in general has been emphasised by many nations. In a softer environment children of feeble constitution who, in harder circumstances would have died, are enabled to survive and themselves to have children. It has even been suggested that in this fact may lie the secret of the eventual decay of nations and of aristocracies which have obtained great wealth.
>
> (ibid.: 117)

Falling intelligence levels can only aid the transition from democracy to dictatorship. Once totalitarian regimes are established in the West, governments will try very hard to meet the basic needs of their subjects who, terrified by the problems created by overpopulation, are likely to demand beefburgers and television before liberty and justice. The life for the thinking and caring minority will be hellish and they may turn to sedative drugs, the use of which will be encouraged by the authoritarian governments to keep them docile.

In the Huxlian scheme of things, allowing unfit social groups to survive and expand will eventually overpopulate the world and this is against the principles of natural selection. Social institutions and attitudes which allow this to happen will eventually collapse under the weight of their creation.

Although powerful and compelling, it may be that there are some problems with the Malthusian theory. As an economic law, diminishing returns – a topic which Malthus explored further in his theory of rent (Malthus 1815) – holds only for a constant state of technology. Today, Western Europe is a small and very crowded region of the globe and one of its problems is not food shortage, but surplus which has come about as a result of improvements in agricultural technology and the substantial farm support packages that have been in existence since the Second World War. In addition, Malthus failed to see that as income and education levels improve, people may change their attitude by restricting, voluntarily, the size of their family – as has occurred in modern Europe. In this the role of family planning technology has been substantial. Various effective birth control methods, including the pill, have helped to stabilise populations in many parts of Europe. Contrary to what Malthus asserted, contraception has turned out to be a practical means of curtailing the population growth in some countries, and in others concerted efforts are being made in the same direction.

Such developments could not have been foreseen by Malthus in the eighteenth century as he pointed out that the superior power of population will overwhelm human societies:

> I see no way which man can escape from the weight of this law which pervades all animated nature. No fancied equality, no agrarian regulations in their utmost extent, could remove the pressure of it even for a single century.
>
> (Malthus 1798)

However, despite social and technological success achieved in the established democracies of Europe, where food surpluses persist and populations are more or less stabilised, it would perhaps be rather too hasty to claim that the Malthusian theory is falsified. As will be shown later on, the Malthusian theory is one of the main ingredients of modern world models in which a less than rosy picture is painted for the future of mankind. Furthermore, some modern Malthusians such as Lester Brown assert that the world as a whole is about to enter the much feared Malthusian age.

3

RICARDIAN STAGNATION

DAVID RICARDO

Ricardo was the son of a London stockbroker who, with his father's help, became a trader on the stock exchange and by the time he was in his mid-twenties had amassed a fortune. In his early forties he retired, as a rich man, to a country estate and devoted his time to economics as a radical thinker. Ricardo was an apostle of capital accumulation and economic growth, who also wrote on international trade and the labour theory of value and rent, including rent of the rude produce of land.

The development of his classical theory of rent, in which Malthus played an important role, emerged from the so-called Corn Law Controversy which began as a result of the Napoleonic Wars. The embargo on British ports during wartime, which kept foreign grain out of England, forced British farmers to increase their production of grain to feed the population. As a result, between 1790 and 1810 British corn prices rose on average by 18 per cent per annum. Land rents also increased, which pleased the landlords. In 1815 the Corn Law effectively prohibited the importation of foreign grain and was in fact one of the earliest examples of agricultural protectionism affecting economic growth and income distribution in the country.

Ricardo was in agreement with Malthus on the basic principles of population and rent (Ricardo 1817). The reason for the increased price of grain is explained by the law of diminishing returns. Ricardo argued that the price of the produce is determined by profits, wages and rent. In a situation where an increase in production takes place on old lands the incremental rent will be zero or near zero, leaving wages and profits as the sole determinants of price. The rent on old lands would increase only when new territories became available for agriculture. In his words, 'When in the progress of society, land of the second degree of fertility is taken into cultivation, rent immediately commences on that of the first quality, and the amount of that rent will depend on the difference in quality of these two portions of land' (ibid.; see also Sraffa and Dobb (1951–5).

Ricardo believed that the growth of capital was the major source of economic expansion, and thus all economic policy should aim to promote it. Like Smith, Ricardo contended that economic freedom would lead to maximum profits which were the source of capital accumulation and that a competitive economic structure would lead to profit-maximising investment decisions and this, in turn, would maximise economic growth.

On the wages front, Ricardo suggested that the Corn Law allowed a rise in wages, but a fall in profits, and thus less capital accumulation took place which slowed down the economic growth. In Ricardo's scheme of things, profits are the engine of economic growth and wages the engine of population expansion. If wages rose above subsistence, the number of heads coming into the world would go up and eventually wages would fall back again to the subsistence level. If they fell below subsistence, population would fall due to malnutrition and wages would rise again to subsistence.

At the time when Ricardo was thinking his theories through there was another controversy in England as to which sector, agriculture or industry, should be promoted. During the French wars, landlords were happy because of the rise in rents. When peace came, the demand for agriculture slackened and the price of food fell. Then, landlords, together with farmers, began to lobby the government to increase import duty on corn because, they argued, a lucrative agriculture was essential for the nation's defence and the maintenance of old English values. Emphasis was placed on old physiocratic ideals that economic growth depended on the natural productivity of the land.

Industrialists, on the other hand, were opposed to the idea of increasing tariffs on food on the grounds that this would increase food prices and, inevitably, the subsistence wage rate which would be reflected in industrial goods sold in national, as well as international, markets. Industrialists argued that the nation's future lay with industrial expansion (which to a large extent depends on cheap labour) not with agriculture. They advocated the abolition of the Corn Laws. Ricardo had more sympathy with industrialists than farmers. In his view, the expansion of domestic agriculture would only benefit landlords, not the farmers who actually grow food. In this way, a larger share of national income would flow into the hands of an essentially parasitic group, some of whom had already made a bad name for themselves with extravagant and scandalous lifestyles. In other words, rent was an engine of pompous living.

Furthermore, cultivation of new and less fertile land would draw capital and labour away from industry by further crippling the sector. High food prices created by tariffs would be an undermining factor for British industry, which was becoming a major force in international markets.

Ricardo's theory was much more than a treatment of a contemporary policy issue. Fusfeld (1977) argues that if it was so, it would have died as interest in the problem petered out. Although encouraged by the problems of his times, Ricardo took his analyses much further and generalised them into a theory of economic growth which dominated the thinking of economists many years after his death. In his theories there is a conflict between wage and profit levels. When wages are bid well above subsistence, profits will be squeezed to a minimum, then capital accumulation will, temporarily, cease. The next thing is that the population will continue to grow due to above-subsistence wages, forcing earnings of workers back to subsistence. When this happens, rising profits will increase capital accumulation and this in turn will initiate growth, and so forth. Eventually, this process will come to a rest at the point where profits, due to diminishing returns, can no longer be increased – no capital accumulation, no growth, wages at subsistence and the economy in a stationary state.

At the centre of the Ricardian model there is the notion that economic expansion must eventually peter out due to scarcity of natural resources. By looking at the Ricardian theory from the viewpoint of agriculture, envisage that the entire world is a giant farm of fixed size on which capital and labour (population) are used as inputs to produce grain. In Figure 3.1 population is measured along the horizontal axis and output along the vertical axis. We exclude the landowners because the size of land and its ownership is fixed. The output curve is OP and the subsistence curve is OW. When the population is OK, the subsistence wage will be KR and profits TR. The slope of OW is, of course, the wage rate, which is measured as KR/OK, i.e. total wage bill divided by number of workers. The working of the model is as follows: the profits will initiate growth, then the wages will go up above subsistence and thus encourage population growth. As output expands along OP, population will move along the horizontal axis, eventually lowering the wage to subsistence at some point along OW, say R'. At this point the level of output and population are higher, but the profit rate lower than R, the starting point. But there is still profit in the system which will move the economy further along until we get to the stationary state at D. Here wages are of subsistence, profits are squeezed out of the system, population and output levels are constant, all due to natural resource scarcity.

However, Ricardo was aware that technological improvements would bring greater rewards by shifting the output curve from OP to OP' but would not be able to eliminate the tendency towards diminishing return. At D' the output is higher but population is greater than that of K' and there is no change in the subsistence level. Given the scarcity of natural resources as entrepreneurs (driven by self-interest) invest dutifully, workers keep on breeding whenever the conditions permit and eventually the wheel of economic progress grinds to a halt.

The parallel between Malthusian and Ricardian theories is obvious as both highlight the crucial importance of population growth in bringing the economic expansion to an end with unenviable results. On the way to the final destination there are likely to be famines, wars and epidemics. Edel (1973) contends that both the Black Death and the Irish Potato Famine may have been provoked by the land ownership structure inherent in Ricardian

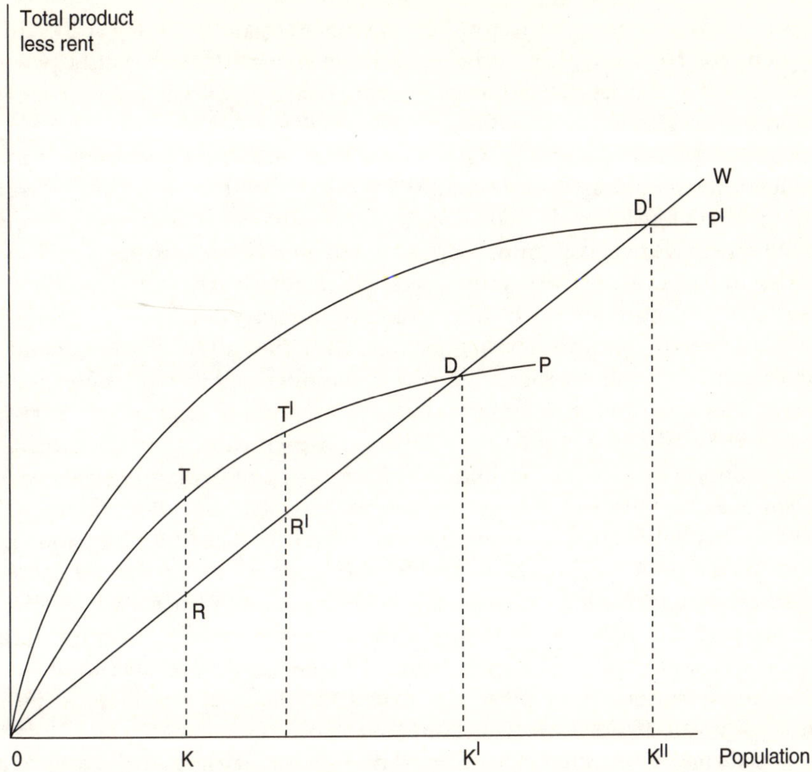

Figure 3.1 Ricardian model of economic growth and stagnation

analysis. In Ireland, for instance, the local population was forced on to marginal lands by the ruling classes who kept the most fertile areas for themselves. Although Ireland had a grain surplus which was shipped out by colonial landlords to England, most peasants relied on potatoes, which were a non-native species originating in Peru. Unlike potatoes grown on native land, those grown in Ireland were all genetically similar, crowded together on poor soil by Irish peasants, and this created conditions for the rapid spread of blight. 'Biological theory would consider the virulence of the blight, once it started as highly probable. However, the conditions that made it probable were economic' (Edel 1973: 32–3). Famine culled the Irish population by about a quarter.

Ricardo also wrote quite a bit on the economics of the extractive sector in which he criticised Adam Smith's theory of rent. Ricardo's definition of rent, which now appears in many modern economics textbooks, is: 'it is that proportion of produce of the earth which is paid to the landowner for the use of the original and indestructible powers of the soil.' He levies a criticism on Adam Smith's argument in which rent is attributed to payment to the landowner for removing wood from the land. According to Ricardo, this is payment for timber and is nothing to do with rent. If, however, a payment was made to the landlord for using the land for afforestation, then this would be called rent.

Ricardo was in agreement with Smith that, just as in farming, return on the least fertile mine deposit would regulate the rent in all other mines. But he challenged Smith's position that marginal land will always capture a rent whereas marginal mine deposits will not be able to do so. In other words, in Ricardo's theory rent operates in exactly the same way for the rude produce of land as it does for agriculture. Apparently, there is a contradiction in Ricardo's writings regarding rent. On the one hand, he argues that payment to the landlord for removing timber or mine deposits is not rent but, on the other hand, he maintains that mining rent is explained by the same rule that explains agricultural rent. According to some economists such as Cannan (1917) one way of explaining this contradiction can be found in the use of language by Ricardo who, compared to many of his colleagues, did not have an extensive literary education. Later on Cannan (1964) emphasised that Ricardo was aware of the fundamental difference between rent in mining and rent in agriculture. When Ricardo was writing on rent, he was thinking in terms of diminishing returns which were prevalent in agriculture. In the extractive sector, however, increasing returns prevailed as the prices of precious metals were falling. For a wider discussion, see Robinson (1989).

As for the price trend in the extractive sector, Ricardo argued that it is influenced by two opposing factors. On the one hand, prices will tend to fall as a result of new discoveries and improvements in extraction technology and transport; on the other hand, prices will be pushed up due to increasing costs when the work moves deeper into the ground and consequently intrusion by water becomes detrimental. In the long run, due to increasingly inferior mineral deposits, rising costs are likely to outweigh the improvement in extractive technology and the transport network. Here Ricardo, with his emphasis on the ultimately diminishing returns in mining, differs from Smith's essentially optimistic view which envisaged increasing returns due to abundance and progress.

OPPOSITION TO RICARDIAN STAGNATION

Henry Carey (1793–1873), son of an Irish immigrant in the United States, began his writings in economics at the age of forty-two. His first book, *Principles of Political Economy* (1837), challenged head on the Ricardo–Malthusian theory that a growing population in the face of the law of diminishing returns would create stagnation and dismal living conditions for mankind in future years. According to him, historic facts in agriculture, as well as in mining, pointed towards increasing return, and capital accumulation levels showed a pace faster than population growth. His father, Matthew Carey, also a writer with a publishing business, was a great advocate of protectionism with a view to developing the American economy to her full potential, a process which, according to him, should not be undermined by foreign competition. Henry Carey's main preoccupation was the same as his father's – protectionism – but in his first book he mainly challenged the views of pessimists such as Malthus and Ricardo.

Carey argues that the development of agriculture all over the world shows a pattern from high-cost to low-cost operation with increasing return to scale. This is because when man first adopted a settled lifestyle he chose lightly wooded regions on high ground where soil types were poor. Cultivation began on the immediately accessible territory. In time, growing population, accumulation of capital and technological development led him to unlock the most fertile soils of the lowlands. This process, which according to Carey is a historic fact, led to the growth of agricultural output way ahead of population. The only advantageous factor attributable to the old lands was accessibility, but as social infrastructure such as roads and canals developed, a much better quality of land became available with improved technology.

A similar situation of increasing returns can also be observed in mining. At the early stages of settled life, substantial mining was not possible because of scarcity of capital. As agriculture began to create a surplus, investment in social infrastructure and mining operations grew. As mines opened up, increasing returns, not diminishing returns, were realised due to a number of factors. First, more intensive application of capital led to greater productivity:

> Increased capital enables the miner to descend double the distances and the value is now greater than at first. A further application of capital enables him to descend successively 300, 500, 600, 1000 or 1500 feet, and with every successive application the property acquires a higher value, notwithstanding the quality of coal that has been taken out.
>
> (Carey 1858)

Second, improved extraction technology enhanced greatly the yield in mining operations – that is, increased quantity and quality of capital which allowed deeper deposits to be mined and at the same time prevented the onset of the law of diminishing returns.

The third factor was the growing opportunity for association, co-operation and commerce prompted by economic expansion. These factors allowed the operation of new mines which had previously been considered worthless. Carey used examples of coal, limestone and granite deposits to prove his point. Even with no change in capital intensity and extraction technology, the third factor tends to make mining operations more and more profitable. 'Every mine that is opened, tends to facilitate the further progress in the same direction because each and every one of them tends to promote association and combination' (Carey 1858).

As for the reward to ownership of the land, i.e. rent, Carey argues that David Ricardo was wrong in his analysis. According to Carey there is, essentially, no difference between mining, forestry and agriculture, which are linked firmly to the productive powers of the soil. If one must establish a difference, the emphasis should be on a matter of degree rather than on kind. For example, timber is no different from corn as far as the productive power argument goes except that the former takes much longer to grow. A payment to a landlord for either timber or corn is the same; they are not for the material removed from land, but for permission to use the productive powers of his asset.

It must be pointed out that there is a substantial difference between the harvesting of timber and the harvesting of corn. The time to harvest the latter is known to the farmer with a high degree of accuracy. For the forestry sector, however, this is not the case. This is a subject which has been debated in the literature for more than hundred years.

At the time when Carey was developing his theories, Martin Faustmann (1849) was grappling with the difficult problem of identifying the optimal cutting age for trees. If left undisturbed, many commercial tree species will grow for more than a hundred years until physical decay sets in. Should the forest owner then wait until such time in order to obtain the maximum volume of wood? Faustmann argued, although in a rather vague manner, that in identifying the optimal cutting age the owners of trees should take into account a host of factors such as expected revenue from the sale of timber, rental value of land and the commercial rate of interest, for it was highly unlikely that the optimal felling age would coincide with the maximum sustainable yield.

More recently, in an attempt to clarify Faustmann's theory, Samuelson (1976) has argued that many well-known foresters, as well as economists, have erred in their analysis of optimal cutting by prescribing a single rotation model, and in doing so they have misled their profession. He suggests the correct solution to the problem is that of multiple rotation latent in Faustmann's analysis.

In Carey's theory, a somewhat similar argument applies to coal mining, where it takes many centuries for the material to mature. Furthermore, agricultural land is just as destructible as mine deposits. If a farmer uses productive agricultural land in a reckless fashion, its fertility will decline and eventually the soil will become worthless. Therefore, agricultural lands are as easily depleted as mine deposits. According to Carey, there is no fundamental difference, in essence, between forestry, short rotation crops and mining as each activity yields a rent.

Carey's theories found some support in the economic literature. For example, Cannan (1917) asserts that Carey was correct to point out that, on the extensive margin, the agricultural industry had not experienced diminishing returns in the past, but that Carey took his optimism too far with regard to the advantages of a large and growing population. Schumpeter (1954) contends that there is a case for Carey's hypothesis of increasing returns to scale, especially in the United States, but that ultimately this does not disprove the Ricardian theory – the cultivation of poor lands first does not necessarily prove that Ricardo was wrong. Schumpeter argues that Henry Carey was not a good analytical economist, but a great visionary. With regard to the views of Mill and Jevons, it is also worth noting that there is a considerable difference between mining and agriculture, as will be explained in the following section.

Ricardo–Malthusian pessimism was also criticised by economists with strong religious beliefs. As Schumpeter (1954) says, 'At the early stages of the development of economic ideas theology was the guiding force.'

CLASSICAL ECONOMISTS MOSTLY IN SUPPORT OF STAGNATION: J. S. MILL AND W. S. JEVONS

John Stuart Mill was a philosopher and an economist who wrote on logic, international trade, political economy, welfare economics, money, banking, agriculture and natural resources. In *Principles of Political Economy* (1848), unlike Carey, he draws a distinction between agricultural produce and mining as the fruits of the land. He points out that, first, coal and metal deposits are more limited than agricultural land but if there is no effective demand for some deposits their market value is zero or near zero. Second, mineral deposits are exhaustible and thus, in the long run, more prone to the law of diminishing returns in cumulative extraction. On the other hand, however, the mining sector is more susceptible to technological developments in cutting the cost of the operation than agriculture. Furthermore, a sudden discovery of superior deposits also counter-balances the progress of existing mines towards exhaustion. Thus, his overall position regarding the long-term prospects in mining seems to be more optimistic and reflects the earlier views of Smith and Carey (Robinson 1989). In his analysis, Mill also mentions fisheries along with mining, suggesting that the superior quality of those already in use are likely to be improved. In this respect he differs from Ricardo.

Another notable point in Mill's writing is that, for the first time, the idea that agriculture is fundamentally different from mining is discussed. He suggests that, unlike farming, mining is characterised by a trade-off between present and future productivity and this requires an optimal time profile in operation which involves a user cost. As we shall see later, this idea is crucial in the development of the fundamental principle in mining economics.

Mill provides two scenarios for the extractive sector as a whole. First, the natural sequence of events will gradually lead to diminishing returns on the extensive margin and the user cost will become substantial. Second, this process – i.e. 'the natural course of events' – could be interrupted by the discovery of superior deposits which would reduce the price, leading to the abandonment of existing high-cost low-grade mines. In this respect, it could be argued that for the extractive sector Mill takes up a position between Smith and Ricardo; certainly, he seems to be more optimistic than his predecessors in the development of the extractive sector.

At a much broader level, involving population growth and economic progress as a whole, Mill appears to be on the side of Malthus and Ricardo. Mill points out that growth in nature is not an endless process; every growth, including the economic one, must eventually come to a lasting equilibrium. According to him, a period of sustained growth did take place in the eighteenth and nineteenth centuries because of mankind's fierce struggle for material advancement, but essentially this is not sustainable, nor is it desirable.

Only foolish people will want to live in a world crowded by human beings and their material possessions. Solitude is an essential ingredient of human well-being. There is no point in contemplating a world where every square metre of land is brought into cultivation, every flowery waste of natural pasture is ploughed up, every plant and animal species exterminated as humanity's rival for food, and every hedgerow or superfluous tree rooted out. It will be the ultimate waste if the earth loses that great portion of its grandeur and pleasantness so that we can support a large population on it. 'I sincerely hope, for the sake of posterity, that they will be content to be stationary, long before necessity compels them to it' (Mill 1848).

Although Mill's views on human well-being are more than one hundred years old, they are supported by most conservationists, who believe that economic growth will neither solve our problems nor improve future conditions. His views are also a challenge for some welfare economists who argue that social well-being will be maximised when the greatest consumption capacity for the greatest number of individuals is attained. In the tradition of Mill, economic growth is essential only for the developing nations. In the developed nations, however, the real issue is the distribution of income, not its growth. Mill was unimpressed with the idea – which was fashionable then as well as now– of the importance of sustained growth and capital accumulation above anything else. He believed that the struggle to progress in terms of material goods in which people compete against one another is neither natural nor desirable for mankind and will end up in failure.

William Stanley Jevons is regarded by many as one of the economists who pioneered neoclassical thinking by his theories on the marginal utility of consumption. However, his work on coal is more in the spirit of the classical tradition. Unlike Malthus and Ricardo, Jevons lived at the time when rapid industrialisation was well under way in Britain. In addition to his marginal utility theory, he wrote on a number of areas of economics including resource exhaustion and a theory of business cycle relating to sun spots. In his theory of resource exhaustion, Jevons made the extraction of coal a central point by emphasising that it was one of the most important constraints on Britain's economic development. According to him, rapid industrialisation was already depleting the rich and easily accessible reserves and forcing miners to extract from less easily accessible stock.

From 1850 onwards there was a rapid increase in both coal output and price in Britain. Table 3.1 shows the output and price trends of coal between 1850 and 1869.

Jevons made the rising price of coal an ominous issue in his book *The Coal Question: An Inquiry Concerning the Progress of the Nation and the Probable Exhaustion of our Coal Mines* (1865). He emphasised that coal was of central significance in Britain's economic supremacy: 'coal alone can command in sufficient abundance either the iron or the steam; and coal, therefore, commands this age – the Age of Coal.' Then he added that the hasty depletion of our most valuable seams was taking place everywhere and soon coal reserves would be exhausted or costs increased to a point where industry would no longer operate:

Table 3.1 Annual estimate of coal production, 1850–69, and index of pithead prices

Year	*Tons (million)*	*Price (1990 = 100)*
1850	62.5	38.5
1851	62.5	37.7
1852	68.3	35.4
1853	71.1	43.1
1854	75.1	49.2
1855	76.4	49.2
1856	79.0	48.5
1857	81.9	46.9
1958	80.3	43.3
1859	82.8	44.6
1860	89.2	46.9
1861	91.1	48.5
1862	55.7	45.4
1863	99.1	44.6
1864	102.1	48.5
1865	104.9	53.8
1866	106.4	59.2
1867	108.2	57.7
1868	110.9	54.6
1869	115.5	50.0

Source: Church (1986)

> I must point out the painful fact that a state of growth will therefore long render out consumption of coal comparable with the total supply. In the increasing depth and difficulty of mining we shall meet that vague but inevitable boundary that will stop our progress.

Nevertheless, time has proved that the exhaustion of British coal deposits did not in fact take place. True, some mines were exhausted, but many rich deposits were discovered along the way. Today, coal is one of the most abundant fossil fuel deposits in Britain. Unfortunately, it has become a politically sensitive and even troublesome commodity, especially since the end of the Second World War, and some have used the commodity as a political football to further their positions. In the 1950s, government encouraged coal production by way of various measures such as subsidies and its use in power stations. In the 1960s and 1970s, coal miners became a major political pressure group creating problems for both the Labour and Conservative governments. In 1984, the Conservative government took on the striking miners who were attempting to bring down the elected government. The strike ended with the defeat of the National Union of Miners which lost considerable sums of money in fighting the strike. Its membership shrank as many miners accepted redundancy and left the industry. The Coal Board lost twenty million tons of deep-mined output; seventy-three coal faces were closed and many others damaged. The result was a great political victory for the Conservative government and since then the coal industry has been in continuous decline. The government argues that there is insufficient demand for British coal at competitive prices to justify its exploitation, a view not everybody would accept.

The current 'coal question' is quite different from that predicted by Jevons. However, some believe that Jevons was somewhat agitated by the idea of the exhaustion of resources and was given to exaggeration (Hutchinson 1953). Humorously, Keynes has pointed out that Jevons held similar ideas about paper and hoarded large quantities of packing and writing paper – to the extent that fifty years after his death his children had still not used up the stock (Spiegel 1952).

AN ALTERNATIVE VIEW OF SCARCITY: THE AMERICAN CONSERVATION MOVEMENT OF 1890–1920

The concern expressed by classical economists such as Malthus, Ricardo, Mill and Jevons on population growth, resource availability and economic progress became well known among a wide range of intellectual groups in the second half of the nineteenth century. However, some natural scientists felt that the views held by economists on resource scarcity were an obstruction and gross over-simplification. For example, Marsh (1865) argued that the natural environment is one of great diversity, interdependence and complexity which cannot be reduced into inputs and outputs; nor can the role of man, as part of the living environment, be simplified as that of producer and/or consumer. In the words of Barnett and Morse (1963), 'One might as well, we gather from Marsh, describe man as a quantum of weight or a linear dimension and not to mention that he is a living organism, or characterise a Rembrandt painting as a mineral-vegetable deposit, or reduce nature to the classical economic quantum land.'

The natural resource universe is in a process of continuous evolution which is extremely complex and diverse and Marsh argues that if, in a continuous process of interaction, man is capable of changing nature, nature in turn will change man. There are many possibilities, therefore, to this balance of man and nature – some desirable, some undesirable. Thus, the stagnation doctrine of Ricardo and Malthus is at odds with nature and cannot be a credible theory.

Marsh was one of the pioneers of the Conservation Movement of 1890–1920 which focused mainly on issues concerning the United States of America. The movement argued that scarcity is a fact of life; it can reveal itself as a regional or even global physical availability at a given point in time or over time. For example, fossil fuel deposits must ultimately be fixed in quantity. A new discovery of rich deposits should not create a wrong impression of abundance and give way to irresponsible utilisation, as what is burned now for trivial purposes will not be available for something very important in the future. Metal deposits, although recyclable, are also subject to exhaustion due to a variety of factors such as corrosion, wear, damage and loss.

Apart from Marsh, other influential personalities behind the American Conservation Movement were Henry Thoreau, John Muir and George Santanya. Thoreau, who is now recognised as one of the earliest ecophilosophers of the Conservation Movement, was highly critical of his country's preoccupation with economic growth and consumerism (1854). He believed this would greatly restrict human freedom, which can only be achieved in harmony with nature. Sessions (1995) contends that some of Thoreau's expressions, such as 'In wildness is the preservation of the world', provide a foundation for modern environmentalism as well as for the nineteenth-century American Conservation Movement. In his time, Thoreau was virtually alone in his views.

John Muir, the Scots-born American explorer and naturalist, remained a mystery figure for a long time after his death as his family denied researchers access to most of his writings. As a young man he used to walk through the North American wilderness deep in thought about nature and life.

On one occasion during a walk through a swamp he saw a wild orchid hidden from human eyes. This made him realise that, contrary to the ideas of anthropocentric theology, things do not exist for humans, but for themselves. (This issue will be discussed in some length in Chapter 11.) Despite a Calvinistic upbringing, his ecocentric view gathered strength during a thousand-mile walk to the Gulf of Mexico. He reached his philosophical position by experience in nature, not by way of a dogmatic teaching.

According to Sessions (1995), the ecocentric pantheism of Thoreau and Muir had made a sharp break from anthropocentrism. Like Thoreau, Muir developed an understanding of nature by the use of participatory scientific method – for example, lying down on glacier-polished granite in order to 'think like a glacier'. Muir was a leading activist who cultivated American interest in the protection of the wild, and was chosen to be the first president of the Sierra Club in 1892, a position he held until his death in 1914 (for more on Muir's influence on the American Conservation Movement, see Turner 1985).

In the twentieth century George Santanya, a Harvard philosopher, was another influential writer who was disillusioned by his colleagues' preoccupation with economic growth. In his retirement speech at Berkeley, he pointed out that if the Western philosophers since Socrates had lived among the mountains of California their systems of thought would have been different. They would see clearly that man is not and has never been the centre and the pivot of the universe. Calvinism saw both humans and nature as sinful in need of redemption. Transcendentalism, on the other hand, saw nature as a beautiful commodity which was a systematic subjectivism, a sham system of nature. Both Calvinism and Transcendentalism failed to provide restraint on exploiting the nature. Instead they provided a justification for the technological domination of nature.

According to the pioneers of the American Conservation Movement scarcity is permanent. It occurs even under conditions of extreme frugality, but the extent of scarcity is gravely aggravated by waste, which the movement condemned as both selfish and foolish behaviour. Economic concepts such as consumer sovereignty and laissez-faire often undermine the wise use of natural resources. According to Ise (1926), who studied the conservation literature, free market economic philosophy encourages competition without sufficient public intervention and glorifies consumer sovereignty by making individuals apathetic. With regard to natural resource scarcity, this had no following in the movement.

The conservation doctrine identifies a number of wasteful activities, including reckless behaviour towards natural resources such as polluting rivers, destroying forests that maintain ecological balance, allowing pastures to be overgrazed, and excessive reliance on fossil fuel for electricity generation even when hydro-power is readily available. Even if these deeds are dictated by the pressure of competition or cost-cutting, they cannot be condoned. The conservation doctrine refuses to acknowledge societies which create market structures that generate unnecessary natural resource scarcity.

Activities which fail to attain maximum physical yield are also condemned. Some of these are: leaving whole or parts of crops to perish in fields; letting fruit go rotten on trees; premature closure of oil, gas or coal fields; not producing hydroelectricity at full capacity and relying in part on fossil fuel. In other words, obtaining inferior results from nature is also wasteful. This view contradicts the Faustmann–Samuelson solution to the optimal forest rotation in which the maximum sustainable yield is condemned. Mismanagement of natural resources such as allowing forest fires to take place, or allowing coal mines to flood is considered another form of waste, as is the misuse of end products, such as not turning off lights and heating when they are no longer required.

American Conservationists also believed that without sufficient public control forces of the free market would not only intensify scarcity, which is a permanent feature of nature, but would create large monopolies to dominate the ownership of the natural resource base. In this way, unfair profits would be generated by a few at the expense of the majority. The rich have always had a tendency to indulge in extravagant and wasteful living which creates envy and discontent.

According to Hays (1959) the Conservation Movement was initiated largely by middle-class city dwellers who witnessed the effects of rapid industrialisation on the natural environment, as well as on American society, and did not like what they saw. The organisation of labour and business communities into opposing groups not only created a situation of conflict, but also undermined individualism. Furthermore, life in large and ugly urban developments destroyed the community atmosphere and weakened religious beliefs and traditional American values. The movement started out with a true doctrine focused on scarcity, but in later years, in order to gather political support, it was broadened to include diverse issues such as immigration, child labour, anti-trust legislation and anti-industrialisation. This created internal contradictions and, as a political movement, the doctrine became compromising. Furthermore, the movement was dominated by the cult personalities of its leaders, who included Theodore Roosevelt.

Another of its leaders, Pinchot, identified five items of material as indispensable to the American civilisation; these were water, coal, timber, iron and agricultural products (1910). Barnett and Morse (1963) argue that this approach has separated the Conservation Movement's view of scarcity from that of Malthus and Ricardo. In the former, scarcity is multidimensional, type and quality specific. One type and quality of resource may be more scarce than others, there may be great regional variations in needs as well as supplies. The classical scarcity of Malthus and Ricardo is highly aggregated in the form of agricultural land.

At the 1908 Governors' Conference in the White House, a decision was taken to make an inventory of the natural resources of the United States; this resulted in numerous estimates in later years. The movement adopted a line of rational and thrifty use of all the nation's endowments by taking into account the needs of future generations.

The Conservation Movement emphasises the interdependence in nature of attaining a dynamic equilibrium. Biological organisms and geological and atmospheric features interact in the form of overlapping systems of interdependence. A given state of equilibrium can be altered by man as well as nature and it is this equilibrium which determines the limits of scarcity.

One of the weaknesses of the movement was that it did not, at any time during its existence, use any form of economic analysis to study scarcity. Furthermore, by and large, the movement side-stepped the economic history of the nineteenth century, a period in which rapid industrialisation and urbanisation took place. Economic concepts such as consumer sovereignty, cost efficiency, competitive behaviour, which can be very useful in studying the phenomenon of scarcity and environmental quality, were dismissed as, at best, irrelevant or, at worst, harmful to the movement. For example, maximum sustainable yield in resource use, which underpins policy recommendation by the American conservationists, is a defective concept in sectors such as fishery and forestry. Economists, in their analyses, take into account the cost of maintaining, say, fish stocks, at maximum sustainable levels. If the cost is a rising function of the fishing effort, as it must be, then it would be best to maintain catches at a lower level (Kula 1994). Likewise, removing the last cobble of coal, or extracting the last barrel of oil from the resource base does not make economical sense if their extraction turns out to be more costly than the value of the output.

It could be said that American conservationists broadened and popularised the Ricardo–Malthusian concept of scarcity despite the fact that they had reservations about various aspects of it. Members had the advantage of at least a hundred years of hindsight regarding the effects of improving agricultural technology and the limits of arable land. Unlike economists, the movement did not make any precise recommendation about resource depletion ratios, but instead advocated frugal and responsible utilisation at all times. Scarcity existed well before Ricardo and Malthus were born and it will exist well after the Conservation Movement has gone; in fact, it will exist forever. In the view of Barnett and Morse (1963), despite its shortcomings, the American Conservation Movement was a political and social success. Although its impact was not immediate, the movement laid the foundation of environmentalism for later years.

4

SOCIALISM, MARXISM AND THE ENVIRONMENT

EARLY SOCIALISTS

Just as the liberals had prepared the ground for Adam Smith's theory of free enterprise, the early socialists did the same for Karl Marx's *Das Kapital*. The Marxist theory did not develop in a void, it had forerunners not only in the classical economists but also in the early socialist movement, which was sharply critical of capitalist practice.

The early critics of the capitalist system launched their attack on two fronts. First, the development of a privileged capitalist class that had given rise to the creation of an acutely underprivileged working class which intensified as the process of capital accumulation gathered pace. The rise of capitalism meant poverty, hard labour, dangerous working conditions and harsh supervision, not only for the workers, but also for their wives and children. To them the market mechanism in which they had weak bargaining powers appeared to be as harsh as a feudal and tyrannical landlord. Second, the pace and rigorous methods of capitalism, which swept away without scruples the old institutions and modes of thought, especially liberal thinking, troubled some writers. It had done all this in the name of humanity by promising freedom, equality, justice and wealth for all, but the truth was different.

Sismondi, in his *New Principles of Political Economy* (1951) [1827], argued that, essentially, political economy has a moral purpose. Its aim is not the creation of wealth as such, but the relationship between wealth and people. Therefore, the distribution of wealth for the purpose of achieving social justice is as important as its creation. In his travels to England, Germany, Italy, Belgium and Switzerland, Sismondi noticed that expansion of productive forces did not create an equivalent increase in the well-being of the masses. He saw a bleak future for mankind with this type of 'progress'. Small farmers, workshop owners and similar operators were disappearing due to the activities of large-scale enterprises and capital was being concentrated in the hands of the few. Labour and ownership became almost entirely separated.

Sismondi also noticed an inherent weakness in the capitalist mode of progress whereby intense competition would lead to overproduction of goods which could not be sold while, with declining demand, neither capital nor labour could be easily withdrawn from industries. The workers could not remain the producers of everything and consumers of only a small part of the output. This process was unsustainable. Unlike Malthus, Sismondi did not believe that population would overrun the means of subsistence. When a worker was truly free he would have control over his situation; he would judge his present condition and, furthermore, he would calculate his future choices. Therefore, he would determine when to marry and how many children to have. Sismondi wanted to see the revival of small farmers and artisans as an alternative to the system existing at that time.

Proudhon, although characterised by Marx as a petty bourgeois, was a leading figure in trade unionism and in the anarchistic doctrine. His main objective was not to establish a dictatorship of any kind, but a social system which would give justice to all without the state imposing rules and regulations, which he believed would only create oppression. In his book, *Economic Contradictions and a Philosophy of Misery* published in 1846, he pointed out that contradictions were an eternal human condition. He set out to discover the right idea which would abolish contradictions, at least in theory, and help to create a better society than the existing one.

Although Proudhon stated that 'property was theft', he regarded private property as an essential condition for freedom. He thought that labour was the only source of wealth, yet it received little or none of what it created. All individuals, labourers as well as others, should be able to enjoy the fruits of their work. Extraction of rent, interest and profit ought to be abolished because they were earned without work. Furthermore, land and raw materials were provided by nature. Unlike Marxists proper, Proudhon did not suggest common ownership of the means of production. His suggestion, like Sismondi's, was that agriculture and industry ought to be parcelled out between numerous small producers. However, he realised that large-scale industry could not be abolished entirely, and thus had to be integrated within the 'new society' of small farmers and artisans.

Other writers with socialist convictions who lived in the late eighteenth and nineteenth centuries, such as William Thompson, John Gray, John Bray and Thomas Hodgskin, shared a number of common ideas. For instance, they all accepted that the amount of labour embodied in any product was a measure of its exchange value and, further, that the wages paid to labourers by the capitalists were always less than the value of the product. This was nothing more than the theory of surplus value which in later years was tortuously developed by Karl Marx.

A further point of consensus between these writers was that they all disliked the capitalist system of private property and the distribution of income. There was also general agreement with the utilitarian doctrine advocated by Jeremy Bentham (1748–1831) that the proper objective of all conduct and legislation was 'the greatest happiness of the greatest number', since this view had an egalitarian flavour. For example, Hodgskin argued that the capitalist system deprived labourers, the sole creators of wealth, of their surplus value by instituting claims on land and capital. This not only created unnatural justice, but misery for the masses. A capitalist system, therefore, could never achieve the greatest happiness of the greatest number.

KARL MARX

The effect of Karl Marx on the political and economic life of the twentieth century has been profound. No other economist has had such an impact on the lives of billions of people. His theories on economics and social engineering eventually led to the division of the world between communist and non-communist nations, to many wars between and within nations, to the nuclear arms race which brought humanity to the threshold of total destruction, and, last but not least, to environmental abuse which has no parallel in human history. Many wicked deeds have been committed in the name of Marxist ideology by his followers and consequently by his opponents. Stone (1996) argues that the Marxist experiment led to the direct killing of fifty million people by Stalin in the Soviet Union and 100 million by Mao in China alone. Karl Marx's walk on this earth was eventful.

Ironically, Marx was a well-meaning thinker. His writings contain care and compassion for the oppressed masses for whom he genuinely tried to construct a social theory for a better world.

Although the industrial revolution of the nineteenth century provided improved living standards for a substantial number of individuals, for a few it created a lot of wealth and prestige. As far as the socialist school was concerned, industrial revolution was, with some justification, a hell on earth for the working class. Pay was very poor, hours of work were long, women and children as young as nine or ten were employed in large numbers in harsh and dangerous sweatshops. Working and living conditions were particularly difficult in England, where Marx wrote his major work *Das Kapital*, the first volume of which was published in 1867. The second volume was edited by Engels and published in 1885; the last part was not issued until 1894 (Marx 1867, 1885, 1894).

Poverty was not a new phenomenon in England when Marx was constructing his theories. The industrial revolution which was taking place in a laissez-faire atmosphere promised abundance. For the first time, it seemed that mankind would rise to a much higher standard of living thanks to the fruits of the market revolution in progress. But the vast slums of British industrial towns where poverty was endemic were telling a different story. Many socialists, including Karl Marx, believed that private ownership, which enabled the capitalist class to reap rich rewards and sit back taking the profits while the workers slaved away, was at the root of this great misery. Furthermore, wealth gave capitalists political power. With this they defended their privileged positions and the existing political system rewarded them handsomely.

Karl Marx was the son of a German civil servant of Jewish faith. He studied law, philosophy, politics and religion at German universities with a view to becoming a lecturer. But events led him to become a journalist, first in Cologne and then in Paris, where he married his childhood sweetheart, the daughter of a German aristocrat. At the early stages of his career Marx was impressed by Proudhon and, in particular, with his views that the ownership of property was theft. In later years Marx became critical of Proudhon's views, especially the idea that population growth was responsible for low wages and dismal living conditions. The real villain, according to Marx, was the oppressive capitalist system. In Paris, Marx met Friedrich Engels, a wealthy philosopher, who supported him morally and financially for the rest of his life. Marx was expelled from France at the request of the Prussian government, due to his radical writings, and went to Brussels where, with Engels, in 1848 he wrote his famous *Communist Manifesto*, in which he invited workers of the world to unite in revolution to overthrow the capitalist system.

According to Marx, economic relationships are the fundamental driving force in any society. Individuals, especially in industrialised countries, are motivated by their economic interests. In a capitalist production structure interest groups can be put into two conflicting camps, workers and capitalists. One group can prosper only at the expense of the other and workers are not the most favoured species of the capitalist system (Marx 1859; Marx and Engels 1948). For example, in the *Communist Manifesto* it is stated that:

> The history of all hitherto existing society is the history of class struggles. Freeman and slave, patrician and plebeian, lord and serf, guild master and journeyman, in a word, oppressor and the oppressed, stood in constant opposition to one another. . . . The modern bourgeois society that has sprouted from the ruins of feudal society has not done away with class antagonisms. It has but established new classes, new conditions of opposition, new forms of struggle in place of the old ones.

Das Kapital, which is a long and highly intricate work, has implications for resource use and the environment in which these issues are seen from the viewpoint of class struggle. It contains writings on natural resources in a number of places, especially in Volume III, but a more extensive analysis of the extractive sector can be found in another work, *Theories of Surplus Value*, which was published after Marx's death (for an English translation, see Marx

1951, 1969). Extractive sectors, such as mining, fishing and quarrying, are characterised by labour intensity as they are low on application of capital. According to Marx, labour is the only source of wealth creation and thus in an ideal society it should reap all the benefits of production. Because of its labour intensity, the extractive sector has the highest surplus value creation and it is in this sector that workers are most vulnerable.

However, Marx notes that due to the ease with which production is realised in the extractive sector, and with intense competition between operators, the output is sold rather cheaply. Therefore, the resulting benefits to owners in the form of rent do not represent the true surplus value of labour. In other words, low rent is a feature of the extractive sector in general. Mining is a special case where capital requirement is higher than in other extractive industries. This view, however, is not maintained throughout Marx's writings. In the *Theories of Surplus Value*, he argues that coal mining has low capital intensity. Furthermore, Marx does not make much distinction between branches of natural resources such as quarries, fisheries and forestry in that they are treated alike in spite of the fact that they have different properties.

Another point which is overlooked by Marx is the user cost in the mining sector. That is, present extraction deprives owners of future profits had extraction been postponed. Robinson (1989) notes that the main reason for this is the position taken by Marx that these resources are available in abundance and thus the user cost is zero, or near zero. In line with Adam Smith and Henry Carey, Marx takes the position that in the natural resource-based sector there is no tendency for decreasing return to scale. Thus, abundance rather than scarcity is likely to be the case in future years. There are a number of reasons mentioned for this. First, progress in science and technology would outpace physical difficulties encountered in natural resource-based sectors, including farming. Poor soil can become viable as agricultural technology improves. Less easily accessible mineral deposits could be put into operation with improved extractive technology. Second, improved communication methods may bring better soils, as well as richer mine deposits, into use. Third, institutional changes can expand production; for example, the release of previously unworked communal land may be put into use.

On the Ricardo–Malthusian idea of the increasingly diminishing returns of land as less and less productive soil gets dragged into operation, Marx takes the opposite view. According to him, differentials in rent are due to varying quality of soil and the expansion of agriculture does not necessarily require a movement from the best to the worst quality land.

Marx notes that the capitalist mode of production is likely to degrade the soil. For example, in Volume I of *Das Kapital*, he boldly states that progress in capitalist agriculture not only robs the labourer of surplus value, but robs the fertility of the soil as well by reckless exploitation:

> Capitalist technology, therefore, develops technology and the combining together of various processes into a social whole, only by sapping the original sources of wealth – the soil and the labourer.
>
> (Marx 1867)

So, in Marxist theory, capitalism is bad news for the environment as well as for the working class.

A cornerstone in Marxist analysis is the labour theory of value which is comprised of two parts: use value and exchange value. The former relates to commodities' material qualities. Different use values exist due to the different material qualities of commodities which realise their purpose in consumption. Labour, although the producer of this value, is not the only source as human effort cannot be exercised without natural resources. Differences in use value embody different ratios of labour and nature and the latter must always exist.

The exchange value relates to the amount of labour that a commodity contains in its production. This amount can be measured by the labour time each commodity requires to be produced. It is important not to think that the less skilled or the slower the worker the greater the exchange value. In its measurement we need to consider the average degree of skill and speed that is necessary to produce a commodity in a collective, or social, production arrangement under normal conditions.

It is important in Marxist analysis to give labour a social significance as the worker is part of the social network. In this the individual worker is generalised to become a part of a social production arrangement. This applies to both use and exchange values. For example, a simple peasant family's needs are satisfied by producing, say, potatoes, clothing and shelter as a collective family effort. The labour of each individual is a part of the common effort by the family. Likewise, in a more complicated and integrated society each labourer is an organ of the common labour power. The capitalist economic system relies upon private means of production, individual enterprise and private exchange. According to Marx, the social labour can be apportioned by way of exchange value.

> The farm which this proportional division of labour operates, in a society where the interconnection of social labour is manifested in the private exchange of individual products of labour, is precisely the exchange-value of these products.
>
> (Marx, Letters to Dr Kugelmann, pp. 73–4, quoted in Roll 1953)

Exchange value, in a way, is a relationship between individuals but is concealed behind other things. The labour time is the measure of the exchange value of the product and the social relationship of the producers takes the form of a social relationship of products. As stated above, in a capitalist system, every commodity has use and exchange value. In order to acquire the former, a commodity has to meet a special need, not necessarily for its owner. For example, for a baker a loaf of bread is a means of economic relation but for a customer it becomes a use value. In the process of exchange it also becomes exchange value.

Natural resources such as land, which Marx regarded as a gift of nature, on which no human labour has been expended has substantial exchange value. In Marxist thought there are four possible theories of rent: monopoly theory, differential rent theory, capital theory of rent and Marx's own theory. In the first one, rent comes about from the monopoly price of agricultural commodities and the monopoly price from the land ownership. The price of agricultural produce is higher than its value because its supply is below the demand. This arises due to the law of diminishing returns and thus the supply cannot keep up with demand. The second theory coincides with the first one in that differentials in rent are due to the variations in land fertility. The third relates to the use of capital on land in order to improve its fertility. Here, rent is linked to the interest on capital equipment used to enhance productivity. However, this theory is incapable of explaining the rent of land on which no capital has been used.

In Marx's own theory, rent is linked with private ownership of land which, according to him, does not invalidate the labour theory of value. Rent is a form of surplus profit. Competition creates a single price for the produce regardless of whether it comes from highly fertile or less fertile land. If the market price turns out to be favourable for the capitalist because he happens to own fertile land, then he will obtain a surplus above the average rate of profit. The lower the cost of production the higher the surplus profit.

The Marxist theory of economic development involves a continuous accumulation of capital which is created and re-created by the labour. That is, accumulation is transformation of surplus value into capital. In the process of continuous capital accumulation, more and more labour is required alongside more and more natural resource-based commodities. Labour is given subsistence so that workers can sustain their physical capabilities and reproduce. Capitalists take whatever they wish to consume and the rest is reinvested. But here there is a conflict in the capitalist mind between accumulation and consumption as proceeds become available. The rate of accumulation intensifies with more labour and also longer hours coupled with harsher conditions imposed on workers. Increase in demand for labour may at times exceed the supply, pushing up wages, but this will only be temporary. On the other hand, improved production methods will curtail the demand for labour, creating surplus labour, the industrial reserve army, from which labour power can be drawn when needed.

Neither Marx nor Engels were impressed by the Malthusian theory that output can be increased by an arithmetic progression. For example, Engels (1844) argued that:

> Since increase in knowledge is at least as much as population, the latter increases in proportion to the size of the previous generation, since it advances in proportion to the knowledge bequeathed to it by the previous generation, and thus under the most ordinary conditions also in geometrical progression. And what is impossible in science?

Nevertheless, the capitalist system perpetually robbed workers of the benefits of technology and production, as the system ensures that workers are paid just enough to maintain their work effort and support their families in a most spartan fashion, so that a new generation of workers can be produced. Workers had no choice but to accept the wages and work conditions offered by the capitalist. First, they had no alternative prospects as they were driven from the land to the cities by a multitude of factors, as mentioned in Chapter 2, such as the enclosure movement. Second, workers were so numerous that they were in competition with one another for jobs in the cities, which did not improve their bargaining positions. However, Marx conceded that wage rates may not be established at biological levels on every occasion. In addition to the biological requirements of workers, the class struggle was another factor in determining the wage levels. For example, workers could be successful in gaining wages above the minimum *socially* acceptable levels, but, in return, capitalists for their part would increase the length and intensity of the work. In the event, what was given by one hand would be taken back by the other, leaving the workers in a no-win situation.

Marx saw capitalism in a state of perpetual growth in order to accumulate more and more wealth for the capitalist. There is a strong desire to invest by the profit-takers for greater and greater rewards. As he put it: 'Accumulate, accumulate. It is their Moses and their prophets' (Marx 1867). In addition to the capitalist psychology, there was the pressure of competition which made the system grow until its inevitable breakdown.

Marx suggested a number of reasons for the unsustainability of the capitalist mode of production. First, as the output expanded there would be a glut due to lack of purchasing power as workers are deprived of their surplus value. Then production would be cut back, unemployment would rise and surplus value, i.e. profit, would decline bringing economic expansion to a temporary halt. After the surplus commodities had been disposed of the system would move again until the next crisis. But, in the long run, the process of boom and bust would become more severe and unmanageable as capitalism developed.

There is a stark difference between the thinking of Marx and Ricardo about how the crises develop. Ricardo's explanation of falling profits is based upon the law of diminishing returns of the soil, whereas in the Marxist analysis crises are inherent in the structure of capitalist industrial progress. Second, as the economy grows in a cyclical fashion, more and more wealth is concentrated in the hands of fewer and fewer groups as small businesses and artisans perish and join the ranks of the workers. Furthermore, technological innovations would diminish work opportunities for workers as their jobs would be taken over by machines. Third, environmental factors, especially when soil is used in a most reckless fashion would make the system unsustainable.

Marx believed that although capitalism was a historic fact, sooner or later, through revolution, it would give way to a classless communist society in which there would be abundance and happiness for all. Ultimately, income distribution would be based on the principle that from each according to his abilities, to each according to his needs. Marx was optimistic about the future state of the environment and adequacy of natural resources in the new classless society which would be built from the ashes of capitalism. Fruits of scientific progress would make greater wealth available, which then would be distributed according to need. In view of Marx's optimism regarding future prospects, Robinson (1989) put him into the same group as Adam Smith and Henry Carey.

A LEAP IN TIME: THE MARXIST EXPERIMENT AND THE ENVIRONMENT

The Marxist ideology led to seventy years of uninterrupted experiment in Russia and forty-five years in the eastern European countries, with disastrous results for the environment. The 1990s began with the disintegration of communist regimes in Eastern Europe and the Soviet Union, with one country after another abandoning communism in favour of free market and pluralist democracy. The collapse of communist systems and gradual opening up of these countries has led to scandalous revelations about the conduct of former communist governments. The abuse of the environment, as well as of human rights, in these countries was common knowledge, but what has startled the world was the extent of incompetence and callousness of the former governments in dealing with their people, the economies and the environment.

Article 18 of the last Soviet Constitution, now defunct, stated that all necessary steps would be taken to protect and make rational use of the country's land, its mineral and water resources and the purity of air and seas, for the well-being of future as well as present generations. However, the regime left behind an appalling catalogue of environmental blunders; the reversible ones will take decades to sort out.

Russell (1991) contends that the extent of environmental problems is multidimensional and stems from almost total neglect. One reason for such a neglect was the domination of supply-side economic management in which nothing was allowed to stand in the way of quantitative fulfilment of numerical production targets. Pearce and Turner (1990) argue that another important reason for failure was that the Soviet territory was fragile and planning blunders quickly broke its back. Only about 10 per cent of the country was suitable for lucrative agriculture and only 1 per cent of this received annual rainfall of 70 cm or more. The bulk of the Soviet agriculture was conducted on arid or semi-arid lands supported by massive irrigation programmes which were fundamentally flawed. As for heavy industry, since planners had decided to locate industrial plants in and around population centres, this required large quantities of mineral and energy deposits to be extracted and transported from distant regions. Concentration of population and industrial activities in such centres led to excessive land and air pollution. However, the aridity and vastness of the former Soviet Union cannot be shown to be the major factors for environmental devastation as the situation was equally bad in small but fertile countries such as Bulgaria and Romania.

Perhaps one of the most important reasons for environmental failure was that the communist governments failed to respond to the needs of people. Furthermore, they failed to motivate workers, including managers of economic units, to act with due regard for good husbandry of the natural resources and the environment. There was total control of the media by the Communist Party, which tried to conceal the growing environmental and other problems until the whole system collapsed.

In the early stages of the communist experiment in the Soviet Union, planners made heavy industry and collectivisation of agriculture top priority. Consequently the Stalinist era of 1928–53 witnessed a process of heavy industrialisation, collectivisation and militarisation which inflicted great pain on the Soviet people. In 1948 Stalin launched his plan for the Transformation of Nature with grandiose projects designed to conquer nature 'scientifically' and ultimately to overpower the great 'enemy of mankind', capitalism. After this, the Soviet economy began to grow rapidly. The launch of Sputnik into orbit in 1957, followed soon after by the flight of Yuri Gagarin, the first man in space, marked the heights of Soviet success.

The process of relentless militarisation and industrial push took its toll on natural resources and the environment. In the 1960s the Soviet population constituted less than 1 per cent of the world population, but the Soviet economy was using up natural resources quite disproportionately to its size in human numbers. Table 4.1 illustrates this point.

There were many environmentally unsound agricultural projects which involved the diversion of rivers. The most ambitious ones aimed at taking water from the northward flowing rivers and diverting it to the more arid and warmer regions of the south. In European Russia, the Omega, Sukhona, Pechara and Vychegda rivers were diverted, and in Siberia the natural flowing patterns of the Ob, Irtish and Yenese rivers were modified (Gerasimov and Gindin 1977; L'Vovich 1978). In central Asia, the Aral Sea project involved diverting waters from the Siri Derya and Amu Derya rivers to irrigate large areas, mainly to grow cotton.

Table 4.1 Non-renewable resource consumption by the Soviet Union in the 1960s

Resource	*Soviet Union's consumption (percentage of world total)*
Aluminium	12
Cobalt	13
Iron	24
Lead	13
Petroleum	12
Zinc	11

Source: US Bureau of Mines (1970)

These agricultural projects turned out to be environmental disasters on a colossal scale. North-to-south river diversion schemes disrupted the ecology of the entire region and concern has been expressed for wider consequences, particularly on the Arctic Sea ice. The Aral Sea has lost more than half of its water since the establishment of irrigation projects and a salt desert has formed on the dry seabed; the wind carries the salt and dust long distances, affecting crops and human health in a wide area. Today, camels walk and beached ships lie on the exposed bed of the Aral Sea, which was once the fourth largest inland sea in the world. A much diminished fishing fleet now docks 40 km from its original harbour. Some reports suggest that resulting changes in rainfall pattern affect food supplies as far away as Pakistan and Afghanistan.

Further to the north-east, Soviet planners established large-scale wood-processing industries around Lake Baikal. These plants discharge effluent either directly into the lake or into rivers feeding it. Furthermore, large-scale logging operations around the lake have increased silt deposited in the lake. The global water system has natural mechanisms by which it regulates and cleanses itself of pollutants, but waters of enclosed seas and aquifers turn over very slowly; for example, the Baltic Sea is replenished only once every eighty years. Thus, the problems resulting from the pollutants dumped there by communist governments will remain longstanding. Even if effluent discharges around Lake Baikal are stopped now, the pollution problems will remain a burden for many generations to come.

Perhaps one of the most worrying legacies of the communist era is actual and potential nuclear pollution. The White Sea is already contaminated by nuclear discharge (Gore 1992). Recently, alarming reports appeared in the Western media that the Soviets have dumped large quantities of highly toxic nuclear waste in inadequate containers in and around the Barents Sea. In 1993 the signing of the historic Start II Nuclear Disarmament Treaty by George Bush and Boris Yeltsin was an important step forward towards the reduction of the world's nuclear arsenal. However, dismantling nuclear arms and storing radioactive material is a very expensive business (Kula 1994).

One wonders how the Russians, who are going through a very lean period in their economic history, are going to be able to afford safe disposal.

The nuclear accident in 1986 at Chernobyl, in the Ukraine, is a constant reminder of what could happen in other parts of the former Soviet bloc, which houses many unsafe nuclear reactors. The Chernobyl accident contaminated a wide area and has affected, and will continue to affect, the health and safety of many generations to come. Recently, press reports contained revelations by Russia's former chief nuclear safety inspector, Vladimir Kuznetsaw, that Moscow has fifty secret and essentially unsafe nuclear reactors and a huge waste dump located next to a military airfield (Campbell 1993). These reactors, constructed mainly for research purposes, have no protective covers, and staffing levels and safety precautions are inadequate. Alarm systems do not work, and some safety equipment has been deliberately tampered with to make it insensitive because the alarm systems were going off all the time, annoying staff. Following his criticism of the safety of Russia's nuclear installations, Mr Kuznetsaw was forced to resign from his post in 1993; he predicted that sooner rather than later an accident would happen with frightening consequences.

The Soviet Union was the major supplier of fossil fuel, which was produced in abundance, especially in the 1960s and 1970s to her East European comrades. Table 4.2 shows the dependence ratio of six former communist countries with respect to coal, oil and natural gas. The prices of Soviet energy resources were stable and cheap compared with world levels, which made it easy to develop energy intensive industries such as iron, steel, cement and aluminium. However, the production technology used in these industries was outdated, wasteful and generated excessive pollution. It was estimated that heavy industries in eastern European countries had one of the highest per capita energy consumption rates in the world (Russell 1991).

In return for cheap energy supplies, the Soviet Union has provided a market for a whole range of industrial and other goods produced in former communist countries. Towards the end of the 1980s, due to increasing economic pressure on the Soviet Union, oil supplies to eastern European countries were becoming unreliable. In 1991 Russia demanded payment in

Table 4.2 Share of imports from the Soviet Union in energy consumption

Country	*Coal*	*Oil*	*Gas*
Bulgaria	44.0	100.0	89.0
Czechoslovakia	4.5	100.0	94.0
Former GDR	4.7	100.0	77.0
Hungary	9.0	84.0	39.0
Poland	-	86.0	48.0
Romania	10.0	8.0	4.0

Source: Russell (1991)

hard currency for oil sold to former satellite states. This led to a move towards energy generation using lignite, which is environmentally objectionable.

Another problem has been the state of the residential sector. During the communist era, numerous new towns were created all over the Eastern bloc countries in which house design and heat insulation were very poor. This sector used mostly poor quality lignite or coal for its heating and lighting. While the highest grade material was exported, the poorest quality was burned in power stations and in domestic hearths. For example, Poland has traditionally been a coal exporting country. The domestic sector was, and still is, as bad as the industrial sector.

After the collapse of communism in Romania, media reports revealed that in the town of Copsa Mica the trees and grass were so dark that an outsider would get the impression that someone had deliberately painted the whole area black. The health of the people in the region has been extremely bad and yet they have little or no opportunity to settle elsewhere.

In former Czechoslovakia, the air in some industrialised areas has been extremely polluted. In fact, it became so bad that people who settled there were paid a bonus, called by inhabitants the burial bonus. Gore (1992) reports that in some areas of Poland children are regularly taken down into underground mines to have a break from the build-up of pollution in the air above ground.

For more than forty years after the Second World War, the Erzgebirge Mountains in former East Germany provided the Soviet Union with its most important source of uranium. In 1992 German researchers announced that they had registered at least 5,500 cases of lung cancer among former uranium miners working for Wismut, the joint Soviet–German company that operated the mines. Trade union officials now argue that between 300,000 and 350,000 people living in the Erzgebirge area have been exposed to excessive levels of radiation. The German Society for Work-Related Medicine recently described the Wismut operation as one of the world's worst radiation disasters after Hiroshima, Nagasaki and Chernobyl.

Where do the former communist countries go from here? Russell (1991) recommends prioritising in managing environmental and resource problems, some of which are urgent. Some important questions are:

> Which type of problem should be dealt with first and by whom?
> What does environmental clean-up officially mean?
> How will the rate of improvement be decided, and by whom?
> Should financial resources be directed towards preventing intensification of existing environmental problems by improving environmental standards in problem-creating industries or should the money be spent in closure of such units?
> Should the development of renewable energy resources be activated immediately or slowly?

Should water pollution problems be addressed before air pollution?
To what extent should neighbouring countries co-operate in dealing with common problems?
Should international aid be directed towards the solution of specific countries or to solving problems in a particular region?

Russell also warns against vested interest groups in the Western world which are likely to benefit from the environmental improvement in Eastern countries. Recent reports on money spent on environmental improvements have been bewildering and even alarming: 'The motivation of the wide variety of interests currently espousing impressive-sounding numbers in dollars is open to question' (Russell 1991).

Karl Marx, like Adam Smith, was essentially an optimist about the future of mankind. The latter required that in order to improve human welfare the role of the state in economic life must to be minimised. The former, on the other hand, required a workers' revolution to overthrow the capitalist system which was not sustainable, in any case, due to its internal inconsistencies. Marx viewed capitalism as a harmful structure for the environment as well as for workers.

On the exploitation of mineral deposits, both Smith and Marx felt that diminishing returns would not be compelling on the extensive margin. The user cost in the extractive sector would therefore be zero or very low. On the issue of agricultural rent, Marx did not agree with Malthus or Ricardo that, in the progress of society when inferior quality of land is taken into cultivation, rent would commence immediately on the old and fertile land. Marx realised that differential rent could develop in a reverse order from bad to good soils. Furthermore, in addition to its fertility, various locational attributes of land could contribute to rent.

Judging purely by the results of the communist experiment in many parts of the world, it would be impossible to claim that Marxism could be an environmentally friendly ideology. It is true that the resource use in the capitalist United States has been as extravagant as it has been in the Soviet Union, an issue which will be explored further in Chapter 8, but nevertheless the former has a lot to show for it whereas the latter has not.

5

NATURAL RESOURCES AND THE ENVIRONMENT IN NEO-CLASSICAL TRADITION

In the neo-classical tradition the emphasis is on laissez-faire, giving only a limited role to government for intervention in the economy, and this is reflected in the writings of economists who deal with, albeit briefly, natural resources and the environment.

Another important aspect of neo-classical economists is that they replaced the supply-orientated theory of value with a demand-orientated concept of marginal utility. Unlike classical economists who focus on the supply side, neo-classical writers stress the importance of demand in determining the value of goods and services. A rational individual with a certain amount of income would be in a position to choose from a wide range of goods and services available in a market economy. If the individuals are utility maximisers, as they must be according to neo-classical economists, then they would allocate their money in such a manner that the last pound spent on one item gives no more or less satisfaction than the last pound spent on anything else.

Jevons, whose name was mentioned in Chapter 3, is regarded by a good number of economists as being a neo-classical writer, especially for his contribution to the theory of marginal utility. He argued that the more consumers have of one commodity, the less satisfaction they will acquire from consuming another unit and the less they will be willing to pay for it. He then concluded that essential but abundant commodities would be cheap because an extra unit would not be worth a great deal to purchasers. Scarce items, on the other hand, would be expensive because consumers would pay a high price for extra units even though they may be non-essential to life. Contest for acquiring an extra unit by buyers, coupled with rarity, would yield a high market price for items such as diamonds and silver.

Walras, by arguing along the same lines, contends that the entire economic system is tied to the spending decisions of the consumer. This include raw materials and capital goods as well as consumer goods.

BÖHM-BAWERK

Towards the end of the nineteenth century an Austrian economist, Eugen von Böhm-Bawerk (1894), broke tradition with Ricardo by pointing out that it would be more appropriate to consider land together with capital in the division of factors of production. Böhm-Bawerk's main focus was the development of a theory for capital, but his argument was later used by Gray as a starting point for a solution to the issue of whether surplus should be taken as rent or royalty.

Böhm-Bawerk argued that, theoretically speaking, land and capital were essentially members of the same class of durable goods. Therefore, rent from land and the royalty from mine deposits should, theoretically, be treated in the same way. The fact that a given stock of mineral deposits may be exhausted in, say, fifty years, while land under proper cultivation could stay in productive condition for a very long period of time should make little difference. The rent is due to the productiveness of a peculiar kind of durable good, land. Böhm-Bawerk believed that rates of return from mines were partly depreciation and partly interest on their capitalised value. The former reflected the fall in the value of mines as extraction progressed. The latter was essentially the same as net return from land.

SORLEY

Sorley was the first neo-classical economist who explicitly dealt with, in a marginalist spirit, the value put upon the extractive sector. Following on from Mill's idea of the opportunity cost in mining, Sorley explained the theoretical foundation of mine deposits (Sorley, 1889). He took an interest in this subject largely as a result of depression in the coal and iron industries in the 1880s which led to criticism of the owners that their royalties aggravated the situation. He placed payments to landlords in three groups: dead rents, unit royalties and wayleave. The first group were fixed periodic payments without regard to the level of production. Unit royalties were justified on the grounds of deterioration of the mine resulting from extraction. Wayleave was payment for right of way to gain access to mines.

Fixed periodic payments protected landlords against a fall in the overall value of the mineral deposit. However, under the Ricardian assumption such a fall would be an exception rather than a rule since as more and more inferior stocks came into operation the value of existing mines would increase. If the reverse was true (a theory suggested by Carey) more fertile land and richer deposits would become available; indeed dead rents would give some protection to owners even if the person who mined the resource did not put it into any use.

In his discussion of the royalty system, especially in the iron and coal sectors in Britain, Sorley pointed out that during falling profits and wages landlords still received uninterrupted fixed sums, which was unfair. Furthermore, since landlords did not put minerals under the soil, what justification could there be for them to claim royalties? Sorley outlined the reform for the royalty system that existed in Britain at the time which made British mining operations less competitive in markets as continental royalties were much lower. He dismissed nationalisation and abolition of royalties as a means of reforming the system. His main recommendation was the introduction of a royalty based upon each unit of mine extracted, i.e. *ad valorem* royalties.

Sorley's main contribution in the theory of natural resources is his analytical ability to further Mill's idea that there is an antagonism between present and future production from mines. Furthermore, he pointed out that the Ricardian theory of agricultural rent cannot find its application in mining, as inferior mines cannot be sustained indefinitely whereas inferior land can. The ultimate exhaustion justifies a royalty even for the worst mine that will enter into the price, whereas the worst farm cannot pay a rent. On the differential rents or royalties, he contended that such differences will depend upon their cost advantage in relation to the worst mine. According to Robinson (1989), Sorley employs a methodology here which is more classical than neoclassical in its approach in that differential royalties are price determined rather than price determining.

MARSHALL

The classical theory of value contends that price, and hence the value, is based upon the cost of production which is ultimately linked to labour. On the other hand, during the last thirty years of the nineteenth century economists such as Menger, Jevons and Walras were arguing that value was utility–demand determined. It was Marshall (1890) who reconciled these two approaches by pointing out that value was determined by both supply and demand, and because of this he is considered to be the father of modern micro-economics.

On the theory of mining and agriculture, Marshall was more in line with the classical school than the tradition of his time (Stigler 1946; Schumpeter 1954). He draws a distinction between the two sectors in the sense that a given plot of agricultural land, if properly utilised, would retain its productivity forever whereas in mining, exhaustion would be the end result for any given deposit. However, as agriculture expanded, he seemed to be more in favour of Carey's position than the Ricardo–Malthusian theory. In mining, he considered that the opening up of new territories and the discovery of fresh deposits would involve increased difficulty and thus this sector would display diminishing returns in the long run. However, improvements in technology would mitigate this, though he offered no opinion as to what extent.

In the short run, the Marshallian theory implies that most mines are likely to experience a constant return to scale. He implies that, since the output of a mine is like a flow from a reservoir in that it becomes deeper to reach over time, the unit cost tends to increase slightly. When the total contents of the reservoir are considered this cost becomes independent of the rate of extraction. Scott (1967) criticises this by arguing that, although in the short run the Marshallian assumption may hold true – namely, that the cumulative cost curve in extraction may not change much – in the long run it is likely to shift upwards as extraction becomes increasingly difficult. In agriculture, where cultivation is carried out on a fixed territory, an increase in factors such as labour and capital on it would yield markedly diminishing returns if the agricultural technology remained unchanged. Furthermore, in agriculture output is further constrained by the cycle of nature, whereas in mining there is no such impediment. On the issue of rent, Marshall contends that, due to exhaustibility in mining, mineral rents are, or should be, calculated on a different principle from rents in agriculture. A farmer contracts land to return in a condition as good as when first rented, but in mining, the operator cannot do this as royalties must be paid to the owner in proportion to the irreplaceable deposits taken out. This payment, royalty, is not a rent which is linked to the exhaustibility of mineral deposits. Marshall concludes:

> the marginal supply price of minerals includes a royalty in addition to the marginal expenses of the mine. . . . But the royalty itself on a ton of coal, when accurately adjusted, represents that diminution in the value of the mine, regarded as a source of wealth in the future, which is caused by taking the ton out of nature's storehouse.
>
> (Marshall 1890)

Although, as Marshall says, mine deposits are a present and future source of wealth, his analysis is static in nature. Unlike the theories of Gray and Hotelling, it does not take up the idea of the mine owner operating in a given optimum time-frame. Robinson (1989) suggests that the significance of Marshall's writings in the extractive sector lies in the authority of its author and the wide dissemination of his work.

Marshallian Externalities

At a much wider level concerning environmental pollution, noise and congestion, Marshall made the first attempt in economic analysis by introducing the concept of external economics. Although Marshall had in mind only the benefits that accrue to the economic units through general industrial development, the concept of externalities contains the key to the economic analysis of environmental problems. The advantages referred to by

Marshall are enjoyed by businessmen without payment and outside the market (Marshall 1890).

Later Pigou (1920) realised that the concept of externalities is a double-edged sword containing not only benefits, but costs as well. As an example of negative externalities, Pigou uses the case of woodlands damaged by sparks from railway engines. He makes it clear that not only can the production conditions of third parties be influenced outside the market, but also the welfare of private persons can be seriously affected, both in terms of costs and benefits. Elsewhere, Pigou (1935) gives a number of examples for externalities which create a gap between aggregate costs and benefits. These range from a factory chimney that increases washing bills in the vicinity to excessive drinking which imposes extra cost on the police.

The first substantial treatment of externalities was by Kapp (1950), who anticipated the far-reaching adverse consequences of economic growth on the environment. The social costs, which are defined as all direct and indirect burdens imposed on third parties or the general public by the participants in economic activities are the central point in Kapp's analysis. He explicitly mentions all costs emanating from productive processes that are passed on to outsiders by way of air and water pollution, which harm health, reduce agricultural yields, accelerate corrosion of materials, endanger aquatic life, flora and fauna, and create problems in the preparation of drinking water.

Externalities occur when activities of economic units (firms and consumers) affect production or consumption of other units where the benefits or costs which accrue to these units do not normally enter into the gain and loss calculation. In other words, these effects, although noticed, are left unpriced and hence the bearers, usually, uncompensated in the private market environment. If externalities are priced and the bearers compensated then they are said to be in internalised (see also Scitovsky 1954).

Some economists such as Bator (1958) emphasise that externalities are a market failure. They arise largely due to the failure to define property rights in certain areas of economic activity. The absence of property rights to air space and water courses may lead to a situation in which some individuals may abuse these resources which are shared by many. Advocates of free market economics believe that the absence of private property rights in certain spheres is responsible for most of our environmental problems. The problem can be solved by creating well-defined, transferable and marketable property rights in all areas of economic activity. That is, the root of most environmental problems is the failure to apply capitalism fully. This view is explored further in Chapter 7.

At the other end of the spectrum, economists who belong to the socialist school argue that public ownership of productive property such as land and capital is more desirable than private ownership. They believe that capitalist ideals would lead the owners of property to produce results which would impoverish the masses, as pointed out by Marx (see Chapter 4).

The importance of externalities is well recognised in current economic literature. Buchanan and Stubblebine (1962) argue that external effects violate the conditions for optimum allocation of resources in the economy. However, it has also been realised that complete elimination of externalities is neither possible nor desirable as economists try to identify the socially optimum level of side-effects by using Marshallian principles. To see this, let us look at Figure 5.1 where marginal gain and loss are measured along the vertical axis and the scale of activity, which is degrading the environment, along the horizontal axis. Two parties are involved: gainers and losers. The former are those who benefit from the industrial activity, e.g. wage earners and profit-takers; the losers are the public at large who suffer from the external effects generated by industry.

The two groups have conflicting interests. From the gainers' viewpoint, OB is the best situation; they will want to push the level of activity to B at which point the marginal gain is zero. On the other hand, the best position for the losers is the origin where the loss is zero. It must be pointed out that this analysis somewhat over-simplifies the situation. First, from the gainer's viewpoint the external effects of, say, pollution, would be zero at the origin, but this would imply no industrial activity. In this situation the public at

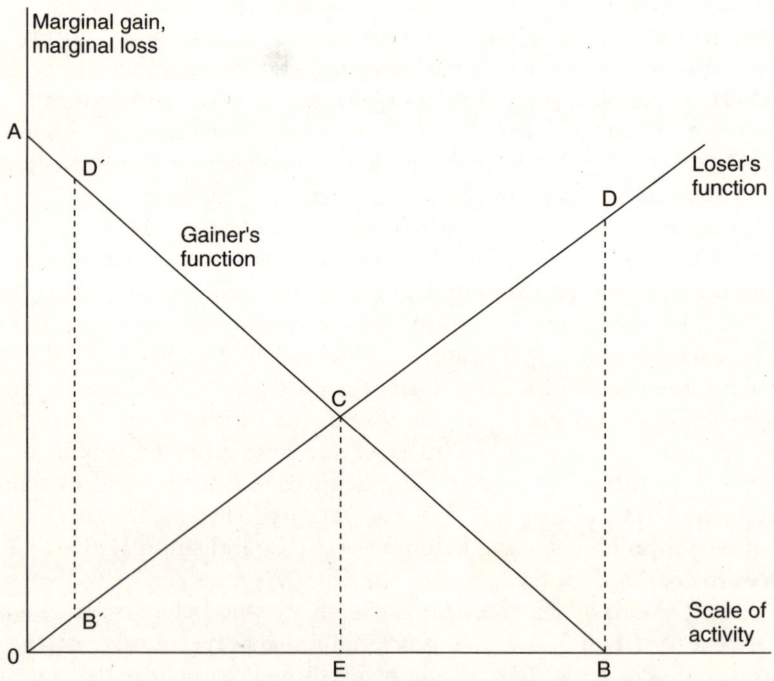

Figure 5.1 Marshallian analysis to determine socially optimum level of external degradation

large, including the victims of the pollution, would stand a loss since they are the beneficiaries of industrial activities as consumers. Furthermore, since wage earners and profit-takers are also part of the community, they too are likely to suffer from external effects created by their own activities.

In a situation where one party (gainers) does not have to pay compensation to the other (losers) the scale of activity is likely to be expanded to point B. Here we would have:

Benefit (gainers)	=	OAB
Cost (losers)	=	ODB
Overall gain (community)[1]	=	OAD'B'

The society gains overall and OAD'B' represents the scale of gain with the maximum level of industrial activity.

If, however, the gainers were to reduce the scale of activity from B to E, the gain to society would increase quite considerably. At point E:

Benefit (gainers)	=	OACE
Cost (losers)	=	OCE
Overall gain (community)	=	OAC

OAC is greater than OAD'B' by B'D'C. So there is a social advantage when the scale of industrial activity, which is causing environmental degradation, say by polluting the atmosphere, is reduced to E, which is the socially optimal level.

This analysis to identify the socially optimum level of external effects is entirely in the tradition of Alfred Marshall. First, just as in bringing together supply and demand conditions to determine the value of marketed commodities, here the two items involved in environmental valuation, i.e. costs and benefits, are brought together. Second, in determining the optimum scale of operation, marginal rather than total gains and losses are considered. What sort of policy instruments can be used to achieve point E is a different subject which will be considered later on in the book.

GRAY

One notable contribution from L. C. Gray (1913, 1914) is his distinction of the mining sector from agriculture or manufacturing, for which he used the work of Böhm-Bawerk, mentioned earlier in this chapter. In his view, the farmer and mine operator deal with two essentially different kinds of assets – the land and the mine. The former resembles factor labour in the sense that the sustainability of its services is possible and desirable. If land and labour

1 OAD'B' = OAB - ODB, since OCB is common to both areas we need to subtract CDB from OAC.

are not used for a considerable period of time they tend to lose productive capacity. Mine deposits, on the other hand, are subject to exhaustion only when they are used or operated. In other words, the use of land and labour maintain, or in some cases improve, their productivity, whereas mining operations depreciate the value of the deposits. Non-operation of mine deposits today means a postponement of utility or income. That is, present and future utilities from mine deposits are antagonistic. In agriculture there is no such issue, and thus land and mine deposits are fundamentally different resources.

For example, let us say that prices of mineral deposits are rising fast and owners anticipate much higher prices in future years. It will be sensible, then, for mine owners to postpone their operations if they are profit maximisers. A similar increase in the price of agricultural produce will not require a postponement of farming operations. On the contrary, rising prices in agriculture will call for intensification of farming as soon as possible. Conversely, if prices of mineral resources are expected to fall in future years, mine operators should intensify operations now in order to take advantage of favourable current prices.

A large part of the economic literature gives credit to Harold Hotelling as the founder of modern micro-economics for the mining sector. Hotelling established the rule in mining that, for the extraction to be justified, the net market price of the resource (net of extraction cost) must rise with the market rate of interest. This rule, which is called the 'fundamental principle' makes it explicit that, *ceteris paribus*, there is a trade-off between present and future profits in mining operations. However, Robinson (1989) suggests that some credit must go to Gray as he argued essentially the same point some seventeen years before the publication of Hotelling's paper (1931).

As for Ricardian rent, Gray contends that indestructibility of land is not a characteristic which separates rent from other forms of yield and thus he feels there is a need for an alternative theory of rent. Indestructibility of land is not essentially a basis for rent which, in any case, is not easily separable from its other yields. Managed properly, land would have an infinite productive life. Present income from land is best considered to be an interest on infinitely productive resources. In mining, however, the asset has a finite productive life. The present yield must partly relate to exhaustion, which is to be called rent, partly to be seen as interest, to be called royalty. Both rent and royalty are to be measured by the surplus over cost of extraction.

Going back to Gray's view that present and future yields in the mining sector are antagonistic, there are some technical problems to be considered. Let us say that a mine owner abandons operations on a marginal coal deposit with a view to restarting it at some future date when prices are more favourable. Cessation of activity may create subsidence or flooding, which may make future operations very costly, or even impossible.

TAUSSIG AND CASSEL

F.W. Taussig was an influential figure in the development of the economic discipline at Harvard University. In his *Principles of Economics* (1915), Taussig differed from his contemporaries when they described clean air and water as abundant and free goods. In determining the price of the commodities, neo-classical economists put an emphasis on the marginal utility of commodities and argued that due to their scarcity non-essentials will have higher marginal utility and thus will command higher prices compared with essential but abundant resources which may carry a zero price tag. Taussig, by looking ahead, implied that as industrialisation intensifies, clean air may one day become less abundant.

As for the mineral resources, Taussig was rather optimistic about their future availability. On the issue of rent and royalty, commenting on Marshall's thinking, Taussig contended that Marshall believed that rent was a surplus over the minimum royalty earned by the marginal operations. Robinson (1989) argues that although this interpretation of Taussig has gained some credibility, it was essentially incorrect. This is because the surplus that accrues to more productive as opposed to marginal deposits is simply a reflection of the superior resources which are taken out of the ground. In other words, surpluses that relate to fertile mines above the minimum royalty are simply further royalty. When mining operations began in new territories or countries, owners would commence a payment even on marginal deposits. According to Taussig this is unlikely to happen in old countries.

Gustav Cassel, writing at the same time as Taussig and Gray, focused mostly on the mine deposits and, to a lesser extent, on agricultural rents in economics of natural resources (Cassel 1918). In dealing with rent, he contended that it is essentially a return from all kinds of durable goods, including land, but noted that as far as the destructible resources were concerned a very large part of the yield relates to the consumption of such resources. For example, in coal mining, its price includes cost of extraction and transport to cover the payments of labour and capital, and a small part of the price is in relation to the *in situ* deposit itself. Robinson (1989) points out that Cassel's view that a large part of the price relates to extraction and transportation implies that opportunity or user cost must be considered to be very small.

Since exhaustion of a sizeable mine deposit takes a long time to complete, Cassel sees that rent of a deposit corresponds to the present value of the stream of returns over its operating life. Rent of a mine, therefore, is similar to interest payment for any long-living asset such as buildings and machinery. The present value of the mine can be altered by changing the time horizon to deplete the resource which is determined by the mine owner. For example, the present value could be increased by shortening the exhaustion period, provided that no substantial increase in cost of extraction takes place.

Cassel also considers the effect of changing interest rate on operations, although this point was taken up more rigorously by Hotelling in later years. For example, a rise in the interest rate, *ceteris paribus*, will tend to hasten the operation in the mining sector as it will decrease the net present value of the asset. Another important factor which is likely to bring operations closer to the present is that of uncertainty. Discovery of much richer deposits or development of substitute material in the future are possible and such thoughts guide the owners to bring production forward in time. A monopoly cartel over the resource would have the opposite effect in restricting current consumption and hence make the resource last longer.

On the development of agriculture, Cassel somewhat took sides with the optimism of Carey as he envisaged that opening up new territories to agriculture need not be more costly than using the old ones. When new territories are opened up, all grades of land come into use – some very fertile, some less so. When capital is scarce and interest rates are high, labour intensive techniques will be used on most lands, new as well as old. But when interest rates fall, more capital intensive operations will take place which may become a catalyst in the development of more efficient agricultural machinery to improve yields. Advancements in irrigation, drainage, the use of better seeds, etc. also improves agricultural yields on all areas.

HOTELLING

As the neo-classical age was closing a new breed of economist was beginning to emerge. These were mathematical economists such as Hotelling, Ramsey and Keynes. Although the seeds of this movement had been sown much earlier by Fisher (1892), these three displayed much more rigorous characteristics in their handling of economic issues and building models. They were, in part, influenced by philosophers such as Bertrand Russell and Alfred Whitehead (1926) in believing that a good proportion of verbal statements or arguments of logic could be converted into mathematical models and developed rigorously to their logical conclusion (see Kula 1996). According to Ormerod (1994), this movement started a dark age which intensified as time progressed.

Hotelling built his mathematical models in a number of fields such as a theory of depreciation (Hotelling 1925), the economics of exhaustible resources (Hotelling 1931), and even pioneered the construction of models for the recreational benefits of environmental attributes (Hotelling 1947). However, he has become well known for his modelling of the so-called 'cake-eating' problem associated with destructible resources. A number of contemporary economists such as Solow (1974), Devarajan and Fisher (1981) highlighted the work of Hotelling as being seminal in the development of exhaustible resources. In the 1920s there was a great deal of concern about the exhaustion of the world's limited resources (see, for example, the section on Arthur Pigou in Chapter 6) and Hotelling's paper was largely a response to it.

Hotelling's central preoccupation was with the identification of the optimal depletion rate at which non-renewable resources should be exhausted over a period of time. He looked at the optimal 'cake-eating ratio' from the viewpoint of the government who wanted to maximise the social welfare in depleting non-renewable resources. Hotelling showed that a competitive industry consisting, as government, of many firms with identical extraction costs and demand conditions and having information about resource prices, will arrive at exactly the same extraction path. That is, the optimal extraction rate determined unilaterally by each firm would yield the socially optimal result in perfect competition.

In the optimal cake-eating model there are two distinct costs involved: the marginal extraction cost arising from current operations as labour and capital are used and the marginal user cost arising from foregone profits had the extraction been postponed. Hotelling's model suggests that the revenue which would arise from current extraction should be high enough to cover both costs. This leads to the so-called 'fundamental principle' in the extractive sector that for the operations to be justified the net market price of the resource (net of extraction cost) must rise in line with the market rate of interest. This principle can be easily understood by imagining two situations:

1 Assume that market price minus extraction cost is rising at a rate higher than the interest rate. What is the best course of action? The owner should leave the resource in the ground as it would represent a superior investment to the alternative available. In fact, during the second oil crisis of 1978–81 when the price of the commodity was rocketing, many producers stated that in a situation like this it would be better to 'leave the stuff in the ground'.

2 Now let us say that the net price is rising more slowly than the market rate of interest. What is the best course of action? If the owner is a profit maximiser, as must be the case, the stock should be extracted and sold as fast as possible and the proceeds invested elsewhere, say, in a time deposit.

Therefore, a net price increasing at the same price as market rate of interest is the equilibrium condition. Formally, the equilibrium condition can be expressed as:

$$P(t) - C = \lambda(1+r)^t \qquad [5.1]$$

where

> $P(t)$ = price of extracted commodity
> C = extraction cost, assumed to be constant for computational convenience
> r = interest rate
> ^{t} = time, normally expressed in terms of years
> λ = is a constant

The left-hand side of the equation is the net price of the deposit (net of extraction cost) and the right-hand side is the resource rent. This shows that the net price must go up in line with the market rate of interest.

Hotelling was in line with many of his predecessors in believing that first the high quality and easily accessible resources will be worked out. His publication pioneered many research papers in later years on policy matters concerning conservation measures for destructible resources. For example, if a government feels that the nation's destructible resources are being depleted too fast, then one form of action would be to impose an excise tax on extraction. To see this, let us consider a non-renewable endowment, say, oil, to be depleted by a profit-maximising owner in line with Equation 5.1. Also, assume that extraction is carried out at a constant cost and is uniform at all points of extraction. That is, there is no difference between the first and last barrels of oil extracted.

Figure 5.2 assumes that the entire oil industry is facing a downward sloping curve (diagram on the left). According to this schedule the greater the industry's output the lower the price. At the point where the demand curve touches the vertical axis, where the price of the commodity is measured, the demand will be zero. That is, at price level *P*, output demanded, which is measured along the horizontal axis, is zero. In order to command higher prices in line with Equation 5.1 the industry must reduce its output per period of time. Therefore, extraction next year must be less than this year's output to ensure that the price goes up just enough to satisfy Equation 5.1.

As the price reaches *P* over time, no one would be willing to purchase the commodity at that level, the choke-off price. Therefore, the resource owner would want to exhaust the stock just before the price level becomes *P* and would thus work out a plan to decrease the level of output at each point in time, which in turn will determine the price path. In Figure 5.2 this is shown on the right-hand side. The choke-off price on the left becomes the ceiling for the figure on the right. The cost of extraction, which is assumed to be constant, is illustrated by the horizontal line, *c*; *ab* is the price path which is achieved by reducing the level of output in each period of time. The difference between *ab* and *c* is the resource rent which increases at a rate equal to the market rate of interest in a perfectly competitive world.

Now let us say that the government feels that the nation's oil deposits are

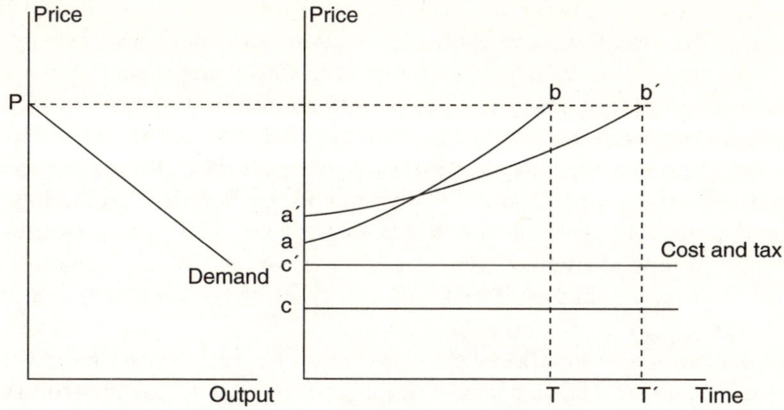

Figure 5.2 Tax on extraction used as policy variable for conservation measure to make oil deposits last longer

running down at a fast rate and thus imposes an excise tax on extraction. For the owner of oil deposits a tax on extraction is a cost which will reduce the level of current extraction and increase the depletion time. With the tax, the new cost curve becomes *c'* on the right-hand side of Figure 5.2. The new price path is now *a'b'* and the depletion time will increase from *T* to *T'*. As the extraction cost goes up due to taxation, the rent will be squeezed. In response, the owner will reduce current output and this will increase the initial price from *a* to *a'* and the new price/output path will become *a'b'*.

Another factor which would affect the deflation rate is a change in interest rate. When the interest rate goes up, *ceteris paribus*, this will increase extraction levels which would shorten the depletion time. Higher interest rates would mean that returns on alternative money markets, say, time deposits, in the financial sector would be higher. If the owner of oil deposits does not make any alteration on the previously worked out plan, the stocks will be earning a sub-optimal rate of return over time. The way to avoid this loss is to shift production to the present. That is, the owner will extract and sell more now, which will drive down the current price. Thereafter, less will be extracted so that the net price on the remaining deposits can rise at a higher rate. However, if the rise in the rate is substantial, it impacts cost so that the effect of a too high interest rate on depletion is not clear. If the interest rate comes down, exactly the opposite will happen. The starting price will go up as the owner shifts output towards the future by reducing current output. This means that the time to depletion must go up (Herfindahl 1967).

Theoretically, the 'fundamental principle' is a neat model, but its operation will be severely restricted in the real world due to a number of factors. First, take the market rate of interest. If it comes down, *ceteris paribus*, the extraction rate will slow down; if it goes up, the pace of extraction should increase. It is well known that market rates of interest change quite sharply over time. For example, in the United Kingdom, during the last twenty-five years, the rate of interest has not at any time stayed the same for two years running. It is quite unrealistic to expect an automatic response by resource owners to changes in interest rates. Let us say that the market rate of interest has risen quite considerably, causing owners to increase the pace of extraction so that the proceeds can be invested in high return bank deposits. Normally, an increase in output levels in the extractive sector requires an expansion of capacity, which takes time. Furthermore, the high interest rate may not last long, which will make owners think twice before engaging in a costly exercise of capacity expansion.

Similar problems can arise with regard to excise duty levied on extraction. National tax policies in democratic countries change with the government in power; thus resource owners cannot be certain about the longevity of a particular tax policy. If capacity levels are based on current tax legislation, owners may be left with excess or inadequate structures to operate optimally when legislation is suddenly changed. Another important factor is technological development which may reduce the demand for a particular resource. To give an historic example, in the ninth century, whale oil became widely used in Europe for lighting purposes because of its clean-burning properties, thus leading to an expansion of whaling. Increased pressure on the whale population forced animals to migrate towards less accessible parts of the sea, such as the Arctic, which made capture costly. Due to increased demand for whale oil, and with improvements in navigation and shipbuilding, whaling continued, leading to a severe depletion of the whale population by the eighteenth century. Due to scarcity, the price of whale oil increased by more than 400 per cent between 1820 and 1860 and, as a result, users were looking for substitutes. This led to the use of gas lighting in many European cities and drilling for oil intensified as a source of another substitute. By 1863 there were about 300 experimental refineries in the United States producing kerosene. A few years later, kerosene had almost replaced whale oil, and in 1870 its price struck a historic low. Similarly, a technological breakthrough in tapping solar power may reduce the demand for fossil fuel substantially. In other words, there are uncertainties regarding future demand conditions that would impact upon the decisions of resource owners. In addition to the 'fundamental principle', resource owners are also guided by the maxim 'sell your stocks now while customers exist'.

In addition to technological uncertainties and future demand, there is the ownership uncertainty when extraction companies operate in a politically unstable region where resource appropriation may look threatening. This possibility tends to make resource owners very nervous indeed, leading them to extract hastily and get out. Even in established democracies such as Britain, nationalisation of fossil fuel deposits took place in a relatively short space of time during the administration of socialist governments.

One last point worth mentioning is that of impatience. For various reasons, a resource owner may be in great need of cash, which could either be acquired by selling the property rights, or by hastening the extraction. When stocks are owned publicly, selling property rights may be politically difficult and the government may decide to deplete stocks fast for early cash. For example, in the 1980s two major oil producing nations, Iran and Iraq, were engaged in a long and costly war. During this time, both countries were in need of hard currency to maintain their costly war efforts. This money was largely raised by selling their oil.

Because of all these reasons the 'fundamental principle', which is largely attributed to Hotelling, is unlikely to be the driving force in real world decision-making. Furthermore, Hotelling's 'cake-eating' model implies that prices of destructible resources must drift upwards over time in line with Equation 5.1 (above). However, the work of some resource economists in the 1960s revealed that prices of almost all natural resource-based commodities have not been rising, but falling, over a long period of time (Potter and Christy 1962; Barnett and Morse 1963). Has Hotelling's theoretical model any relevance at all in the real world? This has been tested by Slade (1982) by assuming technological progress in extraction and a change in the grade of deposits. Slade has studied price trends for all fuels and major metal deposits over a long period of time in the United States. If we slightly modify Equation 5.1 by allowing the cost of extraction to change over time, then:

$$P_{(t)} = C_{(t)} + \lambda (1 + r)^{t} \qquad [5.2]$$

where

$C(t)$ = cost of extraction at time t which could rise or fall.

Slade permits a fall in price by arguing that although $(1 + r)^t$, which is rent, is normally rising, then $C(t)$ may fall substantially, yielding a declining price trend. At the early stages of extraction, a decline in costs may outweigh the increase in rent, but later on its power may diminish yielding a U-shaped price path. For example, between 1900 and 1940 the price of copper in the United States fell because of the advent of large earth-moving equipment, which made possible the strip mining of extremely low-grade ore bodies, and the discovery of froth flotation, which made concentration of inferior sulphide ores economical. Thus overall costs fell up until the Second World War, by which time the switch to new technology had reached its natural limits since the decline in unit cost had moderated, giving rise to an increase in price trend (see Figure 5.3).

Slade's data covers the period 1870–1978 for all major metals and fuels with the exception of gold. Annual prices are deflated by the US wholesale

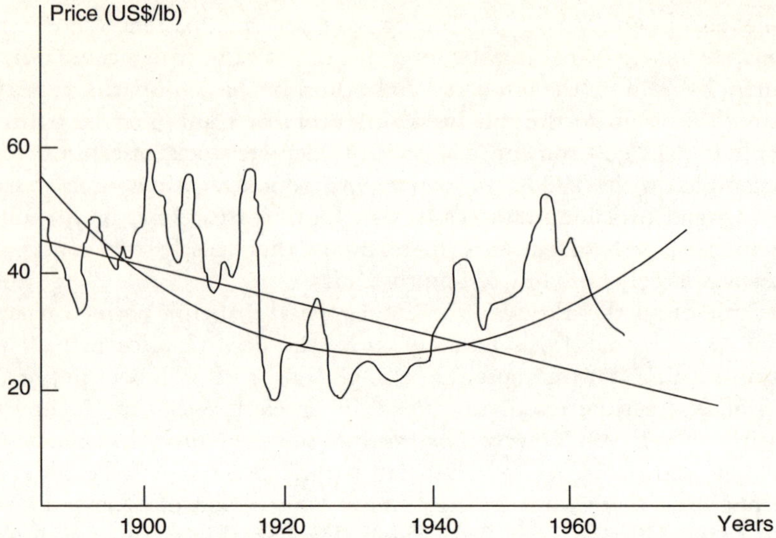

Figure 5.3 History of deflated prices and fitted linear and U-shaped curves for copper
Source: Slade (1982)

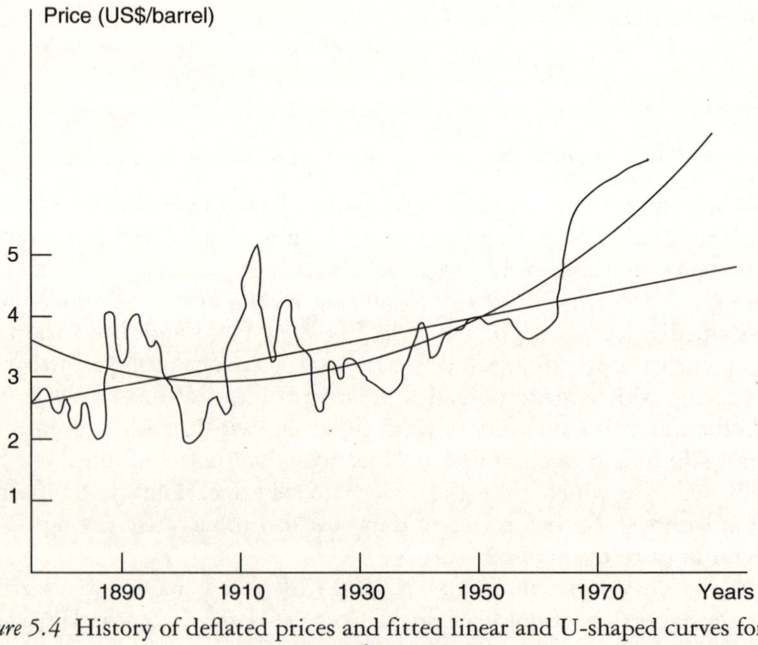

Figure 5.4 History of deflated prices and fitted linear and U-shaped curves for petroleum
Source: Slade (1982)

price index in which 1967 was taken to be the base year. Two price trends were estimated for each resource, one where the price trend is a straight line, the other where price is a U-shaped function of time. U-shaped curves tend to fit well into the data. At the early stages of operation the fall in prices can be understood by assuming that technological change off-sets ore grade decline and costs fall. In later years, technological developments reach their limits, ore quality falls and accessibility becomes more difficult, giving rise to increasing cost. Figure 5.4 shows one other resource, petroleum, in which the U-shaped price trend fits better than the linear one. Slade notes that the model over-simplifies the situation as it neglects many important aspects of the extraction industry such as environmental regulations, tax policy, price control and market structure.

As I mentioned earlier, in economic literature the basic theory of exhaustible resources, i.e. the 'fundamental principle', is largely credited to Hotelling, but almost all aspects of it were discussed by Gray and Cassel sometime before the publication of 'The economics of exhaustible resources' in 1931. Hotelling's main contribution to the theory was his formalising of it by the use of mathematical models, which were popularised – some would even say over-emphasised – by mathematical economists such as Solow, Devarjan, Dasgupta and Heal.

Apart from the 'cake-eating' models, another important development in the neo-classical age was the recognition given to externalities and their importance in economic life. This important concept, which was introduced by Marshall, was later developed in various forms by a number of economists, some of whom have been mentioned in this chapter, and others who will be discussed in Chapter 6.

6

THE INTERVENTIONIST SCHOOL ON NATURAL RESOURCES AND THE ENVIRONMENT

PIGOU

In the early part of the twentieth century, various debates were taking place amongst economists as to whether governments should adopt interventionist policies to achieve socially desirable objectives. In the Soviet Union, after the Bolshevik revolution, intensive work got under way to devise a system for complete planning of the economy, mainly to achieve political objectives. Of course, not everybody was in support of the Soviet style of grandiose planning. One interesting idea was that free market prices, for various reasons, do not always reflect their true scarcity values, nor do they fully satisfy consumers or workers and thus governments may wish to compute shadow prices which can then be used in various policy measures as substitutes for imperfect market prices. Tylor (1928) contended that governments, by trial and error, could correct market prices. After that, consumers ought to be left free to spend their money on goods and services that carry corrected price tags. The combined efforts of consumers and governments would be able to clear the markets. Lange and Tylor (1938) went even further, saying that a government, in establishing shadow prices, could take into account true consumer desires and fair profit maximising objectives of entrepreneurs. The result would be maximisation of communal welfare with a mixture of competitive market economy and state intervention in which all markets could be cleared and full employment would be ensured by the correct level of investment.

Pigou (1920) was largely sympathetic to the view that unfettered market economy did not always work well and thus there was substantial room for governments to intervene for the purpose of promoting economic welfare. Pigou believed that welfare was a highly desirable concept with two main properties: first, elements of welfare are states of consciousness, and second, it could be brought under the category of less and more. For its measurement, Pigou argued that money could successfully be used as a measuring rod. That is, economic welfare is a group of satisfactions and dissatisfactions which can be measured with the help of money.

Pigou (1929), in his analysis of the promotion of social welfare, expressed great concern about depletion of natural resources and the claims of future generations on such assets. In this respect, he made a number of observations about human behaviour regarding intertemporal allocation of resources. That is, individuals distribute their resources between present, near future and remote future on the basis of wholly irrational preferences. When we have a choice between two satisfactions, we do not necessarily choose the larger of the two, but often devote ourselves to obtaining a small one straight away in preference to a much larger one in later years. Of course, there is an element of risk and uncertainty involved in intertemporal decisions, but even so the emphasis is still overwhelmingly on the present. Why is that so? According to Pigou, our telescopic faculty is defective and thus we see future events, needs, pains and pleasures at a diminishing scale which reveals a far-reaching disharmony.

The existence of a defective telescopic faculty manifests itself especially in market transactions that are likely to hurt future generations far more than present ones. If communal efforts are to be based totally on current market transactions, the future state of the world will become much less attractive. Take, for example, investment decisions made by individuals. As human life is limited, the fruits of those savings which accrue after a considerable interval are unlikely to be enjoyed by those making the sacrifice. Consequently, efforts directed towards the distant future will hold much less appeal to savers than those directed to the more immediate future. In the latter case, the beneficiaries will probably be the next generation – whose interests may be regarded as of almost equal importance – while, in the former case, the beneficiaries will be more remote in time and/or blood links and will thus be individuals for whom the savers have little concern. As a consequence, the resulting investments and created new capital may not be sufficient for future needs.

Holzman (1958), arguing along the same lines as Pigou, suggests the current markets reveal that individuals' decisions on savings versus consumption which affect future generations are likely to be in conflict with decisions taken by the state. He observes the explicit attempts of many countries to grow faster and increase per capita income. If the rates of saving and economic growth dictated by the free market are satisfactory, why should governments be obsessed with rapid economic development? By doing so do they damage consumer sovereignty? Holzman believes that if governments enforced some saving measures on the community, this would not seriously damage consumers' choices. Just as Pigou accepts the defective nature of the human telescopic faculty, Holzman points out that when looking back on our past decisions many of us regret that these were not perfect. Most people who, having lived through a period of plenty, are now experiencing a decline in living standards, would be more than willing to trade part of that past surplus to improve their present conditions.

Pigou prescribes fiscal measures to encourage individuals to save more.

> In view of this 'natural' tendency of people to devote too much of their resources to present service and too little to future service, any artificial interference on the part of government in favour of that tendency is bound, unless it has compensating advantages on the side of distribution, to diminish economic welfare. Subject to that condition, therefore, all taxes which differentiate against saving, as compared with spending, must diminish economic welfare. Even without differentiation there will be too little saving; with it there will be much too little saving. Property taxes, where they exist, and death duties, obviously differentiate against saving.
>
> (Pigou 1929: 28–9)

Then he states that the English income tax system does not promote social welfare as it falls on saved income and property. In the construction of an optimum tax scheme, the redistribution effects of income and property taxes must be weighed carefully against their adverse effects on saving and creation of capital.

Pigou does not suggest that the government should coerce people with means to save more for their own, as well as their descendants', interests. His point is that desirable redistributive attributes of income and property taxes have a cost in terms of a broader social welfare structure. Therefore, the benefits and costs of such taxes must be taken into account in any fiscal legislation. Furthermore, Pigou states that the government should protect the interests of present as well as future generations against excessive and irrational discounting.

On the issue of destructible resources, according to Pigou, our defective telescopic faculty will lead to reckless depletion:

> Sometimes people will win what they require by methods that destroy, as against the future, much more than they themselves obtain. Over-hasty exploitation of the best coal seams by methods that cover up and render unworkable for ever worse, but still valuable, seams; fishing operations so conducted as to disregard breeding seasons, thus threatening certain species of fish with extinction; farming operations so conducted as to exhaust the fertility of the soil, are all instances in point. There is also waste in the sense of injury to the sum total of economic satisfaction, when one generation, though not destroying more actual stuff than it itself obtains, uses up for trivial purposes a natural product which is abundant now but which is likely to become scarce and not readily available, even for very important purposes, to future generations. This sort of waste is illustrated when enormous quantities of coal

> are employed in high-speed vessels in order to shorten in a small degree the time of a journey that is already short. We cut off the time of our passage to New York at the cost of preventing, perhaps, one of our descendants from making the passage at all.
>
> (Pigou 1929: 28)

Market forces often are not conducive to either preservation or creation of natural resource-based capital. In projects such as development of water resources and afforestation, as net returns are distant they are handicapped by the slackness of desire towards distant satisfactions. Pigou states categorically that the government is the trustee for the unborn as well as its current citizens, to watch over and act, by legislation if necessary, to defend the exhaustible stocks of the nation from rash and reckless exploitation.

Pigou suggests basically three policy instruments for the rational use of exhaustible resources, protection of the environmental quality, curbing wasteful consumption, promotion of saving and above all prevention of harmful short-sightedness. These are:

- State subsidies
- Taxation
- Legislation

A leap in time – Pigovian policies in action

The Pigovian policies discussed above have been extensively used for the promotion of the forestry sector in Britain and Ireland for some time. In forestry, the time interval between planting a tree and felling it for timber could be long for some species. Long gestation periods that dominate the forestry business deter many private investors from tying up their money in afforestation. Once the forest resources of a nation are depleted, regeneration could be a long and painful process – as the British experience demonstrates. From the distant past right up to the Middle Ages, the British Isles were clothed with dense forests. From then on, a relentless process of destruction took place for a number of reasons. First, forested land had to be converted into agriculture to grow food to feed the increasing population. Second, the use of wood as fuel and construction material took its toll on forests. This was so extensive in some areas such as Scotland that a traveller there at the end of the seventeenth century noted that 'a tree here is as rare as a horse in Venice' (Thompson 1971). Third, the rise of Britain as a supreme naval force and seafaring nation resulted in the depletion of forest resources for the shipbuilding industry. Finally, wars took their toll of forests. By the turn of this century, these once forest-rich islands had become one of the most deforested areas in Europe.

During the First World War, Britain suffered a severe shortage of timber as the German Navy prevented imports and what little was left by way of domestic stocks was nearly exhausted. During the war years, timber was a strategic commodity used in the construction sector and also in coal mining as pit props – the country's vital source of energy being coal. After the war, the British premier, Lloyd George, admitted that the country had come close to losing the war due to lack of timber. It was largely these supply problems experienced during the war that led to the establishment of the Forestry Commission in 1919. The early objectives of the commission were: to train young men as practical foresters, to create 200,000 acres of new plantations immediately and to restore 50,000 acres of pre-existing forests, and, by the provision of state aid, to encourage the private sector to invest in forestry.

Despite Pigou's specific recommendation to encourage private and public sector forestry, the early objectives of the Forestry Commission were not realised. There has always been an anti-forestry lobby in Britain arguing that afforestation is not a profitable venture. This lobby persuaded the government that forestry was, essentially, unprofitable, and during the 1922–4 period there were cut-backs in which the afforestation programme suffered badly. The advent of the Second World War reminded the government of the reasons why the Forestry Commission had been established in the first place – trees planted in the 1920s were not ready for felling, and bulky timber imports proved to be an easy target for German submarines.

Having had two bitter experiences, after the war further and quite extensive plantations were created in the United Kingdom, and the forestry sector enjoyed slow but steady growth under the protective policies of post-war governments. Today, however, forest coverage in the United Kingdom is still less than ten per cent of the land surface, making it one of the least afforested regions of Europe.

The British government's policy is to expand the forestry sector by using all three Pigovian policies. In this respect, the country's remaining ancient forests are protected by legislation. The Forestry Commission is allowed to use an interest rate as low as 3 per cent – the forestry target rate of return – in its appraisal of new plantations, whereas other tradable public sector bodies are using 8 per cent. Private planters receive cash grants, currently paid in three instalments – 70 per cent immediately after planting, 20 per cent five years later, and the remaining 10 per cent in the tenth year. Last, but not least, the proceeds from the sale of trees are tax free. At the time of writing, the British government has indicated that incentives for private sector forestry will be maintained and planting grants will be improved.

As for the curbing of environmental contamination, Pigovian taxes could be levied on the level of industrial activity which is the source of pollution, or directly on pollution itself. In the former, if we reconsider the Marshallian marginalist analysis explained in Chapter 5, the optimum level of economic activity is the one where marginal benefit function coincides with the marginal cost function. In Figure 6.1 this is identified as OE. In the absence of compensation, it would not be in the interests of the private sector to reduce its level of activity from OB to OE. A Pigovian tax levied on per unit of output can help to reduce the level of activity to the socially optimal point. Taxation equal to T would shift the industry's gain function to the left because it is a cost to the operator. With new net (net of tax) gain function industry will operate at OE, which coincides with the socially optimal level of output.

Alternatively, a Pigovian tax could be levied directly on pollution emissions or pollution emitting substances. For instance, if we take the proposed European carbon tax, which has been studied by the European Union officials as well as academics in many countries, that has already been imposed in countries such as Holland, Norway, Sweden and Finland, and the Danish parliament has passed a law calling for one. In Britain, the Secretary of State for the Environment first indicated in 1988 that a carbon tax may be on the cards. However, thus far there has been no such levy.

One important objective of the proposed tax is to stabilise carbon dioxide emissions in the European Union at their 1990 levels by the year 2000. Originally, the carbon tax was intended to start in 1993 at $3 per barrel of oil, then to increase by $1 per year until it reached $10 per barrel in the year 2000. The revenue would belong to each member state to be used exclusively for environmental improvement. However, in 1992 the European Union shied away from the introduction of a community-based carbon tax; it is quite possible though that in the early part of the next decade a carbon tax may be in force in the Union, levied on fossil fuel and other sources of energy.

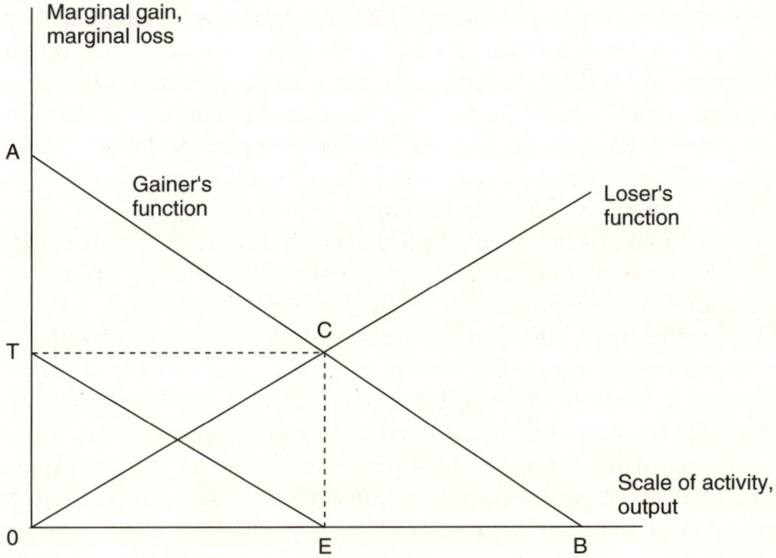

Figure 6.1 A Pigovian tax on output

The tax would have two components: carbon content and energy content. Tax on nuclear energy would relate to the latter, tax on fossil fuel would relate to both the energy and carbon content. Coal is the dirtiest fuel: roughly speaking it is 25 per cent worse than oil, which is about 33 per cent worse than natural gas. Therefore, there is need for a higher tax on coal than oil and a higher tax on oil than gas. A number of studies suggest that the price elasticity of demand for fossil fuel is very low in the short run. That is, in the short run the demand is rather unresponsive to an increase in price. Barrett (1990), using the British government's figures, calculates the effect of a 1 per cent increase in the price of gas, oil and coal.

How hard should each item be taxed in order to curb emissions noticeably? According to Barrett (1990), in order to achieve a 50 per cent reduction in CO_2, in the short term, the government needs to tax gas by 100 per cent, oil by 134 per cent and coal by 167 per cent. Long-term figures would be 35 per cent for gas, 47 per cent for oil and 59 per cent for coal.

In Pigou's analysis, an income tax may be socially desirable from a distributive viewpoint as it takes more from the rich. This view, which has been debated by Baumol and Oates, will be discussed at the end of this chapter. However, Pigou implied that this may slow down the creation of capital, and may be in conflict with the well-being of future generations. Simply put, an income tax which hits the rich could injure future generations.

It has been argued that a pollution tax in the form of the proposed European carbon tax would hit the poor, but would be environmentally beneficial, both for present generations and, especially, for future ones. Since the poor spend a greater proportion of their income on heating and lighting than the rich, the increased price of energy would be regressive. Furthermore, in the United Kingdom, the poor tend to rely heavily on the dirtiest fuel – coal – for house heating, whereas the rich tend to use the relatively cleaner fuels, oil and gas. As pointed out previously, in order to be effective a carbon tax should fall most heavily on coal – the fuel used by the low income groups for domestic heating.

Apart from the equity issue, a carbon tax could create adverse economic consequences, especially by reducing the competitiveness in domestic as well as international markets of those industries using fossil fuels. This is one reason why the British government has backed away, perhaps temporarily, from the introduction of a carbon tax in recent years. Ideally, a carbon tax must be levied globally in all polluting countries – something which will be very difficult to achieve. If a tax were to be implemented by the European Union, it would be borne by the Union members, but the environmental benefits would be spread globally. In other words, unless every country does the same, the citizens of the European Union would be unable to capture the full benefits of the tax.

One factor which could lead to imposition of a widespread carbon tax is that governments need revenue. Pezzey (1989) argues that although industry and households may tolerate a pollution tax based upon a realistic 'polluter pays' principle, they are unlikely to put up with yet another excuse to increase the tax burden. This also happens in another Pigorian tax – excise duty on the output of extractive industries (see Chapter 5, under Hotelling). It is true that this type of tax slows down the rate of extraction, which benefits future generations, but one important reason for this tax is that it brings in quick and substantial revenue to governments. For example, during 1978–81 when OPEC countries substantially increased the price of crude oil by way of taxes, they argued that the cartel was looking after the interests of future generations. Only the naive believed that.

Apart from extractive taxes, despite their theoretical and practical appeal, Pigorian taxes on pollution are not widespread. They are an exception rather than the rule. Why is this so? Pezzey (1989) and Hanley *et al.* (1990) offer a number of explanations, one of which is ignorance, in that policy makers do not know or cannot appreciate the usefulness of pollution taxes. Normally, debates on such taxes take place among economists, who use extensive and often unnecessary mathematics and jargon that keep non-specialists out. Another factor is that policy makers lack information regarding the nature of marginal cost and benefit functions involved in identifying the optimal level. Without a sound knowledge of these functions, it is impossible to devise an optimum tax. Finally, there is institutional resistance to Pigovian taxes. Many pollution regulation bodies in Britain and other industrialised countries were established more than a hundred years ago in response to legislation on public health and safety. Pollution taxes are disliked in regulatory circles, whose members wish to know exactly why the existing system is inadequate and also see the new system of taxes as a challenge to their position and authority.

Clearly, Pigovian policies such as legislation, taxation and subsidies are implemented in many countries. For instance, there is legislation to protect heritage landscape, ancient forests, etc. in force in the United Kingdom, together with subsidies to encourage private sector forestry and tax exemptions for foresters. The Republic of Ireland and Holland, too, provide subsidies to encourage private sector forestry. In most countries, the legislation on many aspects of environmental protection is extensive and growing – if Pigou was alive today, it is likely he would be rather pleased by the wide implementation of his policies on natural resource use.

THE KEYNESIAN VISION OF THE FUTURE

Keynes did not write widely on natural resources and the environment. Rather, he made some profound comments on population growth, natural resource adequacy and the future of mankind in general. Although, judged on his publications, Keynes cannot be described as having been a big influence on environmental matters, he has been a dominant figure in the economic policy making of many countries for a large part of this century, which has impacted on all aspects of economic life – including the environment.

John Maynard Keynes (1883–1946) was a member of the social and intellectual elite of his time. He was educated at Eton and Cambridge, where he studied philosophy and economics and was taught by Marshall. During the First World War, he worked at the Treasury; after the war, he argued that the economic problems in Europe were more important than boundaries and national aspirations of individual countries. He was also highly critical of the British government's domestic economic policy, especially its efforts to return to the gold standard. Although there was a noticeable conservation movement in the 1920s, Keynes' attention was taken by much more pressing problems of the time such as war reparations, gold standards versus a managed monetary policy, disparity between saving and investment and, above all, the mass unemployment which came about after the crash of the stock market.

Keynes believed that the Western world had the resources and ability to solve the pressing economic problems provided that an appropriate economic structure could be constructed, one in which the state should intervene to achieve economic goals, especially when the markets fail. He saw unemployment and poverty as real, but temporary, problems which have affected much of mankind throughout recorded history.

Keynes, like many other thinkers and intellectuals, such as Smith, Malthus, Ricardo and Mill, had a 'vision of the future' which was profoundly optimistic. In his *Essays in Persuasion* (1931), written during a period of general gloom and pessimism, he envied the future – not the very distant future – but a hundred years from his time. There were two main forces in progress which led him to express such optimism: the rate of capital accumulation and technological progress.

Until the sixteenth century, Keynes argued, human progress had been very slow – in parts of the world it was not happening at all. The modern age had begun with the process of accumulation of capital in the sixteenth century, and the power of compound interest over two hundred years had led to the availability of a substantial amount of capital when it was most needed at the beginning of the great age of scientific development and technical inventions in the eighteenth century. As an example, Keynes pointed to the value of Britain's foreign investment in the 1930s, which amounted to £4 billion at the time. He traced this to 1580 when Drake stole treasures from Spain and brought them home to Queen Elizabeth I. After the use of spoils for various things, an investment of £40,000 was made to create the Levant Company, which in turn led to the creation of the East India Company. Profits from these two great business ventures led to the creation of numerous overseas companies and, by accumulating at a 3.25 per cent interest rate, the £40,000 of 1580 became approximately the value of Britain's foreign investment in the 1930s.

Industrialisation gathered pace at the beginning of the nineteenth century fuelled by innovations, the opening up of markets, and the availability of capital. New methods led to mass production in many branches of industry and mining. As a result, in spite of population growth, the average standard of living in the West had risen about four-fold by the 1930s. Although, at times, continuous progress brought difficult and painful problems, Keynes asserted that all economic problems could be solved. On the population issue, Keynes wrote 'from now on we need not expect so great an increase of population' (1931: 363). The pace at which we can reach the golden age will partly depend on our power to control population, which we can achieve.

Keynes considered that, in the long term, mankind would solve all its economic problems: a hundred years on from 1930 the standard of living in progressive countries would be between four and eight times higher – in fact it would not be foolish to expect even greater gains. He maintained that economic problems were not a permanent feature of mankind and that, when solved, man would enter into a new age in which human energy would be spent on non-economic pursuits.

> Thus for the first time since his creation man will be faced with his real, his paramount problem – how to use his freedom from pressing economic cares, how to occupy the leisure, which science and compound interest will have won for him, to live wisely and agreeably and well.
>
> In the new age there will be great changes in the code of morals. Man will be able to rid himself of many pseudo-moral principles and adopt truly virtuous values such as avarice is vice, good is above useful. Also, at the dawn of the moral age as opposed to the economic age, which has dominated our lives for so long, there will be problems. As the affluence begins to settle in man will be deprived of his traditional purpose of relentless work for a living, something which has been bred into us for countless generations. The main problem will be that of adjustment into a more leisurely life in which we must use our freedom wisely. Judging by the problems of some well-to-do housewives who have been largely deprived of their traditional tasks such as cleaning, cooking, mending, etc., and are unable to find alternatives and are thus depressed, the adjustment period which is awaiting us could be a hard one.
>
> To judge from the behaviour and achievements of the wealthy classes today in any quarter of the world, the outlook is very depressing.
>
> (Keynes 1931: 368)

What a contrasting view to the Malthusian vision of the future. We are now only just over three decades away from the year 2030. Is there any sign of the boringly affluent times which will soon greet mankind? On the contrary, according to some (as will be discussed in Chapter 11), in the face of recent evidence, life in the year 2030 is unlikely to be as Keynes predicted. Hence, it could be argued that Keynes was wrong – in some instances very wrong. Take his views about population growth. First, he asserted in 1930 that from then on we need not expect so great an increase in population. In 1930 the world population was about 2 billion, today it is about 6 billion, and by the year 2030 it is likely to be about 9 billion. Even in England, one of the 'sober' countries of the world, the population rose by about 30 per cent between 1930 and 1990.

Second, it was surely a Keynesian pipe-dream to argue that man would live very comfortably by the principles of compound interest on capital, and by reaping the fruits of scientific developments which, around the year 2030, would provide material abundance unparalleled in human history. More than sixty years before Keynes wrote his essay, Mill made it abundantly clear that every kind of growth, including the growth of capital stock, must come to an end (1862). In this respect, in 1966 Kenneth Boulding argued that anyone who believes in exponential growth that can go on forever in a finite world is either mad or an economist.

Third, Keynes implies that virtuous living and adoption of true moral principles can only take place in a state of society when all economic problems are solved. He states quite categorically that all kinds of unjust and distasteful social behaviour, which we maintain now because they are useful in promoting the accumulation of capital, will be discarded in the affluent society. What an amazing piece of nonsensical writing! In effect, most of us know that the most valuable and virtuous deeds are those which take place when things are tight. A just society must be available to mankind at all times regardless of the level of gross national product. Keynes implies that a rich man must have a greater capacity for virtue and just conduct than a poor man!

Another unusual statement made by Keynes was that 'in the long run I will be dead'. In my dealings with some economists, there have been many occasions when they have dismissed long-term environmental problems, such as the full effects of global warming, ozone depletion, nuclear waste storage, and so forth, by quoting from Keynes. Some take the attitude that those environmental problems which are likely to bite harder in the distant future are not really their problem. In the Keynesian scheme of things, the emphasis is and should be on short-term problems.

GALBRAITH

John Kenneth Galbraith, who was born in Canada of Scottish parentage, is one of the best-known economists of the twentieth century. His writings carry the message that the market mechanism is not an effective means of allocating scarce resources and thus there is a substantial role for governments to intervene in order to achieve real prosperity and other socially desirable objectives. He is the author of many best sellers, such as *American Capitalism* (1972), *The Affluent Society* (1958), *The New Industrial State* (1967), *Economics and the Public Purpose* (1974), *The Age of Uncertainty* (1977), and *The Culture of Contentment* (1993). His main focus has been American capitalism which he criticises fiercely. According to him, American capitalism, in its established track, will not only aggravate existing economic and social ills, it will create many new problems, including environmental ones. As an alternative, he proposes a *new socialist system* which would redistribute income, adjust prices, wages and profits, scrutinise great corporations, and nationalise the health service and the armament industry (Galbraith 1972). This is nothing like the collapsed centrally planned economics of Eastern Europe, but a structure in which there are a number of partners such as modern corporations, government, unions and education establishments co-operating in a liberal democratic tradition.

Galbraith holds that American capitalism has not brought happiness to its citizens, but envy, violence, physical and visual pollution and, above all, a feeling of insecurity (Galbraith 1958, 1967, 1974, 1977). As the economy grows, firms, especially large ones, create pseudo-needs by invention, imitation, advertising, salesmanship and envy. In this climate consumers, dizzy under the influence of fierce advertising campaigns and a heightened feeling of envy, can no longer make sensible decisions. As individuals strive towards more and varied, and often trivial, consumption, the free market gives further signals to producers to respond in greater quantities. The most important objective of modern firms is survival, growth and their own aggrandisement. However, managers are fully aware that they must achieve sufficient profits to keep shareholders happy which, by and large, they do. A modern conglomerate achieves its objectives by having a technostructure of experts who operate within a plan. If planning works for giant corporations, it could also work for society provided that it is properly implemented to achieve clear and humane objectives.

In his view, in a modern capitalist society firms are able to manipulate markets to achieve one of their most important objectives, namely, growth:

> Economic growth is the central goal of the firm; from this it becomes a central goal of society. Growth, being a paramount purpose of the society, nothing, naturally enough, is allowed to stand in its way. That includes its effect, including its adverse effect, on the environment, on air, water, the tranquillity of urban life, the beauty of the countryside.
>
> (Galbraith 1974: 286)

Furthermore, he continues, free-market economy stresses individual wants and starves the public sector to the point of social discomfort and even ill health. As private wealth grows, the crisis in the supply of public goods deepens. A civilised society should strike a balance between private and social wealth. Galbraith calls it the issue of social balance. Disparity between the flow of private and public goods is not a matter of subjective judgement as it can be seen and felt daily in almost all parts of America. In all large cities there is a severe shortage of even the most elementary public services: police forces are understaffed, schools are over-crowded with inadequate facilities, streets are full of rubbish, green spaces are insufficient, dirty and dangerous, traffic is congested, air is polluted, and so on. Even the countryside is congested, polluted, and made invisible by the numerous advertising boards which litter every highway in the country.

Since the Second World War, as private wealth has increased, public squalor has become more intense and there is no sign of this being reversed. Galbraith asks: Is this the American genius?

On the issue of population growth, Galbraith acknowledges that the ghost of Malthus is hovering over the Third World and not everyone is certain that the better-off nations are assured of enduring abundance (1958). Curbing the growth of human numbers by way of birth control is already a lost cause in areas where it is most needed. It is such an unrewarding task that governments have usually put their most incompetent ministers in charge of family planning. Pest control officers measure their degree of success by results, i.e. pests killed, but the success of family planning officers is measured by the number of leaflets they distribute and the vigour of their speech (1977: 285). For instance, in India, the voluntary sterilisation policy was at its height in the 1970s when those in charge of it were able to measure their success by numbers. Then things went wrong. In order to increase their degree of success, some officers began to use coercion, which, in the event, brought the policy into disrepute and led to its abandonment.

Galbraith points out that in the 'rich world' people have a style of living to protect and thus families use contraception. Furthermore, in addition to sex, there are a lot of recreational facilities to spend time on such as television, theatre, books, travel, and sport. In the poor world, however, people do not have a high standard of living to protect and sexual intercourse is perhaps the only moment of brightness and escape from the daily toil. It offers immediate enjoyment with consequences to follow months later.

Governments in the Third World are mostly occupied by immediate problems. Family planning, although a 'must' brings benefits and relief years later, long after the decision makers, frequently military dictators, disappear from the scene, so why bother?

Birth control is a hotly debated issue in the Western world where the population is not growing much. According to Galbraith, poor nations believe that family planning is a way of stopping the white race being swamped by the black, yellow and brown. Ideas regarding the expulsion of immigrant communities from Europe and the United States enhance this belief in the poor world and undermine the whole idea of birth control.

He contends that the neo-classical economists (who were discussed in Chapter 5) under-emphasised the importance of externalities. Since growth is the main objective of a modern capitalist economy, the damage to the environment becomes wholly predictable. The greater the growth, the greater the volume of waste to be disposed of in air or water. In his words, 'the greater the wealth the thicker will be the dirt' (Galbraith 1958: 194). True, there are many environmental protection measures, but these are not as important as the growth itself. The claims of the environment can be advanced only in the face of a heavy burden of proof.

Growth-based capitalist economy not only creates innumerable environmental problems, but also discriminates against public services that are needed to ease the burden. New forms of pollution and hazards are constantly being created. For example, in addition to coal-burning power stations which are causing acid rain and global warming, scientists, with the blessing of governments, have created atomic power plants with unknown radiation hazards. There is a concerted effort by the interested groups to play down the environmental effects of such activities. Instead of eliminating harmful operations, the public are told that these things are benign or the hazards imaginary. He cites, as an example, an advertising agency which in 1970 promised to do a major face-lifting exercise for any corporation by way of television commercials for a mere $400,000. In this way, environmental culprits can cheaply rely on the power of television to improve their image.

What then should, or could, be done? Galbraith proposes three remedies – two of which, he believes, are not workable. The first, and most obvious solution, is to limit the uninhibited growth. Since environmental problems are created by economic expansion, putting the brakes on it must be the most effective solution. In effect, this policy (which will be discussed in Chapter 9) has been recommended by the Club of Rome as the only viable alternative to resource and environmental problems. However, Galbraith does not believe that halting growth is an option. For one thing, he says, it is a matter of decades before any alleviation becomes effective. The time frames do not match. Furthermore, reduction of economic growth becomes feasible only after the creation of a more equitable income distribution which is not in sight. Today, more and more people believe that redistribution of income in favour of the most vulnerable groups by way of public assistance do more harm than good. Affluent groups now believe that environmental protection is a much more urgent issue than helping the poor.

The second solution comes from neo-classical economics which, as discussed in Chapter 5, largely sees externalities as a market failure and suggests a process of internalising. In this, either the firm which is creating the environmental damage pays directly, or the community at large picks up the tab for cleaning up the mess. When the firm is compelled to pay, eventually this cost will be passed on to its customers. When the community is required to engage in a clean-up operation, firms, as well as consumers, need to be taxed to raise the required revenue. Who should actually bear most of the tax burden is, of course, likely to be determined politically by the government in power. Galbraith does not believe that the neo-classical approach to environmental problems is sensible, because it rests on the belief of its proponents who find universal virtue in the market:

> there is no good way of making those who smoke in public places pay for the discomfort of those who do not. In the end, one prohibits smoking. To assess to airline passengers the discomfort of the noise of the people below is equally hopeless. To assess the passengers on an SST the damage to the upper atmosphere is not only hopeless, but ridiculous.
>
> (Galbraith 1974: 288)

The neo-classical economists who first discussed externalities, he continues, did not prepare us for the colossal damage that their market system would do to the environment:

> so economists would be wise to be restrained in recommending remedies that grow out of these ideas.

The third and really viable solution Galbraith puts forward is to allow economic growth to continue but to specify *by legislation* the domain in which it can occur. Establishing these boundaries is a major task for governments and the legal profession. The legislation on occasions may involve prohibition of consumption and hence production of certain goods or abolition of harmful technology. It is most important to realise that direct control makes the state, not the market mechanism, the arbiter and protector of communal interest.

Galbraith reports that in the past when public interests (including environmental concern) conflicted with private ones, steps were taken by regulatory agencies with a view to preparing the ground for legislation to protect the public. The regulatory authorities had considerable discretion and power to determine the proper course of action. But when powerful private interest groups such as the chemical, pharmaceutical, oil and car manufacturing industries were involved they were successful in moderating, and in some cases even preventing, the proposed course of action. Legislation became a time-consuming and expensive business and public bodies were accused of trying to put a strait-jacket on business that was in fact providing jobs and income for literally millions of people. Galbraith asserts that this sort of objection should not deter anyone as a strait-jacket is precisely the requirement for protecting the public interest. The quid pro quo for the firms would be full autonomy within the proposed framework.

Legislation should specify the type and level of wastes that can be created and discharged into air and water, but minimum intervention as to how the results are obtained. Visual pollution is no less important and this is allowed to blight our surroundings because modern capitalism assigns a low value to art and aesthetic considerations. Rules for the development within a specific area should be clearly established but, once again, there should be freedom of decision within the rules. There is now a good deal of legislation on environmental protection and development in the United States, but the rigours of these acts do not reach effectively to all corners of the country.

In the Galbraithian scheme of things, private planning to achieve growth objectives should only be reconciled with public purpose by public planning. He also warns us about the dangers of absolutism. Environmental concerns have created deep suspicion about the economic growth amongst a large section of the population and intellectuals. Schools of zero population growth and zero economic growth have become highly vocal in their arguments, but they overlook many things. For example, a smaller number of people in one place may consume twice as many goods and discharge more effluent into the environment than a larger population elsewhere. The environmental strategy proposed by Galbraith does not exclude growth, but requires that growth must be in the public interest. Some conservationists oppose any economic development that can have deleterious environmental effects, largely because of past failures and the weakness of current public sector policy makers. Calls for no oil refineries, no power plants, no more highways, etc. are often heard. There is a great danger in this. As with most things in life, environmental protection has a cost. The benefits from protection must be compared with the costs.

Most of Galbraith's views on the environment are not new. His argument that accumulation of private wealth has not brought happiness to Americans may be true in that it has also brought with it public squalor and feelings of insecurity. J. S. Mill warned us more than a century ago (Mill 1862) that unabated economic growth would not necessarily bring happiness.

J. K. Galbraith has some ideas in common with Arthur Pigou, as both advocate legislation to protect the environment. However, unlike Pigou, Galbraith is not in favour of taxation, which he believes to be largely ineffective and, in certain cases, could become a ridiculous policy. Above all, taxation, by being essentially a market-based instrument, implies that the market is the most efficient and virtuous organisation to achieve social goals. Instead, Galbraith recommends direct control for environmental protection with a clear set of rules for producers as well as consumers. Agents should then be left free to operate within these rules to achieve their goals.

Galbraith strongly advocates that there should always be a balance between private and public wealth. Some writers, such as Benjamin *et al.*

(1973), suggest that this notion of balance should be broadened to include the whole ecosystem of the world, not merely a national boundary.

MISHAN

Ezra J. Mishan's most important works on the environment are *The Cost of Economic Growth* (1967) and *The Economic Growth Debate* (1977). Although the books have a different focus, both depart from the 'conventional wisdom' that economic growth would enhance social welfare. Mishan notes that there have always been economists who have refused to accept the idea that a net increase in goods entails a net increase in welfare even in the absence of externalities. The overwhelming majority of the profession tend to spend almost their entire time immersed in pages of equations and numbers in order to create even more equations and numbers. When they lift up their heads to glance at the real world, they notice with admiration the growing volume of goods but seldom wonder whether there is any sense in this. Even fewer doubts may arise regarding the relevance of their own 'contribution' to the subject they study without the slightest intention of changing their course of research. In *The Cost of Economic Growth*, Mishan recognises the widespread public belief that industrial progress is ultimately beneficial and that often economists tend to hide behind this faith when they advocate more and more growth.

Mishan draws a parallel between his views and those of Galbraith that the 'conventional wisdom' to grow more and faster is flawed. However, he points out that formal economic analysis is still useful in correcting past errors and, in this respect, Galbraith should have analysed his theory of private wealth versus public squalor more formally within the framework of externalities. Perhaps Galbraith eschewed the concept of external effects in favour of a more direct and popular effect.

According to Mishan, almost all environmental problems have occurred as a result of the unrestrained commercial attitude that has been encouraged. Economic activities take place within a legal framework which could be modified to achieve better results.

Like Galbraith, Mishan gives an extensive account of environmental damage and contends that numerous desirable things, which were freely available in the past, have now become scarce and which, with current trends, will be even more scarce in the future. He believes that the damage to the environment has become so great that broadening the concept of property rights to internalise external effects is no longer possible (see also Kapp 1950). Modernisation of the entire institutional framework is now necessary; without this problems will grow even more menacingly.

In the creation of a more desirable environment, protective modern legislation rather than fiscal measures is necessary. For example, environmental rights, similar to, say, property rights for private land ownership, should be instituted. No one should be compelled against their will to absorb harmful substances which are created by others for a profit motive. Nobody should be forced to live in a noisy environment unless this is their choice.

Mishan implies that Pigovian policies such as taxation and subsidies are unlikely to be effective measures as they have been overtaken by the events. The only Pigovian policy which makes sense is legislation to protect the environment for present and future generations. Furthermore in his *Economic Growth Debate* he gives an account of fundamental disharmonies between economic growth and the good life. In addition to the basic necessities of life Mishan draws up a list of items as essential ingredients of good living. Some of these are: good health, enjoyment of natural phenomena, leisure, sense of security, love, trust, self-esteem, adherence to basic moral principles and personal freedom. Mishan doubts whether the unrestricted growth which has taken place, especially since the Second World War, has enhanced these values.

In effect, there is a good deal of evidence which points towards the opposite direction. For example, economic growth, by creating stress, has undermined health, deprived masses of natural habitat, reduced leisure time and created a feeling of insecurity. Furthermore, the relentless search for efficiency created material abundance often at the expense of affection and sympathy between people and diminished opportunities to enjoy the vital experience of love. Good living brings individuals into tolerable harmony with themselves and others. Economic growth, by undermining this, has created disharmony.

A MILDER TONE – BAUMOL AND OATES

In the 1960s and 1970s, a number of economists, disillusioned with the proposed property rights approach, which will be discussed in the next chapter, began to focus more tightly on Pigovian taxes and subsidies as a policy tool to protect the environment. Coase's theorem appeared to be unworkable, partly due to the large transaction costs involved and partly because of the policy makers' inability or unwillingness to grant property rights to all parties concerned.

During that time, Baumol and Oates noticed the increasing burden of environmental externalities stemming from the growth of privately owned goods, which has been emphasised by a number of economists. The problem has also been aggravated by the declining effectiveness of the public services supply, which has largely been determined independent of externalities (Baumol and Oates 1975). In other words, the quality of life has been under attack from two fronts: growing environmental externalities and decreasing effectiveness of public services.

There is a certain parallel between the views of Baumol and Oates and those of Galbraith, who expresses concern about the growth of private wealth in the midst of public squalor. For example, the quality of life in a modern city depends upon the rate at which rubbish has been thrown into the streets by self-serving individuals and the speed and thoroughness with which it has been removed by municipal authorities. Baumol and Oates, therefore, urge economists to study both issues simultaneously. Unlike Galbraith, who favours direct control, Baumol and Oates recommend a tax-subsidy programme, as they believe this to be a practical and effective procedure of intervention to protect the environment.

In their analyses of externalities, Baumol and Oates conclude that in reality the achievement of true social optimum is not feasible, partly due to the information problem and partly due to a degree of arbitrariness that exists in the design of environmental standards. Instead they opt for a 'satisficing' approach in which one tries to find a tax-subsidy structure to improve the environmental quality. A shift from a totally centralised regulation would achieve administrative savings which could then be used to implement fiscal measures.

Although the use of fiscal instruments can be a highly efficient means of dealing with environmental externalities, a complete removal of direct control is not to be recommended. Natural conditions, such as wind and rain, could change rapidly in a region for a while making it administratively difficult to alter taxation/subsidy levels to cope with such emergencies. Instead, it could be quicker and less expensive to make temporary use of the direct control mechanism, despite its static inefficiency. Furthermore, a system of direct control can be extended beyond emergencies to supplement an essentially fiscal structure.

In countries where direct control is the norm, regulators make producers liable for pollution fines only when they exceed the legal limit. These fines are seldom used to compensate the households who tend to suffer most. This implies that it is the state rather than private individuals who retain property rights to environmental attributes. Furthermore, absence of compensation to households is rather fortunate because of the difficulties in calculating the correct compensation which must be almost impossible.

When the marginal damage and benefit functions associated with external effects are not known clearly, a uniform tax on excessive pollution discharge achieves reduction more efficiently than a uniform set of standards on all firms (Baumol and Oates 1971). The tax rate aimed at reducing pollution to a politically desirable level can be achieved by way of trial and error. Tax can be increased if, after its introduction, the overall reduction of pollution is insufficient, or it could be reduced if the cut in emission is excessive.

There may be a substantial gap between the politically and economically desired levels of environmental degradation. No doubt the government will focus on the former and the least cost of attaining this level would be a tax on emission equal to the long-term marginal cost of abatement.

Regarding policy variables, Baumol and Oates prefer taxation to subsidy to protect the quality of the environment. In the latter, firms may have to be rewarded for a reduction in the level of externalities. On the whole, subsidy is an inferior tool for environmental management but on occasions convincing cases can be made for its implementation. For example, a smoking factory originally built away from population centres may, in later years, find itself surrounded by houses. In order to reduce the damage to households, the firm may have to invest heavily in smoke abatement or relocate. In such a case, it would be reasonable for the firm to ask for assistance from the government. Taxation, on the other hand, would be a penalty imposed on the firm for its external effect. Although taxation and subsidy may prove to be equally effective in reducing the emission problem of a single firm, from the viewpoint of the industry as a whole, subsidies encourage the entry of new firms whereas taxes promote their exit.

Equity also features in the analysis of Baumol and Oates, who feel that the rich can be expected to gain more from environmental protection. Ignoring the redistributive consequences of an environmental policy would lead policy makers to harm, although unintentionally, the poor in society. The wealthiest section of the community would be most keen on environmental improvement since the environment is a normal good; people with more money would want to purchase more of it. However, even when environmental improvement measures are financed by taxation, Baumol and Oates are not sure that a progressive income tax would ensure that the rich will bear a suitably proportionate share of the cost.

7

MARKET ENVIRONMENTALISM BASED ON PROPERTY RIGHTS

COASE'S APPROACH

The objective of the interventionist school is to move resource allocation towards the ideal for which some recommend legislation ranging from outright abolition to much reduced activity and fiscal measures ranging from taxation to subsidies. Intervention by the state to correct the shortcomings of the market assumes that governments are essentially efficient and capable of working out solutions to problems (Demsetz 1969). On the other hand, market environmentalists tend to believe that individuals are the best judge of their own welfare. Under a well-defined and free market structure, economic units should be able to take the necessary steps to achieve the best solution for themselves and their dependants.

In order to achieve a socially optimal level of environmental degradation, at least at a theoretical level, Ronald Coase rejects abolition, standard setting, taxation and subsidies as such decisions assume that the government has the articulated knowledge on all aspects of environmental externalities and is capable of internalising them. In the intervention theory, the special knowledge of the few, i.e. communal policy makers, is used to guide the actions of the many, i.e. all users of environmental attributes. In Hayek's words:

> [the] economic problem is not merely a problem of how to allocate given resources if given is taken to mean given to a single mind which deliberately solves the problem set by these data. It is rather a problem of which to secure the best use of resources known to any of the members of society, for ends whose relative importance only these individuals know.
>
> (Hayek 1972)

According to Coase (1960), if a system of property rights is properly instituted and guaranteed by the force of law there would be no need for intervention on, say, pollution; the parties involved should be left to tackle the issue themselves. In a free market environment with well-defined property rights individuals would be able to achieve the desirable level of pollution. In Coase's theorem, it is not crucial which party, polluted or the polluter, holds the property rights.

Under certain assumptions, a desirable level of environmental degradation can be achieved by negotiations between the polluter and polluted. If the polluter has the property rights, he or she could be compensated by the polluted for costs incurred in pollution reduction. Similarly, if the rights are with the polluted, they could be compensated by the polluter for their tolerance of the nuisance. In fact there is no requirement or restriction on the nature of the deal done; it could be a bribe as well as compensation. The assignment of property rights would solve the problem (see also Olson and Zeckhauser 1970; Farrell 1987).

In the bargaining process, the polluted would be willing to pay any money less than the suffering he or she would otherwise have to bear. On the other hand, the polluted will accept any money higher than his or her benefit curve for a unit reduction in the level of activity. Coase's property rights approach becomes appealing when there are a small number of individuals involved in external effects. Interested parties could effectively negotiate a payment scheme to induce those who generate externalities to adjust their behaviour to acceptable levels.

There are a number of well-known cases of bargaining which have taken place between a small number of parties with satisfactory results. The 1939 Trial Smelter Arbitral Tribunal is a case in point. The tribunal dealt with smoke damage caused by a Canadian industrial plant in North America. An international arbitration body found that Canada was liable for the damage caused by the industrial unit located in her jurisdiction and recommended regulation of emission (Trial Smelter Arbitral Tribunal 1939).

Coase's theorem has been criticised from a number of viewpoints. When the number of parties involved is not small, the likelihood of negotiation becomes unworkable due to the administrative cost of co-ordination. Even when the number of polluters in a locality is small, those affected by the emission tend to become large enough to make direct negotiation unmanageable. When the numbers are huge, they will tend to treat the behaviour of all others as beyond their control (see Buchanan 1967; Kneese 1971; Lerner 1971). With such numbers it will be extremely difficult for individuals to establish a definite and clear-cut bargaining strategy. It is inevitable that there will be different interest groups each trying to fight its own corner.

Demsetz (1969) contends that the idea of negotiation between interested parties would be relevant if negotiation costs are small. However, when an agreement is reached, we should not immediately assume that the cost of policing the agreement will be small. The problem will be even more acute in the case of regulation in which policy makers need to take the views of all those affected in the community before implementing and enforcing the policy. That is, cost of negotiation and enforcement for regulation is bound to be enormous and thus the best solutions to environmental problems are the development of property rights.

Coase's analysis that it makes no difference on efficiency grounds which party has the property right is debatable. When such rights are held by the rich and powerful, the outcome is likely to be different from the case in which the holders are average citizens. Furthermore, what if the victims of pollution are the poorest members of society, which may be so in many instances, would it then be morally right to expect the victims to pay the offenders for improvement in the quality of the environment?

There are also cases of external effects which are dispersed over a wide geographical area affecting a number of countries and millions of individuals. For instance, pesticide used by a farmer does not only affect a small group of individuals in the immediate area. It gets transported from its point of origin by winds, rivers and ocean currents and spread throughout the globe affecting countless numbers of individuals. Acid rain is another example of transfrontier pollution in which large numbers of industrial units affect millions throughout the globe. The nature of external effects in these cases makes it practically impossible to use Coase's property rights approach to strike a deal between the culprits and victims.

Furthermore, in the case of intergenerational environmental problems, it is not clear in Coase's theory who would be bargaining on behalf of future generations, especially the distant ones who may be the most vulnerable. In cases such as acute resource depletion, global warming and nuclear waste storage, can future individuals bribe present generations so that harmful activities are moderated or eliminated altogether?

It is also doubtful that individual bargaining power, even if it was practical, would result in a socially optimal outcome. Let us take a case in which a factory is emitting smoke which stays mostly in the surrounding district and individuals who live in that area are paid an amount sufficient to compensate them fully for the nuisance. In this case, since everyone is compensated, no one would have any motivation to live away from the factory. In effect, compensation would create an economic incentive to accept the bad effects of the externality with no offsetting benefits to anyone. In the words of Baumol and Oates:

> An excessive amount of smoke emission and an excessive number of nearby residents should both be avoided. Excessive smoke emission can be curbed by a Pigovian tax on the producer. Now Coase's analysis has suggested that, to prevent too many nearby residents, it may be necessary to impose a tax on those who live nearby. Far from compensating the victim of the externality, Coase's view is that they should be charged for the smoke they inhale.
>
> (Baumol and Oates 1975: 25)

Coase, in support of his position, argues further that the imposition of a pollution tax can itself introduce a set of externalities. In the previous example, let us say that more households move into the region which is affected by the smoke. In this way social damage caused by the external effects will be increased by the decisions of the households as the tax will affect the firm. Increased tax is an externality created by the decisions of the households which will reduce the value of the output produced by the firm. The failure to take account of this cost created by the households is comparable to the cost created by the firm on the households resulting from the emission. However, Baumol and Oates (1975) demonstrate that this type of reverse externality mentioned by Coase need not create resource misallocation because it is a pecuniary externality. Taxation would only change prices of some commodities and affect the financial circumstances of the parties involved. Increased smoke, on the other hand, will increase the cost on resource use as, for instance, households would require greater laundry service.

Recently, it has been argued that with imaginative methods the property rights approach can be extended to many cases. For example, exhaust fumes from cars are a major source of air pollution and a property rights-based approach can be used to moderate the problem. One proposed solution is to privatise major motorways which are the main source of traffic pollution. This would make the owner of the motorway, who was liable for damages, in turn seek measures to reduce this liability. Under this system, cars with better pollution control equipment would be subjected to lower tolls, while tolls at peak times would be made more expensive, thus reducing heavy concentrations of smoke by spreading the emissions more evenly during the day and night (Rothbard 1982).

With regard to pollution generated by industrial units, traces such as colouring agents or isotopes can be used to monitor the emissions and the drift. When pollution is having an impact on, say, property values, then the owners would have some basis for either seeking damages or entering into negotiations with the culprits.

Another market-based approach to minimise environmental problems is that of legal liability. In this, advocates recommend imposition of a legal liability on the activities of potential environmental culprits who pay for damages only when they occur. In this way, a market for damages would be created which would check the behaviour of the operators. The emphasis here is on liability rules rather than property rules (Bromley 1989).

THE MARKETABLE PERMIT APPROACH TO POLLUTION

Despite its apparent problems, the free-market school maintains that the environment will be better served through the exchange of well-defined and enforceable property rights in which there is a role for the government as enforcer. Then, self-interested individuals will engage in a voluntary exchange of property rights in a free-market environment which will promote co-operation and compromises. In the United States, the Nature Conservancy Program, which is based on free-market environmentalism, has yielded satisfactory results in the conservation of environmental attributes. For example, when the Wisconsin Nature Conservancy was given title to a beach some people felt that nature would be well protected, but at an enormous cost. However, the conservancy traded the property for a much larger wilderness area containing many endangered plant and animal species. In the event the wealth of the conservancy was enhanced.

According to Anderson and Leal (1991), the history of market environmentalism in the United States shows a steady progress from management of relatively easy land and energy development projects to more complex water issues. Communalisation, on the other hand, has hindered the full development of market-based environmentalism but subsidised environmental destruction.

It may be possible, by looking at encouraging past events, to move market environmentalism from land and water issues to much more complex air pollution problems. Dales (1968) and Montgomery (1972) contend that by issuing marketable pollution permits the community can achieve a desirable level of air quality. In this, the government allows only a certain level of pollution discharge and issues permits which can be tried on the market.

In order to implement a marketable permit system, the government, which becomes a part of the market-based structure, must first work out the geographical boundaries of the market. Next, the type and the level of discharge must be ascertained. In order to distinguish between various polluters, the government may split the market into a number of groups such as motor vehicles, households and industrial plants. Some polluters may have a negligible effect on the environment in a geographical district and thus the government may decide to exclude them from its scheme.

Should there be an initial price that permit holders must pay or should the rights be given free of charge? Naturally, polluters would favour a free distribution of rights which would give them a form of rent. In some cases, the government may decide to auction pollution rights in order to raise revenue to improve the already deteriorated environment. The system cannot work without enforcement to deter violations. Penalties may involve fines, removal of permits, or even shutdown.

In the 1920s, the US Environmental Protection Agency introduced a few market-based projects to facilitate economic growth without compromising the environmental quality. The Emission Offset Program allowed new firms to enter into an environmentally saturated area provided that they made existing firms reduce their emission. This confirmed a kind of property rights on existing firms for which they were able to extract payment.

According to Baumol and Blinder (1984), this policy did not work very well. Firms obtained permits to construct new plants either by offsetting reductions in other plants they owned or by offsetting reductions in emissions by some government agency.

In 1979, amendments to the Clean Air Act created the so-called bubble policy in which a firm is permitted to satisfy its mandatory pollution ceiling in a way which is most economical. The entire operation by a single firm is considered to be an imaginary bubble. The Environmental Protection Agency requires that emissions from the bubble stay within the required limit; it does not care what goes on inside the bubble. This policy was originally intended for single firms but since then it has been extended to include a host of firms.

Marketable permits seem to have some advantages. First, they can provide a flexible strategy for the regulator. If, for example, a given number of permits are creating an excessive amount of discharge, then the government can buy back some rights. Conversely, if given rights are creating a situation in which the emission is less than the desired level then more permits can be issued. Such permits can be thought of being a vertical pollution supply schedule which can be shifted by way of market operations. Second, permits can give flexibility and low-cost efficiency to polluters. When firms have different pollution control costs there will be possibilities in which low-cost polluters can sell their permits to high-cost polluters and in this way the cost of pollution control can be minimised. Newcomers, as well as established firms, can gain from the market transactions. A new firm will buy rights if it has a high abatement cost, otherwise it will invest in pollution control equipment. Sometimes abatement costs are lumpy; to reduce the discharge it may become necessary to invest in a new type of control process which may turn out to be costly. The firm can reduce its abatement cost by buying permits on the market.

On the negative side, if permits are administered too rigidly, they may give existing firms an unfair monopolistic advantage over newcomers. The holders can use their rights to deter new entry into the area, or even into a particular industry. The barrier to entry can become quite severe in locations where a small number of firms hold all the pollution rights. A marketable pollution permit system would be highly complex when pollution crosses national frontiers, which often happens in densely populated and politically fragmented Europe. Identifying the geographical boundaries of the market can become cumbersome when more than one nationality is involved.

There have been a number of suggestions with regard to the types of permits. In the ambient permit systems, the regulating body determines the areas where the pollution is received. Then the emission allowable in each receptor point, consistent with ambient air quality standards, is determined. Standards may change from one receptor point to another and rights can be obtained from different markets and probably at widely different prices. The regulator does not need to collate information about the abatement cost for each polluter, nor does it need to compute marginal damage and marginal benefit functions for polluters. In a system of fiscal measures, it is necessary to know the shape of these functions. From the polluter's viewpoint, an ambient-based system exhibits some difficulties as each firm would need to have permits for every receptor area that its pollution is affecting. There would be as many markets as receptor areas and polluters might find it quite costly to conduct transactions.

An emission-based system tends to eliminate the problem of multiple markets and prices per polluter. In this, permits are defined in terms of emission levels at source as opposed to the effect of emission or the ambient quality in all receptor areas. Discharges within a particular area can be treated as equivalent, regardless of where they drift. The main problem would be that the system would not discriminate between sources on the basis of the damage due. In order to overcome some of these problems, Krupnick *et al.* (1983) proposed that definition of rights in terms of emissions and trade would take place within a defined zone, but not on a one-for-one basis. No transfer would be allowed unless air quality was preserved at any receptor point. The buyer must obtain enough to satisfy the standard at all points within the area. The offset system tends to combine the characteristics of ambient and emission-based systems.

MARKETABLE PERMITS AND RIGHTS-BASED FISHERIES

Fishery, by its nature, has always been a vulnerable natural resource to the common access problem as in the open sea it is extremely difficult to establish property rights on a resource base. In the past, individuals with the necessary skill and equipment were able to dip into fisheries in many parts of the world. Gordon (1954) argues that despite the fact that the fishery resources of the sea are the richest and the most indestructible known to man, it is a rare thing to identify a rich fisherman or fishing community due to the persistence of common access. The theory of fishery economics was developed against this background in the 1950s by Gordon (1954), Scott (1955) and Schaeffer (1957).

The main preoccupation of the fishery scientists and economists at that time was that, given the open access problem, governments were called upon to regulate fishing activity. The crucial question was what should be the basis for fishery regulation? Fishery scientists were in favour of a concept called the maximum sustainable yield aimed to bring in the maximum catch. Economists were not happy about this concept on the grounds that it did not give any consideration to cost of catching fish. As an alternative, they recommended the optimum sustainable yield which identifies the maximum economic rent by taking account of the cost as well as the revenue. In later years, a dynamic theory of fisheries was developed by Copes (1972), Clark and Munro (1975), Clark (1976) and Clark *et al.* (1979).

In the 1950s and 1960s some governments sought to increase their control over the waters off their coasts, arguing that this was the best way to protect the fish stocks from unrestricted access. In 1952, Chile, Peru and Ecuador extended their fishing territories. In Europe, Iceland was the first country to do so – in 1958 the fishing territory around Iceland was extended to twelve miles and in 1972 to fifty miles. This raised tempers between Britain and Iceland and culminated in the so-called 'cod war' of the 1970s.

As the territorial waters were expanding in the 1950s, the United Nations called the first of a number of Law of the Sea conferences with a view to exploring commercial and legal matters regarding the use of the seas. The third of these conferences, in 1971, produced the Informal Composite Negotiating Text recommending that coastal ocean states should, where appropriate, have exclusive economic zones of 200 miles. Many nations then unilaterally declared a 200-mile fishing limit. The Convention of the Law of the Sea was signed in 1982. Article 612 of this convention states that the coastal states shall determine the allowable catch in their exclusive zones. They should also ensure by proper conservation and management measures that the stocks in the exclusion zone are not endangered by over-exploitation. All the necessary measures should be taken to monitor and restore population of harvested species which can produce sustainable yields as qualified by relevant environmental, economic and social factors.

With the enlarged jurisdiction on fisheries, many nations implemented various methods to achieve the aims of the Convention of the Law of the Sea. It cannot be claimed that all of these methods have been successful. For example, in 1977, the fishery plan for New England, USA, established an annual quota regime for major species without restriction of entry. This did not work because the harvest was taken early in the year and the fishermen remained idle for the rest of the time. The policy in the following year was modified to allow two harvests, but this was not a long-term solution. In later years, quarterly quotas were tried, which again did not work satisfactorily mainly due to natural conditions. Then quotas based on vessel size were tried in which the emphasis was shifted to fishing effort. Most boats incurred high harvesting costs because they frequently rushed to the port to fill their quotas quickly. Owners of small boats felt particularly pinched because they were frequently affected by adverse weather conditions and missed some of their quotas. The policy was revised again, this time based on the size of the crew; this resulted in large crews appearing on each vessel. Additional regulations were than laid down for each type of boat. In the end, the whole system became complex and unmanageable and was abandoned.

The development of the rights-based fishery during the 1980s took place against the management problems described above. Policy makers were beginning to realise that a fishery management scheme works better when authorities do not encourage fishermen to race for the allowable catch. In a rights-based fishery, regulators grant each operator access to a geographical area at certain times, and allow them to land and market certain species of fish and issue permits for the use of vessel and gear. These rights can be traded on the market.

The main characteristics of a rights-based fishing scheme are: quality of title, exclusivity, duration, divisibility, transferability and flexibility. It enables the holder to save fish for harvest in a later year by conservation, minimises rush and unnecessary competition among fishermen to fill their quotas, assists co-ordination among those who hold similar rights, reduces competitive investment which leads to overcapitalisation and allows fishermen to trade their rights. This system has distinct advantages over the old policies of restricted entry and regulation in which fishermen spent a good deal of their time out-racing rivals, outwitting regulators and disputing gear and other rules.

As a criticism against rights-based fisheries, it can be argued that, just as under the old system, quota owners can easily cheat and poach; thus a quota system requires equally extensive monitoring and enforcement. However, this type of criticism assumes that fishermen will continue to behave as evasively as they did under the old regulatory system, although the strength of the quota system is that it creates some incentive for self-enforcement. Retting (1989) believes that a rights-based system developed for close consultation with all the interested parties is likely to be more successful than the one designed by aloof officials or academics interested in furthering their own careers. Furthermore, allocation of rights among people with common cultural and social ties is likely to be more successful than programmes involving highly diverse groups.

The first comprehensive application of a transferable quota system was introduced in New Zealand in 1986. The progress of this experiment is being watched with keen interest by resource economists, fishery scientists and policy makers in all parts of the world. Up until 1963, the inshore fishery in that country was managed under a system of strict gear and area controls alongside restricted entry. In 1963, the inshore fishery was deregulated with a view to attracting fresh investment into the sector. As a result, the industry expanded rapidly and, with the introduction of 200-mile fishing zones in 1978, possibilities for a lucrative fishery sector looked promising.

In 1982, the New Zealand government introduced a limited quota management system for some fish stocks, with transferable rights in the new 200-mile zone. This was the beginning of the rights-based system. In 1986, the economic goals in fishery management and transferable permit system become fully effective. Initially, quotas were allocated for a period of ten years for certain species. Later on, the government allocated these quotas in perpetuity and widened the species. The quotas are currently issued on the basis of past catches. There are three main objectives of the system: to achieve a level of catch which maximises the benefit to the nation on a sustained basis; to achieve an optimum number of configuration of labour and capital; to minimise the implementation and enforcement costs.

Although its implementation has taken place only recently, the conceptual origins of rights-based fishery are old. In the distant past, it existed in various forms in the Japanese, Aboriginal, Nordic and Anglo-Saxon traditions. In the old English tradition, there were complex rules regulating individuals rights to fisheries. Although the development of private fishery rights began early in England, it soon ceased in the tidal and offshore fisheries. Private rights, however, did continue in inland fisheries, based upon land ownership. When private rights to the open seas were ended, the concept of public rights of fishing took over, gradually giving way to the horrors of commons.

8

EMPIRICAL STUDIES ON SCARCITY AFTER THE SECOND WORLD WAR

After the Second World War, Western economies began to grow rapidly putting an increasing pressure on exhaustible resources. Alongside industrial development, growing pollution and ecological damage was becoming conspicuous and creating concern. Energy consumption in the United States, which had been growing steadily since the middle of the nineteenth century, began to accelerate immediately after the war. Nearly all power generated in the United States was fuelled by coal, oil and natural gas and thus ultimate exhaustion looked inevitable as there is no second crop in fossil fuel. The large volume of gases released by burning fossil fuels was darkening the skies in and around industrial centres. Growing car ownership was adding to the problem in a major way.

At a global level, fossil fuel use grew by about 4.4 per cent per annum between 1860 and 1914. Between the beginning of the First World War and the end of the Second World War the annual growth rate was under 1 per cent. In the decade to 1955, the growth rate became very rapid once again, approaching 4 per cent per annum. Figure 8.1 shows the products of energy from coal and oil between 1860 and 1955. Post-war governments welcomed and encouraged economic growth.

THE US PRESIDENTIAL COMMISSION ON MATERIAL POLICY

Alongside growing ecological problems, there was the realisation that the fast-growing economy would become increasingly dependent on the importation of oil and other raw materials. Were the foreign supplies secure enough to sustain the growth in the United States' economy? One of the earliest national studies of resource and environmental problems was carried out by the US President's Material Policy Commission. It published a report entitled *Resources for Freedom, Foundation for Growth and Scarcity* (1952) which revealed that in the United States alone the consumption of fuel and other minerals since the beginning of the First World War had been greater than the total consumption of all the previous centuries put together. The report

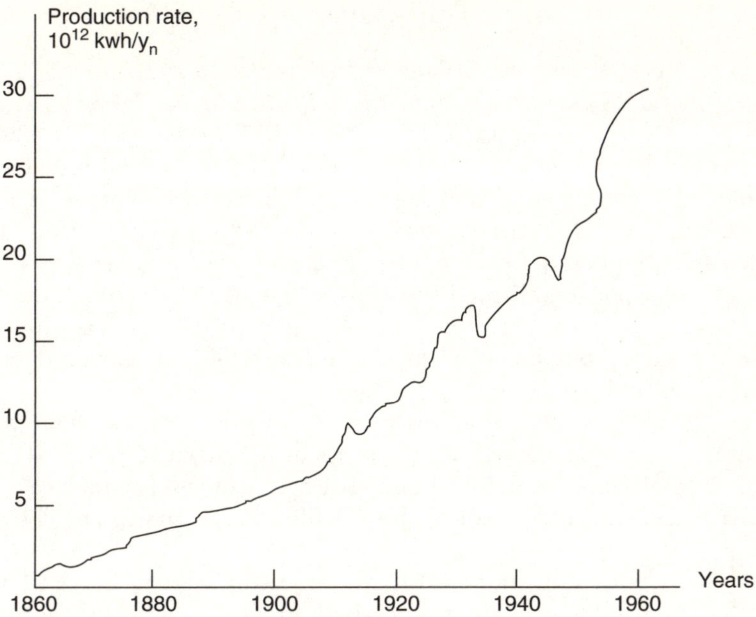

Figure 8.1 World production of energy from coal and oil
Source: Bubbert (1969)

concluded that natural resources are vital to the well-being of the nation's economy and urged the government to make plans for immediate as well as future needs.

The report marks an important landmark in the history of natural resource economics since, for the first time, a serious study had been commissioned by a head of a state. At the outset it states:

> [that] the question, has the United States of America the material means to sustain its civilisation would never have occurred to the men who brought this nation into greatness as the 20th century dawned. But with the 20th century now half gone by, the question presses and the honest answers are not glib.

The United States of America, in maintaining her democracy and fighting evil forces such as Nazism and Communism, needs an ample supply of natural resources. The interdependence between moral values and material base is undeniable in today's world. The report urged that the nation must give serious consideration to the earth's natural resources which are the foundation of freedom and prosperity. Its main recommendation was that the United States should ensure a sufficient and reliable flow of material at the lowest cost consistent with national security and the well-being of friendly countries.

POTTER AND CHRISTY

One of the best-known studies on scarcity is Potter and Christy's *Trends in Natural Resource Commodities – Statistics of Prices, Output, Consumption, Foreign Trade and Employment in the United States, 1870–1957* (1962). The book presents a collection of economic time series data on natural resource-based commodities, consumed as well as produced in the United States. They note that during the period covered in their study, 1870–1957, the United States progressed from being a net importer of capital and exporter of raw materials to a net exporter of capital and finished goods. Furthermore, during the period the population increased fourfold, land used for agriculture almost tripled, wood output increased more than threefold, extraction of iron ore increased 26-fold, crude oil 490-fold and copper 27-fold.

The report by Potter and Christy includes price, output, foreign trade, consumption, employment, and employment to output ratio for 90 per cent of all natural resource-based commodities consumed or produced in the United States. It excludes water and wildlife due to the absence of reliable data.

The most important statistical item to measure scarcity is price levels for the commodities which are summarised in four aggregates: agriculture, forestry, minerals and all resources. Agriculture includes all important commodities such as cereals, meat, dairy products, sugar, tobacco, wool. Likewise, the mineral sector contains the main commodities such as fossil fuels, iron, copper, lead, zinc, aluminium, gold, silver. Forestry includes lumber and pulpwood. In order to obtain real trends, prices were deflated by the Bureau of Labour Statistics' general wholesale price index to remove the effects of inflation.

The summary trends are shown in Figure 8.2 where the vertical axis is measured on a logarithmic scale which gives equal value to equal percentage changes in each series and thus enables the eye to compare the series for completely different magnitudes. The only sector showing a decisive upward trend is forestry, reaching a level in 1957 which is nearly five times higher than in 1870, an average annual increase of 1.9 per cent in real terms. Potter and Christy note that the rise in the price of timber may be understated because of the shift of the industry from the east to the west coast of America, which placed the output further away from the largest consumer market.

In Britain, research by Hiley (1967) confirms that price of timber has also increased on this side of the Atlantic. For example, the annual price increase for imported timber was 1.5 per cent in real terms between 1863 and 1963/4. The other sectors show less than 20 per cent above their 1870–4 level by 1952–7.

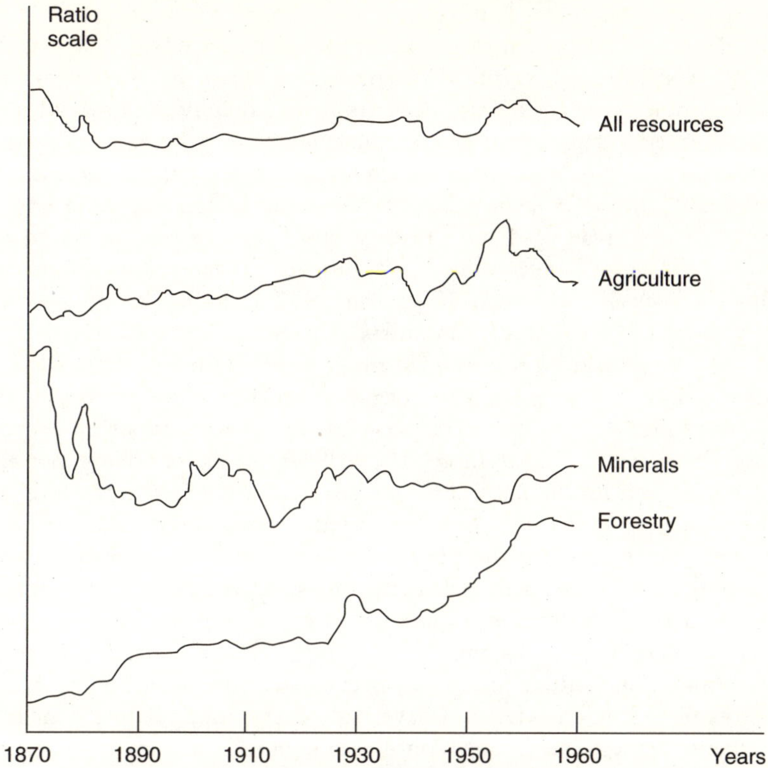

Figure 8.2 Deflated prices in natural resource-based sectors
Source: Potter and Christy (1962)

BARNETT AND MORSE

Working on the issue of scarcity at the same time as Potter and Christy, Barnett and Morse (1963) tested the implications of resource 'shortage' on extraction costs and prices of natural resource-based commodities. Their work, which partly relies on the data provided by Potter and Christy, covers a period between 1870 and 1957 in the United States. The objective of this study was to examine the conceptual and empirical foundations of the doctrine of increasing natural resource scarcity suggested by classical economists such as Malthus, Ricardo, Mill, and others. The problem they treated lies in the realm of historical growth economics rather than static efficiency doctrine.

Barnett and Morse note that the Malthusian problem could only occur in primitive and isolated societies which possess narrow knowledge about resource availability, have limited skills in production methods and also fail to develop taboos to restrict population. Likewise, the Ricardian stagnation would be relevant in a world where resource quality declines as economic expansion takes place with no important technological progress. In other words, Ricardo–Malthusian stagnation can occur in a world which is closed to social, scientific and technical progress. But when social conventions are changing, new discoveries are occurring, technology is improving, and resource substitution is available, stagnation theories based upon a diminishing returns hypothesis will be irrelevant. Even natural or man-made disturbances can have favourable effects on agricultural production. One example is the spread of deltas creating large areas of rich farmland which today support a sizeable section of communities in many countries.

The study period between 1870 and 1957 is long enough to test the scarcity doctrine of classical economists as it covers the most crucial period when the United States progressed steadily from an underdeveloped stage to an advanced economy. Short-term trends cannot be suitable to understand the scarcity doctrine as wars, trade cycles and other temporary events can obscure the picture. Furthermore, the full effects of increasing population and income levels on the natural resource sector can be felt in the long term.

The choice of the United States was partly due to data availability but, more importantly, during the period studied, population consumption and production levels were increased many times, putting heavy pressure on all types of natural resources in the country. As many deposits became exhausted there were substantial new discoveries, technical progress and substitution. The United States has been a free market economy and thus the forces of supply and demand have had plenty of opportunity for mutual adjustment. Sixteen years after publication of the report by Barnett and Morse, Barnett extended the study for another thirteen years, up to 1970 (Barnett 1979).

If the Ricardo–Malthusian scarcity was correct, it would reveal itself in the form of increased cost in output of the extractive and agricultural sectors, especially towards the end of the study period when economic growth was high. Barnett and Morse studied the unit cost of extractive products in agriculture, forestry, fishery and mineral sectors. Unit cost was defined as a weighted labour and capital aggregate divided by net output. That is:

$$C = \frac{lL + kK}{Q}$$

where:

C = cost per unit
L = labour input
K = capital input
Q = net output
l, k = weights used to aggregate labour and capital respectively

Labour input included mostly number of workers employed in the respective sectors. Instead of man hours for labour, for the greater part of the study, persons engaged were used in order to overcome a number of difficulties in data availability as well as in other matters. For capital input, mostly the volume of capital, measured in constant prices, was employed in the respective extractive industries. Most of the data for inputs as well as the relative weighting factors were taken from Kendrick (1961).

However, it should be mentioned at this stage that in addition to unit cost there are at least two other criteria which could be used to test scarcity theories: the real price and the resource rent. In the former, the market price of commodities which actually captures the cost is taken as a measure of scarcity. The main problem with this criterion is that the results would be highly sensitive to the choice of price deflator. The other method, resource rent, could be highly useful as it tends to capture the effects of technological change and substitution possibilities. Some believe that cost or price methods of testing scarcity are likely to understate the situation, especially when substitution between inputs is possible (Hartwick and Olewiler 1986). In addition to unit costs, Barnett and Morse also considered real prices of commodities with the assumption that price trends should follow the cost trend, apart from changes in the degree of monopoly, transport cost, taxation and subsidies. Broadly speaking, price trends confirmed cost trends, with some minor exceptions.

Research by Barnett and Morse revealed that all resources except forestry showed a decline in unit cost, expressed in real terms. For the entire extractive sector, the cost fell by about 1 per cent per annum until 1920 and by nearly 3 per cent per annum from 1920 to 1957. The extractive sector is particularly important because mineral resources are subject to depletion to a far greater degree than most other natural resources, given the fact that demand for minerals increased by nearly forty-fold between 1870 and 1957. During the period, many more new domestic reserves were found than old deposits exhausted. Also, advancement in the extractive technology and accessibility factor, such as off-shore oil and being able to use previously sub-standard deposits, helped to reduce the unit cost.

The agricultural sector, like the mining sector, underwent substantial changes during the period of study. The use of artificial fertilisers, irrigation water, and the substitution of machines for animal and human power became widespread. The substitution of farm machinery for farm animals especially reduced the pressure on land to provide calories for work animals. It also saved more labour per unit than its cost in capital. Improved seeds, weed and insect control and the cross-breeding of livestock increased the yield. There was little change in the total area of agricultural land during the study period: 2,970,000 square miles in 1870, as opposed to 2,971,000 square miles in 1958.

In the fisheries sector, as output went up, labour trended horizontally, with the result that labour cost per unit of output declined. Capital input data were not available for fishing or forestry, but timber output had increased steadily until about 1910 since when it had shown no particular trend upwards or downwards. The labour input increased sharply between 1870 and 1920, followed by a brief decline before picking up again until 1950. For the period as a whole, forestry supported the increasing scarcity hypothesis. Table 8.1 shows the situation in all four sectors.

Barnett and Morse conclude that apart from forestry, the unit cost in all sectors has fallen steadily, implying that natural resources have become less scarce. This is attributed to the discovery of new deposits, advances in exploration, extraction, processing and production, and the substitution of more abundant low-grade resources for scarce high-grade ones. However, it has to be mentioned that the work has some shortcomings. First, unit cost index is essentially a backward-looking indicator as it does not incorporate expectations about the future. It is quite correct that most of us make our decisions on the basis of past observations and beliefs, but sometimes these turn out to be wrong. Second, the unit cost index, in which capital and labour are lumped together, is defective. Aggregation of capital alone is a substantial problem. The correlation between extraction cost and technical progress is quite a problem. As physical depletion comes closer and deposits become harder to find, it may well be that unit costs rise, but this may also encourage efforts to find new deposits and improve technology to cut the cost. In other words, no clear sign can emerge from this measure about future costs and prices.

Table 8.1 Unit cost in natural resources, 1870–1957

Sectors	*1870–1900*	*1919*	*1957*
Agriculture	132	114	61
Forestry	59	106	90
Fishing	200	100	18
Minerals	210	164	47
Total extractive	134	122	60

Source: Barnett and Morse (1963)

NORDHAUS AND OTHERS

Another long-term study to test scarcity is by Nordhaus (1973), who looked at price trends between 1900 and 1970 for a number of commodities. A price analysis is convenient in the sense that statistical data is mostly available based upon the current prices but it must be deflated to eliminate the effect of fluctuations in the purchasing power of money.

Nordhaus deflates commodity prices at the refined level by hourly manufacturing wage rates. The results for some commodities are shown in Table. 8.2. One strength of using the real price data is that it is a relatively forward-looking measure because expectations about future supplies and costs will be reflected in the market prices of the commodities. Hartwich and Olewiler (1986) note that looking at prices decade by decade could be misleading as it does not tell us the whole story. For example, what happened to prices between 1910 and 1920?

The message of Nordhaus is that all commodities became cheaper and thus less scarce between 1900 and 1970.

Another study, which broadly confirms Nordhaus's work, is by Jorgensen and Griliches (1967) who deflated commodity prices by the price of capital. The results for some selective commodities are seen in Table. 8.3. This table also incorporates information from a number of other sources as mentioned in Hartwick and Olewiler (1986). Price trends for three commodities – coal, lead and zinc – do not confirm other trends in the same study, nor do they fall in line with the works of Barnett and Morse, Potter and Christy or Nordhaus as they show a substantial increase before 1940 and 1950.

Statistics presented thus far show a declining trend in costs and prices of natural resource-based commodities. Falling or steady prices, together with booming economies of the world, led to continuously increasing consumption right up to 1973. For example, between 1945 and 1973 global consumption of fuels rose by about 5 per cent per annum. Oil was the most sought after fuel as its use increased more than seven-fold to 2,800 million tonnes from 1950 to 1973. The psychology of falling commodity prices

Table 8.2 Price index, deflated by wage rate for commodities

Commodity	*1900*	*1920*	*1940*	*1950*	*1960*	*1970*
Oil	1034	716	198	213	135	100
Coal	459	451	189	208	111	100
Copper	785	226	121	99	82	100
Aluminium	3150	859	278	166	134	100
Iron	620	287	144	112	120	100
Lead	788	288	204	228	114	100
Zinc	794	400	272	256	125	100

Source: Nordhaus (1973)

Table 8.3 Price index, deflated by value of capital for commodities

Commodities	*1920*	*1940*	*1950*
Oil	547	205	275
Coal	340	195	413
Copper	170	125	129
Aluminium	647	297	217
Iron	216	149	146
Lead	292	211	298
Zinc	301	281	335

Source: Hartwick and Olewiler (1986)

suddenly changed during the first oil crisis of 1973–4 when the price of crude oil rose by nearly four times. During the 1973 Arab–Israeli war, OPEC countries acting in solidarity with the Arab world decided to use oil as a political weapon against the West, hoping that Western nations, especially the United States, would put pressure on Israel. The price of Saudi crude was $2.12 per barrel on 1 January 1973; in January 1975 the price went up to $10.72.

Mineral prices fluctuated quite sharply during the last three decades, but the overall trend has been downward. Sharp rises occurred during the oil crisis of 1973 which also affected other commodities such as agricultural produce. According to Griffin and Teece (1982), the main purpose of the OPEC was not to influence world price per se, but simply to achieve its share of oil rents. Figure 8.3 shows the price trend, adjusted for inflation, for non-fuel minerals. Real prices recovered somewhat in the second half of the 1980s but never returned to the levels that occurred in the 1950s and 1960s. One reason for falling mineral prices is that most producing nations subsidise development of new as well as existing deposits (Young 1981). For example, since the 1920s the United States government has provided generous tax exemptions and depletion allowances to mining companies. In this way, companies have been able to deduct an allowance ranging from 5 per cent to 22 per cent of their gross income, which can be in force as long as the business operates. In the 1980s, taxes lost in this way to the US Treasury added up to $5 billion. Furthermore, based upon the 1872 General Mining Act, companies who discovered metal deposits on public land were able to purchase the land for $12 per hectare or less, and thus the government received no royalties for the minerals taken from the land.

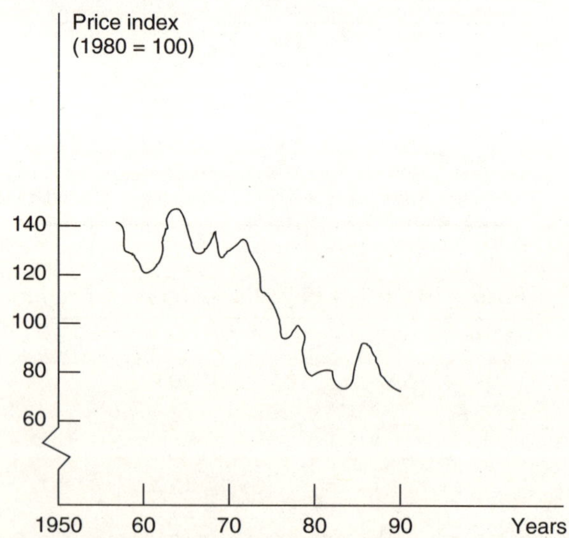

Figure 8.3 Index of real non-fuel mineral prices, 1957–97
Source: World Economic and Financial Surveys (1990)

Other countries, such as Japan, offer tax incentives, loans and subsidies for exploration of domestic resources. Japanese mining companies operating overseas receive low interest loans, loan guarantees and direct state investment. The French government has a number of packages available for mineral exploration, but they are less generous in Germany. These nations justify subsidies to mining corporations on the grounds of national security as they supply raw materials to the armament industry. Today, powerful political and commercial interest groups support the continuation of subsidies in mineral industries. These schemes make the prices of minerals much cheaper than they would be otherwise.

By looking at general price trends, some believe that the pessimistic views of economists and others on resource scarcity have not been substantiated (Soussian 1992). The available mineral deposits are understood to be much greater than was assumed a few decades ago. The collapse of commodity prices created balance of trade problems for producing countries. Today, the problem is not one of scarcity, but of abundance, reflected in prices that are too low.

As for the price of oil, which has become one of the most closely watched items, after two sharp increases in 1973–4 and 1979–80, the price has been in decline. Oil price affects prices of other fuels, balance of payments of many countries and even world economic growth. Figure 8.4 shows the real price trend expressed in US dollars at an average 1986 value. Between 1981 and 1986 the price fell by 75 per cent, hitting a low of $12 per barrel. There are substantial differences in the cost of oil produced in different parts of the world. The marginal cost of producing a barrel of oil in the Middle East is low, below $2, whereas in other places such as the North Sea and Alaska it is high, between $10 and $20.

In the early part of the 1980s, world recession and various conservation measures reduced the demand for oil which created a glut in the market. Brown *et al.* (1987) contends that although pressure on oil prices in the near future is likely to be downwards, sudden increases caused by unforeseen events, such as the Gulf War, could upset this trend temporarily. The prices of oil-based fuels differ from country to country. In most European countries, petrol is taxed heavily, mainly to increase the public revenue. In the United States, however, the oil industry has beaten back government efforts to tax petrol heavily. In many parts of the developing world, diesel and kerosene are subsidised to help consumers of these products. Overall consumption levels in a particular country depend not only on the world price of oil, but also on tax levels (Griffin and Steele 1980). Table 8.4 shows the price of gasoline in a number of countries. The tax could be used as a policy instrument for conservation purposes.

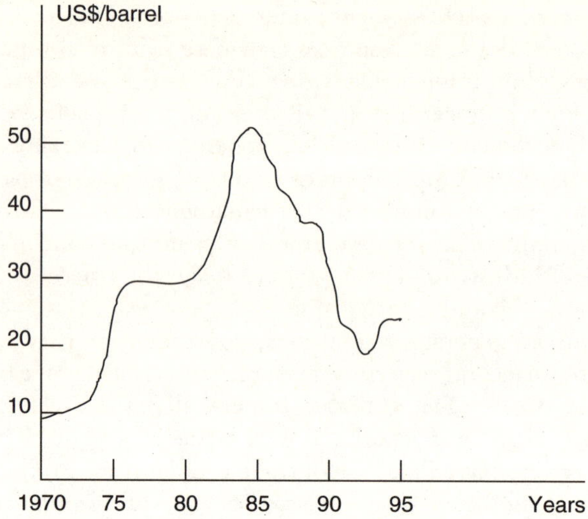

Figure 8.4 Real price of oil in 1986 (in US$)
Sources: US Department of Energy (1987a) and *Basic Petroleum Data Book*, V5, Washington DC

THE US BUREAU OF MINES

As the largely optimistic empirical research on resource scarcity did not convince everybody, some environmental pressure groups, as well as academics, feel that efforts to calculate global stocks as well as demand for every exhaustible commodity should be increased and refined. Only then will we be in a position to understand the extent of the problem. The United States Bureau of Mines has carried out one of the first studies on availability of stocks, demand and resource life.

Table 8.4 Gasoline prices (per gallon) 1982

Country	*Price (US$)*
Mexico	0.71
USA	0.82
Thailand	1.30
Germany	2.09
India	2.17
UK	2.24
Japan	2.89
Brazil	2.94
France	2.95
Denmark	3.58
Italy	3.71

Source: US Department of Energy (1987a)

Table 8.5 shows stock estimates by the Bureau of Mines for some deposits. Figures in Column 3 give resource life based upon constant demand. These are obtained by dividing known stocks by annual demand identified in 1970. According to the table, coal is the most abundant commodity, estimated to last 2,300 years with constant demand. Column 4 shows the annual average growth rate of consumption and the final column gives the length of time stocks will last with growing demand. For instance, with a 4.1 per cent annual growth in coal consumption, the life of known stocks is reduced to 111 years, a huge drop from 2,300 years.

The way in which the dynamic index is obtained is as follows:

$$\textit{Dynamic Index} = \frac{ln\{(g \times s) + 1\}}{g}$$

where g is the annual rate of growth (i.e. 4.1 per cent for coal) and s is the static index (i.e. number of years that known coal deposits will last with constant demand) and ln is natural logarithm.

Example:

On the basis of a 4.1 per cent annual growth in coal consumption, the dynamic index (number of years that stocks will last) for coal is calculated:

$$\begin{aligned}\textit{Dynamic Index} &= \frac{ln\{(0.041 \times 2300) + 1\}}{0.041}\\ &= \frac{ln\{95.3\}}{0.041}\\ &= \frac{4.56}{0.041}\\ &= 111\end{aligned}$$

One should mention that there are some fundamental problems associated with both stock estimates as well as lifespan. Stock figures are normally established by discoveries resulting from exploration. On occasions the information is precise, with a high degree of certainty, but at other times the information is subject to wide margins of error. For example, in estimating coal stocks, two broad reserves are defined: measured and indicated estimates. In the former, reliability is measured by thickness and extent, with seams not less than 0.3 m thick and at depths no greater than 1,200 m (in the case of lignite 500 m). The latter has the same thickness and depth but is only approximately estimated. These are rather loose measures which are open to a wide range of interpretation and estimates in one country may not be comparable with another (Gass 1976).

If information was cost free, it would be desirable to have all possible estimates on existing stocks, but exploration is very expensive and information is treated by agencies as a scarce input. From an economic viewpoint, it would not be sensible to obtain complete information as it would most

Table 8.5 Stock estimates for some resources and number of years they will last with constant and growing demand

Resource	*Known global resources*	*Number of years resources will last with constant demand (static index)*	*Projected average annual rate of growth of consumption %*	*Number of years resources will last with growing demand (dynamic index)*
Aluminium	1.17 x 10^9 tons	100	6.4	31
Chromium	7.75 x 10^8 tons	420	2.6	95
Coal	5 x 10^{12} tons	2300	4.1	111
Copper	308 x 10^6 tons	36	4.6	21
Gold	353 x 10^6 tons	11	4.1	9
Iron	1 x 10^{11} tons	240	1.3	93
Lead	91 x 10^6 tons	26	2.0	21
Natural Gas	1.14 x 10^5 cu ft	38	4.7	22
Nickel	147 x 10^9 lbs	150	3.4	53
Petroleum[a]	455 x 10^9 bbls	31	3.9	20
Silver	5.5 x 10^9 troy oz	16	2.7	13
Tin[b]	4.3 x 10^6 lg tons	17	1.1	15
Tungsten	2.9 x 10^9 lbs	40	2.5	28
Zinc	123 x 10^6 tons	23	2.9	18

Source: US Bureau of Mines (1970)
[a] billion barrels
[b] 1 long ton = 2240 lbs

certainly involve a huge cost to the agency. Globally, it may not pay to eliminate all uncertainties of what the earth contains because a large volume of stocks will not be exploited for many years. Furthermore, development in stock estimates such as using refined satellite data, may make estimates much cheaper in the future. Therefore, at any point in time there must be a sensible or optimum programme of exploration for mining companies as well as for individual nations. This is a rather important issue for nations that invest large sums in exploration with the hope of finding something rich.

The US Bureau of Mines, in defining terms for stock availability, takes two factors into account: the extent of geological knowledge and the economic feasibility of recovery. Geologists are normally concerned with exploration activities that increase the accuracy of our knowledge of stocks, whereas mining engineers concern themselves with improvements in recovery technology in order to bring costs down. Economists bring these two factors together in their analysis to determine the economic viability of exploration.

Alongside the Bureau of Mines there have been other bodies giving estimates of natural resources. The World Energy Conference conducts a survey of energy resources every six years. Table 8.6 shows the situation for hard coal with regard to the year 1970.

Table 8.6 Measured coal reserves and products, 1970

Country/Region	*Coal reserves (10^6 tons)*	*Production in 1970 (10^6 tons)*
North America	110,000	564
USSR	130,000	433
Europe	120,000	488
Africa	47,000	58
Asia	15,000	513
Oceania	10,000	52
South America	5,000	10

Source: Gass (1976)

Another method to estimate the stock life is called the Hubbert criterion which relies on two simple premises:

1 The amount of reserve left in the ground at any point in time is the difference between the initial reserve estimate and the cumulative extraction to date.
2 During the course of operation, the rate of production rises exponentially and after peaking, falls in the same manner to zero. Figure 8.5 shows the situation in which time (say, years) is measured along the horizontal axis and extraction rate along the vertical axis, where:

Q = quality
t = time
P = extraction rate which is dQ/dt

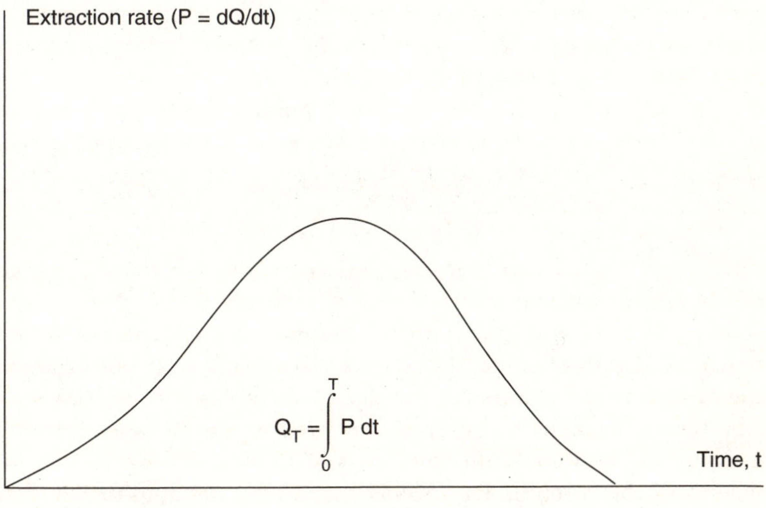

Figure 8.5 Cumulative extraction function

The cumulative production is proportional to the area between the horizontal axis and the bell-shaped production curve up to that time. The sum total of extraction is an integral function which is:

$$Q_t = \int_0^T P dt$$

where T is the time length taken to exhaust the stock. By using this we can predict future production by estimating the amount in the ground and then drawing the production curve so that the area under the curve satisfies the reserve estimate.

INDICATED AND INFERRED STOCKS

Some writers such as McKelvey (1972), Gass (1976) and Rajaraman (1976) contend that in the life of stock, a calculation based upon the known global reserves is over-conservative, even inaccurate. A realistic figure must include not only the known stocks but a guestimate about quantities which are not yet decisively proven. Therefore, stock estimates shown in Table 8.5 grossly underestimate the reality as they are based only upon the proven deposits.

Calculations of total reserves are normally made based upon sample drill holes at the base of the resource. Nevertheless, a sample can give a very biased picture of the total. There are ample cases of mines started up on the basis of sample estimates that proved to be serious underestimates of what is in the ground. In addition to this, total reserves that are worked out are limited by current profitability, which takes into account the present state of technology, costs and prices. Some scientists believe that mankind will never physically run out of mineral resources because the limits of materials in the ground are far beyond the likely economic limits of their utilisation (Zwartendyk 1972). Metal deposits exist in almost all depths of the globe – at what point should we stop counting? Furthermore, some argue that the ultimate stock volume is economically irrelevant as markets tend to behave as if stocks were infinite in supply (Herfindahl 1967; Adelman 1993).

A number of cut-off points have been suggested but there is no agreement upon a particular method. One criterion is to count minerals that can be extracted without crossing an energy barrier – that is, deposits are counted as long as extraction does not use up excessive amounts of energy, where excessive is not clearly defined. This is not a serious problem for fossil fuel because there is a maximum depth in the earth at which they are found. The position taken by 'absolutist' scientists can be described as a physical measure of the maximum stock of any mineral. However, the question is, when will the potential stocks, which may be huge in terms of quantity, ever become actual? Economic measure of a mineral stock must be between the two extremes, i.e. proven and ultimate stocks. Some geologists may have a belief that enormous quantities of metal and fossil fuel deposits exist in the ground but they still have to be discovered.

One way in which inferred estimates are identified is to consider speculative or hypothetical quantities that may exist in unexplored areas. For argument's sake, let us say that one half of Britain was explored for coal and X billion tons were discovered. Inferred estimates imply that in the remaining half there should be another X billion tons of coal, making the total 2X. Table 8.7 compares proven and inferred stocks. There are substantial differences between the two concepts. For example, the inferred estimate for zinc is forty-six times the known stock.

From another source we can see regional differences between inferred and proven stocks. Table 8.8 gives inferred stocks for coal for different regions of the globe.

The stagnation doctrine of classical and other economists eventually led to efforts to test the 'problem' by using the historic price/cost data over a sizeable period of time, which turned out to be inconclusive. Findings of researchers such as Potter, Christy, Barnett, Morse, Nordhaus, Jorgensen and

Table 8.7 Stock life estimates based on proven and speculative reserves

Resource	*Known*	*Inferred*	*Average annual growth in demand (%)*	*Static Index (years)*		*Dynamic Index (years)*	
				Known	*Inferred*	*Known*	*Inferred*
Copper	370	1,700	3.7	54	215	29	60
Lead	144	1,854	2.2	38	488	27	112
Tin	5	41	1.0	18	158	16	95
Zinc	123	5,606	1.2	23	1,038	18	118

Source: Rajaraman (1976)

Table 8.8 Speculative coal reserves, 1968 or 1970

Country/region	*Reserves (106 tons)*
North America	1,200,000
USSR	4,175,000
Europe	135,000
Africa	120,000
Asia	1,150,000
Oceania	30,000
South America	30,000

Source: Gass (1976)

Griliches imply that, judging by past trends, it would be reasonably safe to conclude we are a good way away from the point of stagnation predicted by Ricardo, Jevons, and many others.

On the other hand, the work of the US President's Material Policy Commission and the Bureau of Mines painted a rather gloomy picture. How long and under what conditions can the much desired economic growth continue with finite stocks of in situ resources? The answer by the US Bureau of Mines was, essentially, not very long. However, the bureau also pointed out the importance of the technological and economic circumstances in the recovery of critical commodities. For example, at uranium price of $8 (1970) per pound, 191,000 tons could be produced; at prices between $8 and $10 another 45,000 tons could be supplied; from $10 to $30 another 285,000 tons would become available; and from $30 to $70 per pound another 2.6 million tons would be obtainable. Stocks of non-renewable resources are supplemented all the time by the discoveries resulting from exploration, and thus known stocks to date cannot be a reliable base for forecasting. Other resources such as forests and fish stocks have their own growth or replenishment processes, but even for them exploration and accessibility have been an important source and criterion of new supplies.

9

SPACESHIP EARTH

BOULDING'S ECONOSPHERE

In 1966, Kenneth E. Boulding published a short article 'The economics of the coming Spaceship Earth' in a small book entitled *Environmental Quality in a Growing Economy*, edited by Henry Jarrett (1966). In his chapter, Boulding takes a long view of the state of the world with a critical look at the goals and values which had been accepted without much question for so long. Around that time, photographs of the globe taken for the first time from space showed that our world is a small, self-contained spaceship rather than an endless plain with infinite room to manoeuvre. With growing population, exhaustion of natural resources and restricted space for disposal of all kinds of industrial and agricultural waste, Boulding expressed grave doubts about the desirability of economic growth, which had been one of the most important objectives of all governments.

In his view of an econosphere in which economic activities of mankind interact with local, national and world environments, growth – especially in the way that it has taken place in the industrialised world during the last century or so – is unsustainable. Most introductory textbooks in economics contain a diagram of an economic system showing the circular flow of economic activity in which natural resource scarcity, pollution and waste disposal are rarely mentioned. If they are mentioned – for example, with regard to waste problems – it is implicitly assumed that waste resulting from production and consumption will be recycled by nature to be returned to the land by the natural and indestructible powers of the soil. Furthermore, as firms bring factors of production together to produce goods and services demanded by other firms, as well as households, unlimited natural resource input is assumed to sustain the circular flow. According to Boulding, this is an open system in which a structure is maintained in the midst of a throughput from inputs to output.

The economic psychology which has been developed during the last couple of decades is that of the open system, which needs to be transformed into the closed system – the spaceship economy. Given the exhaustibility of fossil fuel and metal deposits, and the limitation of the world to absorb pollutants, such transformation is essential. If we do not make this move now, when we have relatively more room for manoeuvre, circumstances will force us to do it in the not so distant future under much tougher conditions. The large energy inputs that we have been obtaining from fossil fuel, and the raw materials from other exhaustible resources, are strictly temporary. We will run out of these items eventually. It is rather like the early settlers in America arriving from Europe on the eastern seaboard and moving to the west for further and further settlements in the belief that America is infinitely accommodating. Eventually, this belief was dented when settlers reached the shores of the Pacific ocean.

In the transformation of a system from one form to another there are three essential items: matter, energy and knowledge – the last being the most important. Before anything else, man must have sufficient information about an issue or a problem; then he must visualise a solution. For example, a machine to speed up a production process originated first in the mind of man, then material and energy resources were exploited for its construction. Knowledge and imagination is the key to all kinds of human development including economic transformation and progress. As an example, consider the destruction of capital in Germany during the last war. Because the knowledge of the Germans was not destroyed, the stock of capital was re-created within a couple of decades. In a country such as Ghana, there was no creation of substantial capital because the knowledge did not exist in sufficient amounts. Without credible information about the econosphere, the desire to modify the established patterns of economic behaviour will never take place. This is the first step. The second step is that mankind must then think of ways and means of constructing a new order within the context of a spaceship economy.

Boulding, in colourful language, tries to explain that established measurements of economic success do not make sense in a spaceship economy. For example, the growth rate of the gross national product is almost universally accepted as a measuring rod for the economic success of the nations. Likewise, at an individual level, income and wealth give a person great prestige in a modern consumer society. In conventional economics, consumption and production are regarded as good things and little consideration is given to resource depletion and deterioration of environmental quality which will eventually make both activities unsustainable.

> The success of the economy is measured by the amount of the throughput from the 'factors of production', a part of which, at any rate, is extracted from the reservoirs of raw materials and non-economic objects, and another part of which is output into the reservoirs of pollution. If there are infinite reservoirs from which material can be obtained and into which effluvia can be deposited,

> then the throughput is at least a plausible measure of the success of the economy. By contrast, in the spaceman economy, throughput is by no means a desideratum, and is indeed to be regarded as something to be minimised rather than maximised. The essential measure of the success of the economy is not production and consumption at all, but the nature, extent, quality and complexity of the total capital stock, including in that the state of the human bodies and minds included in the system. In the spaceman economy, what we are primarily concerned with is stock maintenance and technological change which results in the maintenance of a given total stock with a lessened throughput (that is, less production and consumption) is clearly a gain.
>
> (Boulding 1966: 9–10)

Figure 9.1 depicts the circular flow of economic activity inside the Spaceship Earth which contains, in its most simplified form, four sectors: households (or consumers), firms (or producers), exhaustible resources and waste disposal. Traditional economics focuses only on the first two whereas the econosphere considers all four simultaneously. Households provide factors of production (land, labour and capital) to firms, and firms supply goods and services in return. Both households and firms extract from the natural resource sector and both create waste in the course of production and consumption which is passed on to the disposal sector. The main problem here is that as the level of economic activity and population keep on growing, which was highly conspicuous at the time when Boulding formed his ideas, both scarcity and waste problems will get worse unless drastic measures are taken. The conventional system of growth cannot continue because of intensifying scarcity and worsening waste disposal problems. Boulding recommends that the natural resource base must be diligently protected and wastes must be properly managed; our long-term survival depends on our ability to manage these two sectors.

Boulding puts it plainly that, in a spaceship context, production and consumption are not necessarily good things, which is contrary to the wisdom of the conventional economics in which both are encouraged, even at the most excessive levels. The crucial factor in the econosphere is the maintenance of natural capital, which sustains all forms of production, consumption and life itself. In his view, economic welfare should not be measured by depreciation of the natural capital. It would be like measuring the value of housing not by living in nice accommodation, but rather by the rate of depreciation of the property. The less depreciation we inflict upon our house, the better off we are. This is only common sense, but these issues have been neglected with astonishing single-mindedness by economists. Is economic welfare essentially stock or flow dependent? According to Boulding, the stock concept is most fundamental to human welfare. He

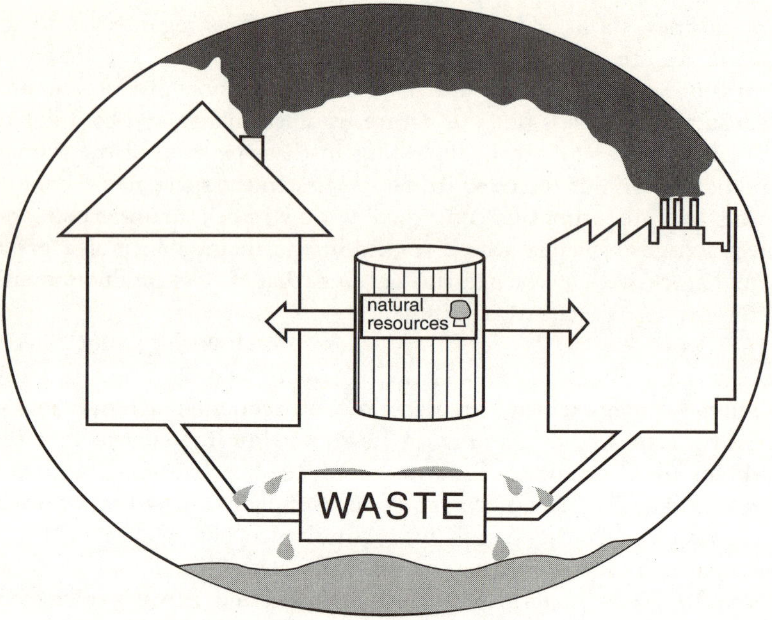

Figure 9.1 Economic activity inside Spaceship Earth

complains that his attempt to call attention to some of these issues has fallen entirely on deaf ears (see, for example, Boulding 1945, 1950).

Boulding warns against complacency in delaying the construction of a structure for the spaceship economy. An attitude such as 'let us multiply, eat, drink, spend, extract and pollute' – i.e. let us grow in the usual way, as the Spaceship Earth is still a good way off – is harmful. In many respects, spaceship economy has arrived, we have already run out of clean air in many industrial cities, many lakes have become cesspools, forests have disappeared from some regions, and once highly productive mines have been exhausted. But the greatest harm will be done to future generations as they are likely to inherit an even more contaminated spaceship, with less and less natural resource deposits in it. For this, there can be no moral legitimacy. A society which loses its responsibility to future generations soon falls apart, as history has demonstrated many times over.

It must be said that Boulding's Spaceship Earth somewhat exaggerates resource and environmental problems. As pointed out in the previous chapter, a group of writers believe that, apart from fossil fuel, the earth is unlikely to run out of natural resources because the sheer limits of materials in the ground are far beyond the limits of their utilisation. In other words, the earth, with some exceptions, is so rich in mineral resources that even cumulative demand will not run it dry for a very long time. If one deposit is depleted then a substitute will be used in its place. On the issue of refuse, given sufficient time, with a few exceptions, wastes degrade over time. That is, they are effectively recycled by nature. Problems exist with non-degradable wastes such as arsenic, etc., but their quantities are not enormous. Nuclear wastes are a different category which could pose serious health and political risks in the future. However, there seems to be no compelling reason, at least at present, for man to rely on nuclear power, especially from an economic viewpoint as, on a full cost basis, nuclear energy appears to be far more expensive than conventional power.

It is also argued that in the spaceship economy production leads to consumption or waste, but an important outcome of the economic system is capital. That is, we convert the iron ore in the ground into steel girders, hammers, railways, bridges, etc., that remain intact for a long period of time. For example, in many regions, houses, bridges and roads constructed a couple of hundred years ago or more are still in use.

However, despite its shortcomings, Boulding's Spaceship Earth concept is an important landmark in the history of economic thought. Its message is simple and powerful – given the fact that the earth is ultimately a fragile self-contained unit, a spaceship, we must protect it for ourselves as well as for future generations. Misuse of our environment has no legitimacy. Boulding's paper contains no equations, diagrams or statistics, but this does not diminish its worth. As we shall see later on, spaceship earth models that contain extensive mathematics turn out to be far less interesting than Boulding's 'plain' article.

In support of Boulding's Spaceship Earth concept, Barnett (1979) argues that the growth of economic activity over the last couple of hundred years has created many environmental problems and made the earth fragile. It is rather like an ant growing to the size of an elephant and becoming highly fragile and immobile in the process. If beings from outer space were to view the human ecology they would quickly observe the rapid damage to the environment which is resulting from unrestricted growth and in which market failure must bear some responsibility. It has been suggested by many economists, as well as others, that the free market economy is one of the most efficient and fair social institutions ever constructed. But it was created by man, not by God, and like all man's creations it is a fallible system. In order to transfer from an endless plain economy to spaceship economy, Barnett emphasises the role of the political leadership in which economics may play only a modest role.

FORRESTER'S SYSTEM DYNAMICS

It was only a matter of time before model builders would capitalise on Boulding's concept of Spaceship Earth and, by using computer simulation technology, would try to predict the future. The first notable model was constructed by an American computer engineer, Jay Wright Forrester (1971) with purely hypothetical, yet plausible, functional correlations between a number of stock and flow variables. Forrester's model contains forty-three variables which are linked together by twenty-two linear and non-linear relationships. Some stock variables are land, exhaustible resources, population, capital stock and pollution. The most important flow variables are food production, non-food production, fabricated goods consumption, and gross investment, all expressed in terms of per capita.

Of the stock variables, pollution depends upon the level of economic activity which creates pollution and undermines the absorption capacity of nature. Population growth depends upon food availability (a positive response), pollution, and human density (a negative response). As affluence grows, human numbers rapidly increase, at poverty levels they decline. That is, population is endogenous to the economic system. Figure 9.2 shows the behaviour of the population growth curve, which is one of the most crucial variables in the model, in response to affluence. Crude birth and death rates are shown along the vertical axis and economic progress along the horizontal one. The process of economic development lowers both birth and death

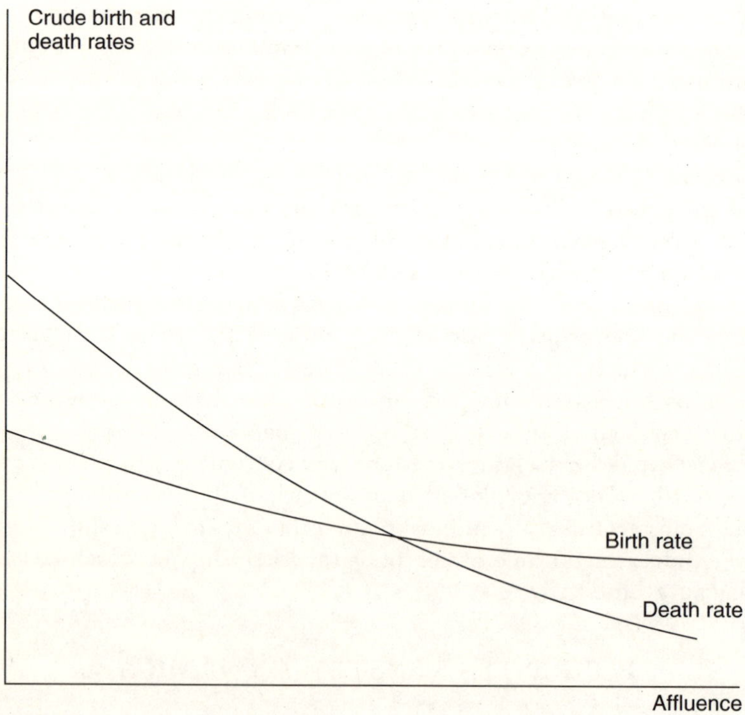

Figure 9.2 Population as a function of economic development in systems dynamics

rates. Eventually, after a brief period, the crude birth rate becomes stabilised above the death rate due to rising incomes. Pulling in the opposite direction, pollution and human density lower net growth of population, but their effects are small.

Forrester assumes that exhaustible resources are about 400 times the current depletion levels with no substitutability between exhaustible stocks. As economic activity expands, exhaustible resources decline on a steady basis grinding the system to an eventual halt. Capital accumulation is a function of per capita investment and rate of depreciation. It saturates at a level which is three times its 1970 figure.

Forrester concludes that quality of life will decline progressively as economic growth continues and human numbers increase. In effect, at present we are enjoying what may be called the golden age of progress in which economic welfare is higher than at any time in the past and higher than what the future is likely to offer. Present problems such as pollution and poverty are small fry compared with what is around the corner. Efforts to control population growth are unlikely to succeed. However, industrial development is a greater curse than population growth in laying the foundation of future misery. There is no hope that the Third World countries will catch up with the standard of living which is now being enjoyed in the West. Furthermore, from a long-term global perspective, efforts by the Third World countries to industrialise are unwise and should not be encouraged.

In order to save the situation, Forrester recommends a number of policies such as: 30 per cent reduction in birth rates; 50 per cent reduction in pollution generation; 75 per cent reduction in natural resource depletion; 40 per cent reduction in capital formation; 20 per cent reduction in food production, as it fuels population growth.

Nordhaus (1973) contends that Forrester's world dynamics has no empirical foundation whatsoever and its assumptions, functional correlations and predictions carry only subjective plausibility. He summarises Forrester's model as *measurement without data*. Furthermore, Nordhaus carried out a number of sensitivity tests on world dynamics and found the model highly fragile.

> the predictions of the world's future are highly sensitive to the specification of the model. Simulation given above indicates that if assumptions regarding population, technological change, or substitution are changed, Forrester's model behaves in a dramatically different manner.

In particular, Nordhaus attacks the assumption regarding the population function in which food and non-food consumption are taken to be positively correlated. In effect, evidence suggests that population growth declines, especially when income levels improve. This type of functional mis-specification has misleading implications. Furthermore, there is no production function in *World Dynamics* (Forrester 1971) and crude aggregation is used in all variables. For example, the population variable lumps people together from Los Angeles to Calcutta and from Sweden to Zaire.

THE CLUB OF ROME

In the spring of 1968, a group of thirty individuals from various countries – including economists, mathematicians, engineers, natural scientists, philosophers, civil servants and businessmen – gathered in Rome under the auspices of Dr Aurellio Peccei, who was one of the leading managers of Olivetti and Fiat, to discuss present as well as future problems of humanity. Out of this gathering, the Club of Rome, an informal think-tank, was formed. Its membership quickly grew to about seventy, and it was decided to freeze the size of the Club at a hundred members. None of its members had official positions and the group decided at the outset not to express any single ideological, political or national point of view.

The issues discussed were broad, including population growth, unemployment, poverty, inflation, alienation of youth, rejection of traditional values, pollution, resource depletion and congestion. They agreed that these contemporary problems occur to some degree in all societies – both developing and advanced – and that they are interconnected. In their view, advanced societies, despite their knowledge and skills, fail to understand the origin of human difficulties because they examine each problem in isolation and thus fail to find an effective response.

The first part of the Club of Rome's project, the predicament of mankind, took shape at meetings held in 1970 in Bern, Switzerland, and Cambridge, USA. At a conference in Cambridge, Forrester outlined a global model which allowed clear definition of many aspects of human problems and suggested a technique to analyse them. The second part of the project was conducted by Dennis Meadows and his team with financial support from the Walksvagen Foundation. The group examined five basic factors that limit economic growth: population growth, agricultural activity, natural resource availability, industrial activity and pollution. In 1972 the Club of Rome published, for general readership, their report entitled *The Limits to Growth* which made front page news in many respectable newspapers around the world (Meadows *et al.* 1972). This report attempts to illustrate, by way of computer models, that economic growth, with or without growing human numbers, is not only a questionable benefit, it is potentially harmful – even disastrous.

By using Forrester's system dynamics as their prototype, Meadows *et al.* constructed more elaborate world models, containing about three times more equations, to examine the effects of economic growth on the world as a whole. Their basic premise is that there are definite limits to growing economic activity, population and pollution because the world has finite arable land, energy deposits, metal ores and pollution-carrying capacity.

The world models contain three groups of items: *absolute variables* such as non-renewable resources, land availability, population, capital stock and population; *changes in the levels of these variables*, and *auxiliary variables* such as industrial output, food production, effect of pollution of lifetime and pollution absorption time. In the first category, land is divided into agriculture, industry and service sectors. Population is divided into various age groups. All variables are measured by index numbers and in terms of growth rates.

The interaction between these three groups of variables is conducted by mathematical equations which include feedback loops. For example, growth in pollution impacts upon agricultural production and population growth rates. Accumulation of capital leads to an increase in living standards which in turn, by way of a different link, affects capital accumulation, a feedback process. For a further explanation of the working mechanism of the Club of Rome's world models, see Cole (1973), Hueting (1980) and Page (1973).

All computer models contain eight explicit variables:

- population
- non-renewable stocks
- individual output
- pollution
- food availability
- services
- birth rate
- death rate

Amongst these, non-renewable stocks always take a negative growth rate, i.e. they deplete. Other items can take positive or negative growth rates depending upon the events taking place in each model, or they can remain constant. All computer models have two distinct phases – past and future. The first one describes trends in all eight variables between 1900 and 1970. The Club of Rome contends that throughout recorded history human population, pollution, capital investment and food production have been growing exponentially. For the future, the world is predicted to be entering into a number of possible shapes, depending upon the behaviour of the variables involved.

All in all, the Club runs fourteen models under various assumptions. In the first model, called the standard run, the proven stocks of destructible resources are taken to be the major constraint on economic growth. The horizontal axis in Figure 9.3 shows a timescale between 1900 and 2100. The vertical axis is adjusted so that the computer makes the best use of the graphs. What is important in the values of the parameters over time are the levels relative to the 1970 figures rather than actual numbers. To the left of the vertical line, historical trends are shown. For example, population rises from 1.6 billion in 1900 to 3.5 billion in 1970. Likewise, industrial production, food supply, services and pollution rise, non-renewable resource stocks decline, and so on. According to Sinclair (1973), the Club of Rome's model, along with Forrester's system dynamics, are most interesting in the sense that quantitative estimation of historic environmental problems appears in them for the first time. In this respect, Forrester and Meadows *et al.* marry the Ricardo–Malthusian theory with a contemporary ecological environmentalism.

The collapse of the world system begins in the early part of the twenty-first century when the food curve falls below the population variable. The system fails because of non-renewable resource exhaustion. The industrial capital stock grows to such heights that it requires enormous inputs of resources. As scarcity bites, marginal deposits become economical and then more and more capital is used for bringing inferior stocks out of the ground, leaving less to be invested for future growth. Capital investment cannot keep pace with depreciation, the industrial base falls apart taking with it agricultural and service sectors that have become highly dependent on modern inputs such as pesticides, inorganic fertilisers, computers, hospital laboratories, and so forth. When the economy fails, the population rises for a short while due to the delays in the process of social adjustment.

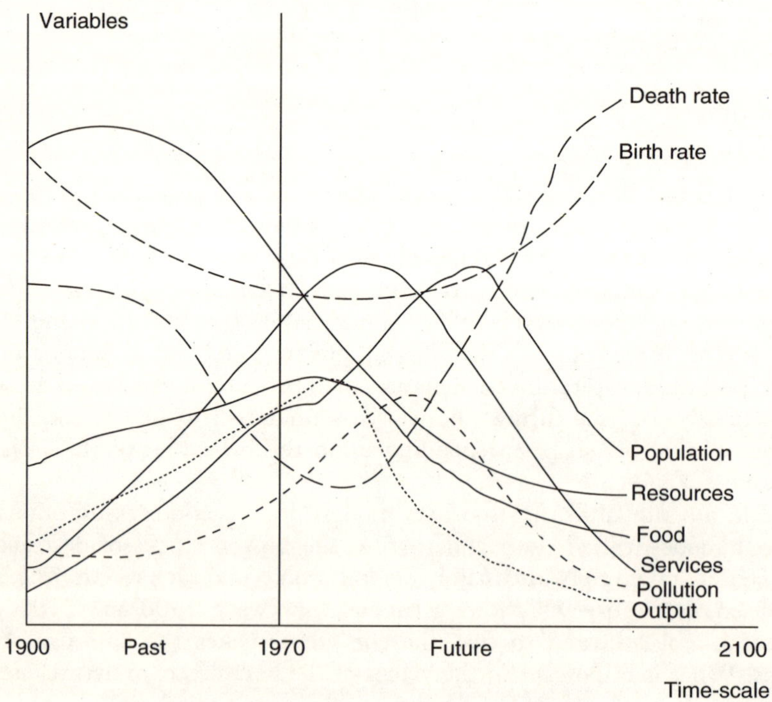

Figure 9.3 World model – standard run

The Club argues that the exact timing of events is not meaningful, given the great aggregation and many uncertainties in the model. What is important is that the economic expansion is stopped well before the twenty-second century. It is further argued that the Club tried in every doubtful case to make the most optimistic estimate of unknown quantities of natural resource stocks. Furthermore, discontinuous events such as conflicts and epidemics were ignored.

That is to say that the model is biased to allow economic expansion to continue longer than it probably can continue:

> We can thus say with some confidence that, under the assumption of no major change in the present system, population and industrial growth will certainly stop within the next century, at the latest.
>
> (Meadows *et al.* 1972: 126)

In the next stage the Club of Rome doubles the natural resource reserves and re-runs the model. The system fails again, but the reason for the failure is the sudden increase in the level of pollution which exceeds the absorption capacity of nature, reducing food output and undermining conditions for human health. It becomes difficult to increase or even sustain food output in a contaminated environment. In the third run unlimited natural resources are assumed, but the system fails again for the same reason – rising pollution.

At a later stage, the Club obtains a stable world model by implementing a number of operations. Population is stabilised by setting birth and death rates equal. Industrial capital, after a natural increase until 1990, is stabilised by setting investment rates equal to the rate of capital depreciation. In order to avoid non-renewable resource famine, their consumption is reduced to a quarter of 1970 levels. Economic preferences of society are assumed to be shifted towards the service sector such as health and education, and in this way levels of factory-produced material goods are reduced along with contamination. Pollution-generating industrial and agricultural output is curtailed to a quarter of its 1970 value. Capital is diverted to agriculture in order to produce food by way of environmentally-friendly methods. Under these assumptions, the Club becomes able to obtain a stable world model as seen in Figure 9.4. Population, industrial output per head, and pollution are not growing. Natural resources are still being depleted but the rate of depletion is moderate so there is time for industry and technology to adjust.

In the next stable model, the Club concedes that a sudden stabilisation of population and industrial capital is rather unrealistic. Instead, they assume that everybody has access to 100 per cent effective birth control. Everyone understands that the desirable family size is two children. Economic agents endeavour to maintain industrial output per capita at about the 1975 level.

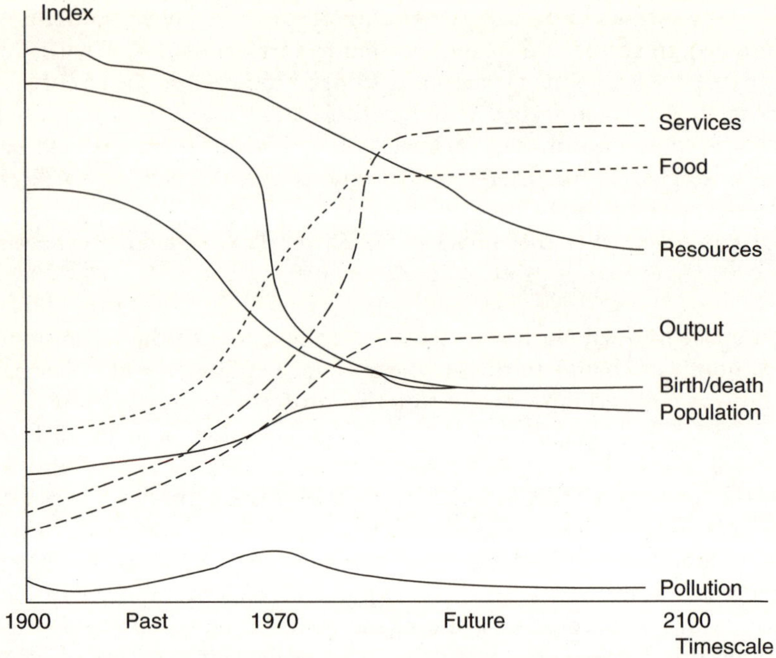

Figure 9.4 World model – stabilised

In other words, the individuals change their attitudes towards choosing stability as a goal but the adjustment takes place as a gradual process. The system achieves stability, but results are not as good as in the previous model as population grows to a much larger size, and natural resources, food, fabricated goods and services per capita remain lower. In other words, the longer the exponential growth is allowed to continue, the fewer possibilities remain for the final stage.

The final paragraph of the book states:

> The last thought we wish to offer is that man must explore himself – his goals and values – as much as the world he seeks to change. The dedication to both tasks must be unending. The crux of the matter is not only whether the human species will survive, but even more, whether it can survive without falling into a state of worthless existence.
>
> (Meadows *et al.* 1972)

A CRITICISM OF *THE LIMITS TO GROWTH*

The Limits to Growth (Meadows *et al.* 1972) is one of the most ambitious attempts to combine classical Ricardo–Malthusian scarcity with contemporary issues such as global pollution, non-renewable resource depletion and technology-led capital accumulation; modern computer methods have been used to construct world models and attention is drawn to the urgency of many environmental and social problems that are growing in complexity as well as in magnitude. However, some authors have demonstrated that there are many serious problems with the analyses carried out by the Club and the conclusions drawn from them.

Although the Club of Rome had made serious efforts to collect information from various sources regarding historic trends, the database for the world models is hopelessly inadequate for the work. Furthermore, the mathematical structures used to describe the history between 1900 and 1970 must be reversible – that is, it should be possible to run them backwards to obtain a more distant view of the past. But when this is done, absurd results are given (Cole and Curnow 1973). If a model fails in its backward operation, it is quite likely to fail in its forward motion, partly because of insufficient and inaccurate data input, and partly because of technical construction problems.

Apart from their data and technical structural problems, the world models were designed in a pessimistic mood to predict a pessimistic outcome. As Cole and Curnow (1973) demonstrate, the outcome of the models can be altered by changing a few pessimistic assumptions. Equally, the same people could have constructed a world model with a number of optimistic assumptions to paint a rosy picture of the future had they wished to do so. Just like Malthus, who was pessimistic about population growth, food availability, and everything else for that matter, *Limits to Growth* has the same outlook (Pavit 1973).

Freeman (1973) describes the work of the Club of Rome as, in effect, Malthus with a computer. In addition to its pessimistic philosophy, *Limits to Growth* tends to put a greater emphasis on the power of computer modelling, as opposed to mental modelling, and in this way a computer fetishism is encouraged to deal with human problems:

> The computer fetishist endows the computer model with a validity and an independent power which altogether transcends the mental models which are its essential basis. Because of the prevalence of this computer fetishism, it cannot be repeated too often that the validity of any computer calculation depends entirely on the quality of the data and assumptions (mental models) which are fed into it. Computer models cannot replace theory.
>
> (ibid.: 8)

Another serious shortcoming of the Club of Rome's work is that all computer models treat the world as a single entity without geographical subdivisions. Rather than being a homogeneous place, our world is extremely heterogeneous in almost every key aspect of the world models, i.e. population growth, level of economic development, resource depletion, food availability and pollution. A population-led collapse may take place in extremely crowded and hard-pressed countries such as India, Pakistan, Bangladesh, Indonesia, Nigeria and Egypt. For example, almost the entire population of Egypt lives in the Nile strip and delta as the rest of the country is not habitable. The situation in Bangladesh is equally drastic.

Population in most parts of Europe is now stable and great efforts are being made to minimise its growth in China as the country implements a single-child-family policy. Most areas where population is growing, such as North and South America, parts of Africa and the Middle East, are still sparsely populated regions of the world.

In *Limits to Growth*, most natural resources are put into the non-renewable category without drawing sufficient distinction between them. Computer models make them disappear over time. In effect, the only non-renewable resources in the true sense are fossil fuels and a few other items such as potash. All metal deposits could be recycled. An effective recycling policy would mean, at least in theory, that the world would never run out of metal stocks. The Club discusses recycling by arguing that it is expensive and uneconomic. Furthermore, a good number of models use actually proven estimates, which is an over-conservative measure. Only a small part of the earth has been explored for mineral resources and only currently economical deposits are being worked out. Some scientists argue that we will never physically run out of mineral resources because the limits of materials in the ground are far beyond the likely limits of their utilisation (Zwartendyke 1972). Page (1973) argues that history proves that new economically exploitable reserves are being discovered all the time as old stocks get exhausted. Given the fact that there are vast amounts of untapped resources in the earth's crust, the ultimate depletion is well beyond the time considered by the Club of Rome. As extractive technology improves and market conditions become favourable, more resources will become available for human use.

A good number of world models fail because of widespread pollution which stems from industrial and agricultural activities. Marstrand and Sinclair (1973) contend that most disasters caused by pollutants are local. The Club aggregates all pollutants and assumes that they behave in some composite way leading to sudden and dramatic failure in the world systems. There are examples of countries such as Switzerland and Austria where industrial and agricultural development has taken place with minimum environmental problems. It could well be argued that if pollution becomes a threat, many affected countries will seek a solution to curb it by regulation, taxation or even by legislation. There are some signs that this is already happening as Green parties are being organised in many countries; a European carbon tax to deal with the greenhouse effect of atmospheric pollution has already been implemented in some countries. It is now true that global pollution in the form of acid rain, ozone depletion and global warming has become a major concern. However, world models advance neither our understanding of these problems nor their interaction with other aspects of world behaviour.

Another shortcoming of the Club of Rome's work is that it ignores the possibility of a technological breakthrough in the energy, manufacturing or agricultural sectors. History amply demonstrates that human development depends upon discoveries and innovations. If we go back to the beginning of the industrial revolution, oil, natural gas and nuclear power would not have featured in an inventory of world energy resources. The modern telecommunications and travel methods that we enjoy now would have been unthinkable even by the most imaginative writers.

The discovery of electricity, the invention of the combustion engine, modern communication and travel methods, computer and microchips have initiated growth and changed our lives. A new technological breakthrough may minimise the reliance on fossil fuels for energy by opening the way to exploit resources such as tidal waves, solar power and wind, which are in endless supply. Surrey and Bromley (1973) argue that, just as the world energy inventory a hundred years ago looked very different from today, a hundred years hence things will again be very different. However, they warn that the assumption of technical progress should not be relied upon to disregard the mounting pressures on current energy resources, but it would be quite wrong to assume that innovations and discoveries will come to a halt. According to them, the real problem is not physical exhaustion of the fossil fuel deposits that we rely on for our energy needs, but the economic, social and technical adjustments needed as they become depleted. The solution to our energy problems lies not with zero growth, as advocated by *Limits to Growth*, but in the development of policies needed to ensure a continuous energy supply when fossil fuel stocks run out.

With regard to the ever-growing demand for destructible resources, *Limits to Growth* underestimates the role of the price mechanism. It mentions that as consumption rates are maintained, despite a rise in prices, exhaustion will be approached very quickly and an example shows that despite a 500 per cent increase in the price of mercury over the twenty-year period from 1950 to 1970, its consumption continued unabated. However, the price mechanism will have two powerful effects: first, the high prices will encourage conservation and the use of substitutes; second, high prices will encourage research, and the resulting technological progress will take consumers away from those commodities that are becoming scarce. The oil crises of 1973 and 1979 demonstrated what high prices a number of developed countries.

It would be extremely naive and damaging to use world models for forecasting or for policy making. Despite the Club of Rome's claim regarding its reliability and recommended policy measures, *The Limits to Growth* was a technical experiment carried out mostly by academics who probably had their own agenda. Mathematical modelling could have some limited use in social sciences, but there are serious dangers in the way these models are often used or misused.

Freeman (1973) points out a number of self-delusions that can stem from similar work. First, the precise correlation between key variables covering the human and natural environment are not known, and in many cases cannot be known. Second, mathematical modelling by gross over-simplification and aggregation creates models which are far removed from reality. Third, omissions from the models, especially with regard to behavioural and policy changes, are a serious problem. If people see that they are going to be damaged by their own actions, then they will make great efforts to adjust their behaviour patterns, and may well succeed. For example, most smokers stop smoking immediately when they are advised by their doctors that if they carry on with it they will die in a few years' time. Fourth, world models make it extremely difficult for the non-numerate to participate in such work, although they may have important contributions to make. Despite the fact that the Club of Rome claims to include expertise from many different disciplines, many find that their work is not interdisciplinary enough. In short, *Limits to Growth* is an attempt to substitute mathematics for knowledge and computation for understanding.

One last point to be made about *The Limits to Growth* is that we cannot know our future. It cannot be predicted by looking at past events. That is, past and future are not samples drawn from the same set of events. Not even the wisest group of academics – or anyone for that matter – can predict the future by looking at past events, no matter how reliable their data or mathematical correlations between the key variables.

OPTIMISTIC PASSENGERS IN SPACESHIP EARTH

Maddox (1972) and Beckerman (1974), unsuppressed by either Forrester's systems dynamics or the Club of Rome's world models, warn all pessimistic writers that mankind has the capacity to solve many problems. Furthermore, it can be argued that economic growth, which is the main culprit leading to eventual disaster in the world models, could create technical as well as financial possibilities to deal with human problems. In other words, the 'problem' could enhance mankind's trouble-shooting capacity. It could become the solution.

In the Club of Rome's second study, *Mankind at the Turning Point* (Mesarovic and Pestel 1974), the future does not look as grim as the first report suggests. In this document, rather than treating the world as a single homogeneous entity, the writers divide it up into ten regions. Furthermore, the mathematical relationships between aggregate growth and ancillary variables are much more sophisticated than in the first document. The view is put forward that a regional or localised collapse could take place in an extremely crowded and food-deficient region, while the rest of the world manages to improve its standard of living. Recent problems in sub-Saharan Africa, Ethiopia, Rwanda and Burundi are examples of such regional economic, social and environmental failures.

Herman Kahn in *The Next 200 Years* (1976) rejects the idea of physical limits to growth. This view was also accepted at the Club of Rome's 1982 meeting in Philadelphia, where the growth potential of the service sector was emphasised. In Kahn's view, the world is just passing through the point of most rapid population growth and this will stabilise at around fifteen billion within the coming century. The main reason for this is that growing affluence and education levels will reduce birth rates, as has happened in contemporary Europe. Even with today's level of agricultural technology it is possible to feed fifteen billion people. Yields of rice in India and other countries could be greatly expanded with current methods of water control, fertilisation and cultivation. There are untapped food resources such as krill, which is abundant in the South Atlantic. Discoveries of miracle grains and pesticides are all genuine possibilities. The only danger to food production would be a chain of weather disasters in several large food-producing countries.

With regard to the availability of natural resources, Kahn believes that there is no early, or even remote, danger of depletion – apart from fossil fuels. He believes we shall soon see the end of the petroleum age. Alternatives to fossil fuel do exist and one, or possibly several, will be developed, whatever the cost may be. For example, hydropower and solar energy could become major sources of energy in the USA. In the past many writers have created false alarms with regard to resource exhaustion. For instance, some of the Club of Rome's statistics were compiled by the US Bureau of Mines. Table 9.1 gives some of these predictions.

According to these numbers, which were calculated in 1970, we should now be out of all these resources but, in effect, the prices of many of these

Table 9.1 Stock estimates for some elective resources and number of years they will last with constant and growing demand

Resource	*Known global resources*	*Number of years that resource will last with constant demand at 1970 level*	*Number of years that resource will last with average growth rate of consumption*
Gold	333 x 106 troy oz	11	9
Lead	91 x 106 tons	26	21
Petroleum	455 x 109 brls	31	20
Silver	55 x 109 troy oz	16	13
Zinc	123 x 106 tons	27	18

Source: US Bureau of Mines (1970)

commodities have been falling during the last few years implying that they are becoming less scarce.

In Herman Kahn's view, regional pollution is not an unmanageable problem as it is possible to eliminate it at a cost of not more than 2 per cent of the GNP of the richer nations. As for global pollution, such as acid rain and the greenhouse effect, he acknowledges that problems do exist but points out that the scientific view on these issues is neither convincing nor conclusive. The need for research and monitoring is great and when we fully understand the problems then solutions will be implemented. Overall, Kahn believes that environmental and resource problems are manageable and there is no need for pessimism. In his view, at the present time the world is simply going through a transition period which is painful, but he considers the future is something to be envied, not feared.

In challenging a rather pessimistic document, *The Global 2000 Report to the President* (Barney 1982), Julian Simon (1984) argued that if current trends continued, by the end of this millennium the world would be less crowded (though more populated), less polluted, more ecologically stable, and less vulnerable to resource/supply disruption than the world was then. Furthermore, people on the whole would be better off and the pressure on natural resources and the environment would lessen. According to him, the main evidence for such optimism was as follows:

- The birth rate in the Third World had been falling during the past two decades;
- life expectancy had been rising fast all over the world – a sign of scientific, economic and demographic success;
- food supply had been increasing steadily for many decades, although there were some regional problems, mainly in Africa;
- fish stocks, after a period of decline, were recovering;
- forest destruction was restricted mainly to the tropics; in the rest of the world, forested land was improving;
- the climate was not showing signs of unusual or threatening changes;
- most natural resources, including oil, were becoming cheaper; and
- threats of air and water pollution had been exaggerated.

As one of the most optimistic writers on population and environmental issues, Julian Simon was unimpressed by the spaceship concept. He seems to have had an unshakeable faith in mankind's ability to solve its problems. Unabashed confidence is useful in environmental debates in the sense that it marks the boundaries of optimism, just as pessimism identifies the extent of worries.

Simon, by using relatively recent but positive events, was trying to throw some light on to the future and in this way was repeating the same mistakes made by the Club of Rome in *The Limits to Growth*. Recent events may not be a reliable guide to discover what is awaiting us in the future.

10

THE SUSTAINABILITY DEBATE

Attempts to define sustainable development have become a favourite pastime for some academics. According to Winpenny (1991), a satisfactory definition of sustainable development is now the holy grail of environmental economics. For example, Pezzey (1989) suggested sixty definitions whereas Pearce *et al.* (1989) put forward about thirty. But elsewhere, Pearce (1993), by focusing on the economic aspect of development, contends that defining sustainable development is not a cumbersome task. On the contrary, it is very simple. The real issue is to outline what has to be done to achieve it once the concept is clearly understood. Then we can use various aggregates for its measurement such as conventionally defined per capita gross national product – a continuously rising consumption per head. Alternatively, we can use some broader measures to include factors such as education, health and life expectancy.

SOME STATED OBJECTIVES

Pearce (1993) also launches an attack on the zero growth school which advocates a change in lifestyle to solve, or at least moderate, ecological crises. According to him the gross national product is the major contributor to human well-being; failure to keep it growing results in poverty and unemployment on a massive scale creating major social problems by widening inequalities. He also finds it a useless idea that the rich half of the world should make a sacrifice on its demand for natural resources so that they can be used by the impoverished nations. This will not work at all, and thus economic growth must go on, i.e. it must be sustained.

It is quite doubtful whether economic growth will solve our social, economic and environmental problems. In spite of exceptional growth in many parts of the world in the second half of this century, poverty, unemployment and the gulf between the rich and poor still persist; in some regions these problems are getting worse. In the United Kingdom, strong economic growth which took place during the 1982–9 period did not narrow the gap between income classes (Stark 1992). When Pearce states that GNP and human well-being are inextricably linked for the vast majority of the world's population, he downplays the fact that the growth of GNP is also linked with environmental impoverishment – a message of many writers mentioned in previous chapters of this book.

More than 130 years ago, J. S. Mill wrote that economic growth will not solve human problems. Furthermore, he pointed out that continuous growth is against the laws of nature as all types of growth, including economic growth, will come to a halt. Kenneth Boulding, a hard-nosed economist who initiated the idea of spaceship economy accuses his colleagues who belong to the relentless economic growth school of madness.

Pearce, by focusing on the word sustainable, contends that its meaning is not debatable; it means enduring, lasting and to keep in being. Of course, one can go on to find other expressions for it such as unabated, relentless or everlasting. But what should be crucial in the sustainability debate is the distinction between relentless efforts to grow and the end result. There are now quite a lot of statistics showing the discrepancy between the GNP per head and a number of broad-based measures for human welfare. For example, Nordhaus and Tobin (1972), by using a concept called measurement of economic welfare (MEW), show that in the United States between 1928 and 1965 as per capita net national product grew by 1.7 per cent compound, the MEW grew only by 1.1 per cent. More recently, Daly and Cobb (1989) constructed an index of economic welfare in which allowances were made for the adverse effects of pollution and destruction of natural resources. The index shows that economic welfare in the United States increased gradually from 1950 until 1961 and then remained stationary for ten years. Since 1980 it has been falling noticeably, even when the GNP per head has been rising.

To many, relentless or sustainable economic growth, no matter how one measures it, appears to be an unsustainable idea itself. Sooner or later it must fall flat on its face. It is true that economic development, even broadly measured, has been achieved in some countries over a prolonged period, and the chances are that it could be maintained for a little longer in places where the population growth is zero or very low. However, one cannot help feeling that the issue is a little like communism – during its height sceptics were considered to be spoilsports at best. Even when progress began to peter out in the communist world some, especially those who benefited from the ideology, maintained that the decline was temporary. This was not the case, however, as the system, with all its structures and ideals, collapsed almost overnight. Like the communist ideals, the sustainable or relentless economic growth theory for achieving full employment and improved standards of living, happiness and equity lacks convincing evidence. Communism gained temporary support, not because it was an appealing theory, but because it promised to the vast majority bread, peace and prosperity. It delivered none of these.

Pearce asserts:

> Failure to keep GNP high shows up in the misery of unemployment and in poverty. Anti-growth advocates are embarrassingly silent or unrealistic on how they would solve problems of poverty and unemployment. Fanciful ideas abound, including one that suggests that economic growth in the 'north' should be sacrificed for the benefit of the 'south', as if not demanding goods and services in the rich countries would somehow release them for poor countries. The actual outcome, of course, is that they would not be produced at all, and everybody loses.
>
> (Pearce 1993: 4)

In this argument, issues which had puzzled economists long ago – such as J. S. Mill – when most of our current ecological problems did not exist, are dismissed straight away . As illustrated by J. Kenneth Galbraith, since the Second World War, environmental and social problems have become worse in the United States, where rapid economic growth has taken place.

Brown (1990) asserts that continuing on a business-as-usual basis virtually assures severe economic disruption, social instability and human suffering. Although Pearce and his colleagues do not support 'business as usual', they maintain that economic growth with some improved conduct is a must. Improved economic behaviour includes reducing material use, cutting down on wasteful energy consumption and avoiding biodiversity loss. Only economic growth will solve our social problems!

SOME DEFINITIONS INCORPORATING FUTURE GENERATIONS

Some writers such as Palmer (1992) and Smith (1993) argue that sustainable development is a young concept which originates from the 1980 World Conservation Strategy of the International Union for the Conservation of Natural Resources. This body contends that sustainability is a strategic concept involving lasting utilisation of natural resources, the preservation of genetic diversity and ecosystem maintenance. In 1983 the United Nations established the World Commission on Environment and Development to formulate a global agenda for change, which was headed by the former Norwegian prime minister Gro Harlem Brundtland. The Commission published its final report, *Our Common Future* (also known as *The Brundtland Report*), in 1987. It took into account three years of special work by experts which included scientific evidence, public hearings, views of world leaders, the business community, and political opinion from a wide range of groups. It defines 'sustainable development' as development that meets the needs of the present without compromising the ability of future generations to meet their own needs.

The Brundtland Report points out the differences between the beginning and the end of the twentieth century during which population increase has reached an unprecedented level. Human activities had only a local impact a hundred years ago; now they have an impact on the global atmosphere, waters, soils and numerous plant and animal species.

The report, although a landmark in the sustainability debate, has been criticised as being distinctly Western in its approach (Palmer 1992). Its definitions of the development and cure of the ecological problems do not sufficiently take into account the diversity of cultural and ethical positions in the world.

Pearce *et al.* (1990) describe how the publication of this report made sustainable development a popular concept among a wide range of disciplines and paved the way to many other definitions. Elsewhere, Pearce defines sustainable development as non-declining human welfare over time. That is, a development path which makes people better off today at the cost of a lower standard of living for future generations is not sustainable (Pearce 1991).

The position of future generations is a cornerstone in the most respectable definitions of sustainability such as *The Brundtland Report*. In effect, the report puts all generations under a moral obligation in that each one should bequeath an undiminished stock of natural resources. Sustainable development should be designed to meet the needs of the current generations without compromising the ability of future ones to meet their own needs.

Some other definitions that give exclusive treatment to future generations are as follows:

> Sustainable development is a development strategy that manages all assets, natural resources, and human resources, as well as financial and physical assets, for increasing long-term wealth and wellbeing. Sustainable development as a goal rejects policies and practices that support current living standards by depleting the productive base, including natural resources and leaves future generations with poorer prospects and greater risk than our own.
>
> (Repetto 1986)

> Sustainability in the purest sense involves embracing ethical norms pertaining to the survival of living matter, to the rights of future generations and to institutions responsible for ensuring that such rights are fully taken into account in policies and actions.
>
> (O'Riordan 1988)

> Sustainable development is that which leaves our total patrimony, including natural environmental assets, intact over a particular period. We should bequeath to future generations the same capital,

> embodying opportunities for potential welfare, that we currently enjoy.
>
> (Winpenny 1991)

> According to the sustainability principle all resources should be used in a manner which respects the needs of future generations.
>
> (Tietenberg 1992)

HISTORIC ROOTS OF THE CURRENT DEBATE

The idea of sustainable development is not a new concept as its roots in farming can be traced to the enclosure movement at the end of the eighteenth century. Arthur Young (1804), in his travels throughout the British Isles, observed the benefits of a change from communal to private farming and was most impressed by the sustained growth in output. Under the old system, large open fields had been farmed in common by local groups. The enclosure movement resulted in individual farms enclosed by a fence or stone wall. Only then did each farmer capture all the benefits from the hard work he put into his land. He was also free to try out new farming methods whereas before he had been compelled to follow the traditional communal farming technology. The result was a sustained improvement in productivity.

In forestry, the concept of sustainable management has been known since the works of Von Thunen (1826) and, in particular, Faustmann (1849) in the nineteenth century. One aspect of Faustmann's work was to identify the optimum cutting age for forests in order to maximise profits over time. He reasoned that in order to achieve maximum benefits the forest estate ought to be sustained indefinitely, which entailed replanting the area after each felling. In later years, Samuelson (1976) elaborated on Faustmann's work by pointing out that many well-known economists such as Hotelling, Alchian, Fisher, Boulding and Goundrey erred in their analysis of forest management by considering a single rotation solution as opposed to multiple rotation. It is worth noting that the intergenerational issue is latent in Faustmann's work. Since the gestation period in forestry is long and replanting is carried out after each felling, future generations will inherit an estate for their benefit, but also will be required to re-create the same thing for their successors.

In the management of fisheries, the idea of sustainable development has been well established since the work of Gordon (1954), Scott (1955) and Schaefer (1957), as explained in Chapter 7. One concept, the maximum sustainable yield, tries to identify fishing effort for maximum catch in the fishery sector and suggests that fishing activity should be planned to maintain this level indefinitely. Another criterion, the optimum sustainable yield, identifies an optimum level of fishing to maximise not the catch but the net revenue or the economic rent over time. In either case, the fishing activity is sustained indefinitely, although at different levels.

It was only a matter of time before the idea of sustainable development, which has been in existence in agriculture, forestry and fishing, would be extended to the whole area of economic activity. Now there is a growing literature on the subject. As Boulding (1978) pointed out, the concept of linear economy moving materials from the soil into product, distributing them for consumption and putting the residue into dumps, oceans and air is a temporary arrangement as this type of activity cannot be sustained indefinitely. Insistence on this process will hit future generations very hard.

Concern for the future has been increasing as our power to alter the environment and hence to change, adversely, the lives of countless generations grows. For example, the creation of highly toxic nuclear wastes, which will remain active for millions of years, has already imposed some degree of risk on the health, safety and civil liberties of future generations. Sir Francis Bacon argued centuries ago that men must pursue things which are just in the present and leave the future to divine providence. However, in his time there were no major environmental problems such as the destruction of ozone layer, acid rain, greenhouse effect of atmospheric pollution, nuclear wastes, relentlessly growing population and a rapid depletion of non-renewable resources. Today's world is very different. The sustainable development debate is essentially about the claims of future generations which have been brought to prominence by environmental problems that have no precedent in human history.

Adam Smith's world was also very different from the current one. In spite of this, some followers of Smith's free market doctrine believe that sustainability is best left to the invisible hand to sort out. If some resources become scarce due to depletion, then their price will increase, encouraging users to develop and utilise cheaper substitutes. As recently as 1974, Robert Solow argued that each natural resource is bound to have substitutes and thus there is no problem of depletion – economic growth alongside developments in science and technology remove the ancient fear of natural resource depletion. 'Exhaustion is just an event, not a catastrophe' (Solow 1974).

Of course, as pointed out by Pearce (1993), the problem with the free market solution is that the resources which are threatened are those without markets, such as atmosphere, ozone layer and oceans. Arthur Pigou (1935) argued that the doctrine of the invisible hand evolving social benefit out of private selfishness was never held by Adam Smith in that absolute and rigid form that popular writers conceive. Adam Smith based his thoughts on his observation that when the public sector intervened to achieve a desired outcome things often turned out to be wrong. Therefore, it was better to leave things alone than hand them over to incompetent bureaucrats. Pigou, however, asserted that this type of consideration is not one that will have the same application at different times and places.

Pigou was one of the earliest economists to defend robustly the interests of the future generations who are likely to sustain injury due to the indulgence of present generations. According to him, it is a part of human nature to underestimate and, hence, under-provide for future needs. Through short-sightedness, individuals often inflict harm upon themselves when they are fully in charge of their own affairs. Furthermore, when they are directly or indirectly dealing with others, say future generations, the recklessness and resulting injury will be even greater. In his own words:

> even though our desires for equal satisfactions of our own occurring at different times were equal, our desire for future satisfaction would often be less intense than for present satisfaction because it is very likely that future satisfaction will not be our own. . . . The practical way in which these discrepancies between desire and satisfaction work themselves out to the injury of economic welfare is by checking the creation of new capital.
>
> (Pigou 1920)

In addition to the failure to create new and lasting man-made capital, there is likely to be further injury to future generations when present individuals deplete the natural capital which is in limited stock. This problem will be more pronounced in countries which are endowed with natural assets such as virgin forests, fossil fuel deposits and fertile soils. Again, in Pigou's words: 'This same slackness of desire towards the future is also responsible for a tendency to wasteful exploitation of nature's gifts (1920).

He identifies two types of capital, natural and man-made, and implies that whereas the former ought to be frugally utilised to leave a sufficient surplus for future generations, the latter should be built up. Market forces that rely upon short-sighted decisions of individual operators are unlikely to achieve either of these and thus governments must act. It appears that Pigou's thoughts have inspired some exponents of the weak and strong sustainability debate. First, his examples of forests, fish stocks and fossil fuels are extended as a logical step to whole economics to identify the natural capital (Pearce 1993). In addition, two other sources of capital are considered: man-made, explicitly discussed by Pigou, and the human capital, or stock of knowledge. Marshall believed that the stock of knowledge is the primary requirements to create and re-create everything. If the world's man-made capital was destroyed, it could be re-created from the stock of knowledge. But if the ideas were lost, then even with an abundance of natural assets what was lost could not be reinvented. The absence of ideas would quickly drag mankind back into the dark ages, barbarism and poverty (see also Pigou 1912).

The overall stock of capital consisting of the three elements – man-made, human and natural – generates output on which human welfare depends (Pearce *et al.* 1989, 1990; Pearce 1993). All three types of capital can be substituted; thus, if one is run down the others should be built up so that future generations receive a constant stock overall. This is the so-called weak sustainability in which the natural stock of capital has no special place (Hartwick 1978; Solow 1986).

On the other hand, strong sustainability places a special emphasis on natural capital, mainly because it is essential both for survival and well-being in general. A proportion of this can be designated as critical capital which is crucial for survival, for example, the ozone layer, carbon cycle, biodiversity, and other natural assets that scientists may identify as vital. Strong sustainability requires keeping at least the critical capital constant. In addition, the overall stock needs to be kept constant, allowing substitution only between human and man-made stocks of capital.

Two further reasons are given for the constant critical capital rule, one of which is irreversibility. That is, once such assets are used up they are gone for ever. The second reason is that of uncertainty; we do not understand clearly the working mechanism of the ecosystem. Perhaps one day we may have a much better understanding of our environment, but until then we should avoid taking unnecessary risks. In addition, sustainable development requires international co-operation as countries depend on one another in the use of primary commodities – trade in finished goods, as well as others, are vulnerable, although at different rates, to the change in atmospheric and stratospheric conditions. In the long run, a strategy to achieve sustainability by one country at the expense of others is not possible.

FLAWS IN THE CURRENT DEBATE

There are a number of serious problems in arguments put forward by the 'sustainability school'. First, the advocates of constant capital rule contend that what is at issue is not the physical stock of capital but its value, and the development of valuation literature is, in part, aimed at addressing this issue. Pearce *et al.* (1990), after mentioning some problems regarding the constant capital theory rule, recommend a combination of physical quantity of productive stocks together with their value, which is a little like summing up grapes and apples. In this way, environmental assets are valued in the same way as human-made assets. With respect to non-renewable resources such as biodiversity, fossil fuel deposits, potash and phosphate and other natural assets (including topsoil, fresh water, and so on), it is virtually certain that, due to population growth, future generations will be worse off in terms of physical availability per capita. Due to scarcity, their prices will be higher in the future and in this way their overall value will be maintained. But this may not be a great comfort to future members of the human race who will have to rely on physical availability for their survival.

As non-renewable assets physically run down and other natural stocks become smaller on a per capita basis, man-made and human capital must be increased to compensate future generations. One assumption here is that man-made and human capital are homogeneous and benign. In fact this is not always so. Take the nuclear industry which is a multi-billion dollar concern. This sector has been creating, for a substantial period of time, substances that are exceedingly dangerous, not only for humans but for all forms of life on this planet. It is estimated that in the United States alone, spent nuclear fuel will increase from 15,903 tonnes of uranium in 1987 to 40,293 tonnes in the year 2000 (Kula 1994). In addition, there are very large quantities of high-level, mid-level and low-level defence and commercial wastes and their volumes are increasing rapidly. There seems to be no clear idea about how to store them safely on a permanent basis. Thanks to our nuclear industry, future generations will inherit a dis-product that our ancestors never dreamed of.

The nuclear equipment itself is nothing like locomotives or ships which, at the end of their useful life, can be melted down and used to make something else, say, razor blades. In effect, the nuclear 'capital' is a highly contaminated structure which must be dismantled and safely disposed of at an enormous cost. In 1990 there were 423 nuclear reactors in various parts of the world providing about 20 per cent of the world's electricity supply and a further 105 units under construction. These plants, when aged, must be returned to green field sites, a process which could take over a hundred years to complete for each one.

Long before the nuclear age, Pigou (1920) argued that identifying and valuing capital is problematic. A motor car, for instance, is capital for a company which hires it out, but it is a utility for a household. In the nuclear age, valuing aggregate man-made capital is even more problematic.

According to Shiva (1992), substitutability of man-made capital for nature is a delusion as money earned from the former, which stays in the circular flow of economic activity, cannot replace nature's flow. As Georgescu-Roegen (1974) puts it:

> If one only looks at money, all one can see is that money just passes from one hand to another; except by regrettable accident it never gets out of the economic process. Perhaps the absence of any difficulty in securing raw materials by those countries where modern economics grew and flourished was yet another reason for economists to remain blind to this crucial economics factor. Not even the wars the same nations fought for the control of the world's natural resources awoke the economists from their slumber.

With regard to human capital, or know-how, it is equally misleading to assume that all is benign. Human knowledge and effort are frequently used for destructive purposes. The best brains and most expensive labour have been used for the creation of weapons of mass destruction, such as nuclear and chemical arsenals. Throughout human history, destruction has taken place by wars in which the best technology available at the time was used. In the recent Gulf War, Saddam Hussein destroyed large tracts of Kuwait, including many of her oil wells, as he was forced to retreat from the conquered territory. Countless other examples could be given.

In the weak sustainability argument, the running down of one form of capital would require increasing one or both of the remaining items. However, it is doubtful whether increased space for, say, cash crops, even if the output could be maintained, would be an acceptable compensation for the loss of tropical forests and the extinction of species.

In strong sustainability, on the other hand, it is required that at least the critical capital must be maintained and, at the same time, the economic activity is encouraged to grow. It has been amply demonstrated by some of the writers mentioned in Chapter 9 that there is a trade-off between economic growth and critical capital. Without substantial energy use, it is not possible to grow; it may even be impossible to maintain economic activity at present levels. An economy based on fossil fuels increases the greenhouse effect. If the energy sector switched, in good measure, to nuclear power, then there would the problem of waste disposal and decommissioning of nuclear 'capital'. What is the alternative? Solar, wind, tidal and hydropower are not available to all nations in sufficient quantities, and so it may be unrealistic to expect growth to continue without fossil fuel or nuclear-based energy.

On the valuation of natural, man-made and human capital, the task, if there is one, is immensely complex. Take the first one. At the outset, one needs to identify all deposits that the earth contains and then value each one. Apart from fossil fuels, metal deposits exist at almost all depths. When do we stop counting? What prices ought to be used to value them? The current market price, or some other measure? Speedy extraction would depress the market price whereas slow extraction, *ceteris paribus*, would have the opposite effect. Or should the valuer use the average historic price? Then there are topsoils, grasslands, forests, freshwater, amenity value of the landscape, wetlands, the capacity of the earth to re-cycle carbon and so forth to consider.

Over the years, economists have not been able to measure even the real income of nations in the coherent and acceptable manner that is necessary for monitoring progress in human well-being. It is a little like an unsuccessful head of a small country who has aspirations to become a world leader and to manage all the problems of all peoples including that of future generations. When Pearce (1993) laments that the British government has, by and large, been deaf to the theories of sustainable development few should be surprised.

One rationale for recommending continuous economic growth, with some improved conduct, is to solve the problem of mass poverty in the Third

World. However, it seems that most countries in the developing world have already adopted the Western style of progress with all its shortcomings, including widening inequalities.

Pearce (1993) implies that the West, by not giving up the perpetual growth principle with its new improved environmental behaviour, should give leadership to the developing world so that they can grow to alleviate poverty. The evidence is very thin on the ground regarding environmentally friendly development and more equitable distribution of income. Furthermore, it is highly unlikely that the Third World will pay much attention to Western writers about good conduct as the West has been so persistent in wrecking the environment and failing to deal with relative as well as absolute poverty on their own territory.

At the conference on 'Saving of the Ozone Layer' in London in March 1988, which attracted more than 120 countries, there was a disagreement between Western advocates of economic development and the delegates from the Third World. Some delegates were sceptical about the good advice given by the industrialised countries. For example, the Chinese delegation pointed out that the present problems of CFC pollution, which have yet to be revealed in full, are overwhelmingly the product of thirty years of environmental abuse in the West, and as a result the Chinese people would probably suffer more than those in the developed world. The Third World will need to be compensated for the damage it will sustain and the development it will have to forego as a result of CFCs and the future restrictions on their use. The Indian delegate argued that the West had a moral duty to consider the way developing countries were being invited to keep their use of CFCs at a level 100 times lower than those which are enjoyed in the West. He pointed out that there was no wish in the Third World that chemical multinationals should suffer, but the entire world should be free from ozone depletion. He urged the setting up of a new fund to help developing nations find alternative substances and for the restructuring of Third World refrigeration industries. He emphasised that this should not be thought of as a charity; there is an excellent principle established in the West – the polluter pays.

Perhaps non-stop economic growth theology, even when it somehow incorporates frugal use of energy and water resources, avoiding forest clearances, improving non-CFC using technology, etc., is not compatible with environmental improvement. For example, in Holland, intensification of agriculture during the 1960s and 1970s resulted in a substantial rise in agricultural yields. But, on the other hand, it created serious water and land pollution. Today, Holland is one of the most seriously polluted countries in Europe with inorganic nitrate and animal waste (Baan and Hopstaken 1989; Stalwijk 1989; Tamminga and Wijnands 1991). As a result, agricultural pollution has been an issue of debate in Dutch politics since the early 1980s. In 1984, the parliament restricted the growth of farming activities on existing farms as well as curbing the development of new farm ventures in poultry, dairy, meat and cereal sectors.

Pearce (1993), in an attack on the change-in-lifestyle school, contends that the only way in which this should happen is by the reduction of current wasteful demands on natural resources. It is possible to maintain economic growth by using fewer resources. Falling, or even a stable GNP per capita, will not be acceptable to the masses due to increase in destitution. Furthermore, the well-off value their standard of living highly and are unlikely to accept a reduction in their position.

When the environmental clouds get darker and lower, those who established a lifestyle on everlasting growth will have to think very seriously about their aspirations. I know of many cases where individuals who had built a lifestyle on drinking and culinary enjoyment, when told by their doctors that they were heading for an early grave, transformed their lifestyles almost overnight. After some years of a Spartan lifestyle, brought about by doctors' orders, they unexpectedly confessed that their new life was much better than they had previously thought possible.

Everlasting economic growth may be an addiction that can be given up. Perhaps we have been conditioned by excessive commercialism to believe that growth is the only acceptable way of living. As Galbraith points out (see Chapter 6), growth is the most important objective of modern corporations and can only take place when households consume more and more.

Cost-benefit analysis has been around for some time to assist the communal decision-maker in assessing the worth of new investment projects which are the engine of economic growth. Without new investment decisions, it is unlikely that the idea of economic growth can be pursued. Perhaps it is at the project level that we should be concerned, not only about the environmental impact assessment, but about the moral questions that individual projects give rise to. Unfortunately, some economists do not appear to be too keen to consider moral issues at this level as they regard cost-benefit analysts as preference counters and number crunchers. For example, Pearce (1983) contends that:

> As a procedure for aggregating the preferences of our set of individuals we establish something of a fundamental importance at the outset: CBA [cost-benefit analysis] makes no claim to produce morally correct decisions. What CBA produces and what is morally correct may coincide if, and only if, we adopt a further rule, namely, that some aggregated set of preferences of individuals is the morally correct way of making decisions.
>
> (Pearce 1983: 3)

The most important ethical concern is the one that relates to future generations who will be affected, in some cases profoundly, by projects initiated by current members of society. Unfortunately, it is now a common practice in cost-benefit analysis to wipe out future consequences of individual projects by way of *ordinary* discounting. As I have demonstrated elsewhere (Kula 1994), health and other costs of nuclear waste storage projects are reduced to minute net present value figures by the process of ordinary discounting even when low rates of discount are used. Pearce (1983) himself demonstrates that the cost of a hypothetical nuclear accident that may take place 500 years from now, and which may impose an economic cost of £10 billion on future generations, will be reduced to 25 pence present value at a 5 per cent discount rate.

I have demonstrated in many publications that *ordinary* discounting is wrong, not only because it discriminates against future generations, but also because it rests upon strange assumptions that individuals live forever or that society is like a single individual who has an eternal life. An alternative *communal* discounting pattern called *modified discounting* has been constructed by assuming that individuals are mortal. (For a summary of various aspects of ordinary and modified discounting methods, see Kula 1994, 1996; for a full treatment, see Kula 1997). In the modified discounting method, the future matters; it is never ignored. Costs and benefits that will fall upon future generations are discounted in the same manner as they are discounted for present members of society, yielding a pattern of discounting which is very different from the conventional method. For example, a discount factor related to an item of cost that will come about in 500 years' time will be 0.00000 in ordinary discounting when a 5 per cent discount rate is used. The factor for the same cost will be 0.26619 at the same rate of interest using the modified discounting method. In other words, the future has practically no economic value and thus it does not matter when *ordinary* discounting is used.

Table 10.1 shows the difference between the ordinary and modified discounting methods for various interest rates and for various years.

In effect, whether the economic activity is sustained or not, it does not matter when ordinary discounting is decision criterion. Provided they are respectable concepts, when the so-called weak sustainability, strong sustainability and constant natural capital rule are seen from the viewpoint of ordinary discounting, their long-term components will be reduced to practically nothing. With ordinary or conventional discounting the focus will be on the present and the near future. That is, economic growth must somehow be maintained in the short run providing material benefits for those who are still alive. Whatever happens after that is of little or no consequence.

Let us say that we have somehow identified and valued the critical, and perhaps some other, capital over a long period of time with a view to maintaining its value for future generations. Finding a net present value by way of ordinary discounting for future capital would yield absurdly low figures – and so why bother? In Pearce's example, £10 billion in 500 years' time is

Table 10.1 Ordinary and modified discounting factors for three different rates of interest for various years

	Ordinary discount factors			*Modified discount factors*		
Year	*1%*	*2.5%*	*5%*	*1%*	*2.5%*	*5%*
0	1.00	1.00	1.00	1.00	1.00	1.00
50	0.61	0.29	0.09	0.79	0.49	0.28
100	0.37	0.08	0.01	0.71	0.46	0.27
500	0.01	0.00	0.00	0.71	0.46	0.27
1,000	0.00	0.00	0.00	0.71	0.46	0.27
2,000	0.00	0.00	0.00	0.71	0.46	0.27
3,000	0.00	0.00	0.00	0.71	0.46	0.27

Source: Kula (1994)

reduced to £0.25 net present value at a 5 per cent discount rate. This means that care for future generations does not exist. This is one of many contradictions and oddities in the writings of some of the sustainable economic development school who, ironically, set out with concepts such as duty, care and consideration for future generations.

Despite an unambiguous statement that cost-benefit analysis does not make any claim to produce morally correct decisions, elsewhere, Pearce and his colleagues define sustainable development as a vector of desirable objectives such as an increase in real income per capita, an improvement in health and nutrition, educational achievement, access to resources, a fairer distribution of income, and increase in basic freedoms. They then state that 'the elements to be included in the vector are open to ethical debate' (Pearce *et al.* 1990: 3). In other words, sustainable development is open to ethical debate, whereas in cost-benefit analysis, where actual decisions are made at micro level, ethical questions are ignored. On the other hand, Turner (1991) emphasises that cost-benefit analysis is an integral part of sustainable resource management.

Perhaps, in a rational and open debate, contradictions and inconsistencies will be eliminated in due course in the sustainable development debate. According to Nove (1992), open debate seldom takes place in economics and those at an advantageous position try to ignore or marginalise those who challenge what has been established even though they may have perfectly valid points in their criticism of the dogma.

Brown *et al.* (1987) argue that sustainable development has already become a transcendent term. Indeed, sustainable development is a highly agreeable term, as is friendship, and thus a good number use it without understanding what it means. Sherman (1990) points out that, instead of focusing on the precise definition, we need to be more concerned with the implication for any given context to which sustainability is applied. The concept is used as a modifier in development, growth, ecosystems, etc., and it is more important to understand the meaning of the term within the context in which it is employed. Most economists relate growth to increase in the GNP, narrowly defined, of the nation, but this process could cause suffering to the majority (Daly 1990; Douthwaite 1992). Smith (1993) suggests that growth of GNP can cost more than its worth. In particular, present patterns of resource distribution in a 'growing' world economy can create more hardship for the poor, which in turn can speed up environmental degradation.

Pearce (1983), with reference to major environmental problems such as nuclear waste disposal and the greenhouse effect of atmospheric pollution and ozone depletion, accepts that there is intergenerational discrimination in economic methods. According to some, the present generations who make the decisions now are the proper electorate and thus they are the ones that matter. 'We cannot take account of costs to generations yet unborn, for to do so is to widen the concept of democratic voting in an unacceptable way' (Pearce 1983: 53).

In order to overcome the intergenerational discrimination problem, Pearce (1983) recommends establishing a compensation fund to benefit future generations for the damage they are likely to sustain from current activities. This must be one of the easiest and painless ways out, or to cop out, from the mess that one generation can create for others. The power of compound interest rate will accumulate vast sums over time which can, in theory, compensate the future individuals. Reversing Pearce's example of £10 billion-worth of damage in 500 years' time, we need to invest only 25 pence now at a 5 per cent interest rate for it to become £10 billion in 500 years! This then can be used to compensate the unfortunate. If the entire British population, some 57 million, each invested £1 now at, say, 3 per cent interest rate this would amount to an enormous sum in 500 years' time. This is economic logic and its roots go back to J. Maynard Keynes, who was mentioned in Chapter 6. The power of compound interest rates not only permits future generations to live in comfort, but also enables us to compensate victims of environmental damage. This type of argument says a lot about the state of economics. Put a few pounds into a bank – it will then 'overcome' future difficulties.

However, Pearce (1983) mentions two problems with this approach; namely, we cannot be certain about the extent of any future damage and interest rates may not remain constant over time. Despite these practical difficulties, he says that the concept of compensation funds is worth pursuing. He also points out that according to some 'hardliners', we may not have to bother with the compensation fund as future generations are already compensated. This is because current projects will add to the capital stock of nations and future generations, with such endowment in hand, will thus be able to engage in welfare improving activities. No distinction is made between railway tracks, nuclear capital, military hardware, etc. I find this line of thought, including the penny-in-the-bank scenario, appalling.

What is the ethical foundation of the arguments put forward by the 'sustainability' school? According to Turner (1991) and Turner and Pearce (1993), the sustainable development debate has a strong ethical dimension as it is based upon the concept of concern for others – namely, that of future generations. It requires a collective action so that generations yet to be born can inherit an environment in which they can generate for themselves a level of welfare no less than that enjoyed by current generations. Sustainable development, therefore, is a kind of intergenerational social contract about the fair use of natural resources over time for the benefit of mankind alone. In this respect, sustainable development is, or should be, anthropocentric, i.e. man-based in orientation.

In the anthropocentric way of thinking, humans are the only species who really matter. That is, those who subscribe to the strong anthropocentric position believe that only human beings possess a quality of life that is worth ethical consideration. Another, and much less strong position, i.e. weak anthropocentricism, allows the development of the concept of stewardship in which humans ought to give some consideration to other species because they benefit humans. That is, man should utilise nature with care and consideration, and without unnecessary cruelty.

At the other end of the spectrum, there are a number of positions, such as the Gaia hypothesis, land ethics, deep ecology, etc., which take a fundamentally different viewpoint. In these beliefs, broadly speaking, non-human species too are worthy of ethical consideration; humans, despite their intellect and ability, are not the central point in creation, but a part of nature. I shall say much more on these views, including the anthropocentric position, in the next chapter. According to some of its exponents, sustainable development ought to be anthropocentric, but should not exclude judgement on behalf of other species (Turner and Pearce 1993).

The non-anthropocentric position, i.e. the bioethical standpoint, is not favoured in the sustainable development debate on at least three grounds. First, it may create social injustice because some resources need to be diverted to, say, animal welfare and to the preservation of some natural phenomena, which may be costly. Second, such diversion of funds and non-use of some species would reduce the economic growth. Third, in dealing with development projects, we only need to incorporate the intrinsic aspects of the natural phenomena in cost-benefit analysis. This approach tries to value a natural attribute the existence of which gives utility to people and therefore it can be expressed in monetary terms. Even if a natural phenomenon is unconnected with the lives of individuals, it still has a value and humans are capable of appreciating this. By using various survey methods individuals may be asked to reveal how much they would be willing to pay to preserve something which may be very remote to them. Then the aggregate sum can be incorporated into cost-benefit analysis as the value of the phenomenon, whatever it may be.

Although the anthropocentric approach, incorporating future generations, is an ethical stance, it is not necessarily environmental. In this, present and future generations care for an environmental attribute solely because it is useful. If the item has no direct or indirect use, then its destruction would be of no consequence. I am not certain that bringing in intrinsic value criteria would satisfy a host of environmental aspirations, as I shall explain in the next chapter.

Although I do not wish to be disrespectful to the ethical position of the 'sustainability' school, I do not find their position strongly environmental. It has been suggested that sustainability imperatives represent high order needs and values (Swaney 1987; Turner and Pearce 1993). I am not sure that most writers in the environmental movement, which will be discussed next, will find the current ethical platform of the sustainability school high enough.

In summary, the arguments of the sustainability school are far from convincing. What has been produced so far is full of contradictions, confusions and internal inconsistencies. Their strongest point, I think, is that the environment is most threatened by rapid population growth (Pearce 1993). After the Second World War, due to labour shortages, Harrod (1952) expressed concern about the declining reproductive rate in England and advised that families should think in terms of four or five children so that the nation would be able to maintain its economic and social progress. Fortunately, economists have moved a long way from this position. Indeed, the most devastating effect of population growth will be the increase in poverty, which in turn will lead to reckless use of the environment out of desperation. But this is hardly a new idea.

11

ETHICAL AND SPIRITUAL DIMENSIONS OF ENVIRONMENTAL EXPLOITATION

As pointed out in the previous chapter, some exponents of the sustainable economic development debate emphasise that, as a concept, sustainability must embrace ethical norms. There is now a fast growing literature on the ethics of environmental conduct. The bottom line on this debate for the economists, I think, must be that environmental abuse hurts people and in this way many moral questions arise. For example, breathing contaminated air or using dirty water makes people sick or even kills them. Mismanagement of nuclear facilities and wastes leads to cancer and genetic deformities for present as well as future generations. Logging in the hills creates soil erosion which silts up the rivers creating floods downstream, and in this way a large number of people die every year in various parts of the world. Overgrazing in fragile regions leads to desertification, which terminates the means of survival for shepherds and their families. Overfishing leads to depletion or even extinction of fish stocks creating hardship and eventual displacement for fishing communities. Countless other examples can be given.

To some economists, it is now essential that we need not only good environmental policies but an underlying environmental ethics for respecting nature. These policies should contain naturalistic, humanitarian and spiritual dimensions, as well as utilitarian ones. Environmental ethics is a term that refers to principles which should guide humanity's relationship to the environment. Menacingly growing population and ecological problems have given fresh impetus to the exploration of the values underpinning human societies. Some of this exploration has been carried out by religious groups, philosophers, environmental scientists and, to a much lesser extent, economists. What is the morally correct economic behaviour impacting the environment? A serious debate is not in sight in the economic profession and I do not think that much will happen in the foreseeable future.

Ironically, economics, as a branch of social science, has an old and rich tradition of just conduct in almost all areas of its jurisdiction. Concepts like just prices, wages, profits, taxation and discounting have been of interest to a great many economists for a long period of time. Take, for instance, the concept of just prices, which has concerned many economists – and others – since the Middle Ages. The early medieval view was that the just price is the one enabling the supplier to live and support his dependants on a scale which is suitable to his status in society (Ashley 1920; Clark 1927; Clough and Cole 1946). Later, a different view developed making the rule of the market the arbiter (Magnus 1894; Kraus 1930). If the market price of a commodity differs from the cost of providing it, suppliers must accept it as being fair, whether or not they gain or lose. Scotus (1894) argues that the fair price is a uniform charge regardless of who is buying and for what purpose. The proper way of looking at the issue is that price is a social phenomenon and should be regulated with this purpose in mind. According to Roover (1970), this idea can be traced back to the Roman times.

The concept of a just wage is as old and varied as that of a just price, and it is possible to trace ideas on it back to the medieval times or even beyond. In the Middle Ages it was accepted that a labourer should be paid enough to sustain him and his family. In order to make this view a reality, guilds were formed for the purpose of achieving just wages and equal opportunities for the workers. However, in the course of time the guilds lost their original purpose. The Marxist school, on the other hand, believe that wages determined in the capitalist markets are profoundly unjust because such markets are based upon the exploitation of the labourers. The marginalist school contend that the just wage is the one that relates a worker's contribution to output at the margin. One of the most famous marginalists, John Bates Clark stated at the beginning of his book (1927) that the main force motivating him to develop a theory of distribution was his desire to find an objective basis for justice in the distribution of income. He reasoned that if the net contribution of labour could be identified in a production process, then its market value would be the just wage.

On the justice of a progressive income tax, Irving Fisher (1927) argued that, since the marginal utility of income is declining as income levels increase, this alone would justify taxing the rich at a higher rate.

Once again, what is the morally correct conduct towards the environment? The economic dimension of this question is undeniable as environmental attributes are exploited for economic gains. Ethical humanists argue that the environment is of value only because it contributes to human welfare. If extinction of a species, deliberate or otherwise, can lead to, say, an increase in economic wealth, we should not worry too much about it. For example, a utilitarian environmentalist would approve of, or even encourage, the efforts to eradicate crop pests completely. To them, responsibility to nature can only be in the light of our responsibility to fellow human beings (Passmore 1980). Consumption, population and pollution control are, and should be, based on human interest alone. By doing this we take responsibility for our own actions, not for the environment. This line of argument is not accepted by everybody, but it is a useful viewpoint as it provides the minimal basis from which we might construct a meaningful policy and a code of conduct (Hooker 1992).

It has been argued that responsibility towards nature is not a clear-cut thesis unless it impacts upon humans, especially in an adverse way. Nature is not a person, nor has it any particular long-term aims that can be accepted universally. To put it crudely, nature is an object. Here, we ought to separate humans and their possessions, e.g. farm animals, pets, land, etc., which are part of nature.

The concept of being responsible to an object– nature – is, and must be, quite different from being responsible to a person in a way that is operationally inactive. However, one can take a caring attitude towards nature in a variety of ways if it is required by law, by God, or by the subject's own deep personal convictions, i.e. conscience. Responsibility to nature is an extremely difficult concept; it is doubtful whether there can be any generally accepted view on it. In order to be responsible towards something in a true sense we have to be involved in its creation, understand its basic process and, last but not least, we must have the capacity to do good rather than bad. Therefore, before leaping into action on environmental responsibility we should think carefully about what is intended by the idea (Hooker 1992).

Responsibility to humans is a different matter. Environmental problems created by reckless behaviour harm mankind. As mentioned before, air pollution creates respiratory and other health problems, water pollution poisons our drinking water and fish stocks, and our crops and forests, while destruction of biodiversity removes opportunities for the development of new medicines and accelerates the greenhouse effect. These are universally acceptable reasons, 'the bottom line', for protecting the environment and, in fact, they play a leading role in formulating current environmental policies. In this, there is no ethical responsibility to the environment as such but there is an ethical responsibility to fellow human beings, including future generations. For one thing, future generations will be created by current ones and we must take responsibility for them. We should therefore pass them a world in good order so that they can fulfil themselves as human beings. Hooker (1992) argues that although this position is an ethical one, it is not intrinsically environmental. The scope and complexity of ethics is vast. A narrow view of the concept would be concern for things we deeply value. The traditional ethical stance is man-based in which the environment should be protected for mankind. At a broader level, it can be defined as the pursuit of goodness in a way which transcends individual interests and human imperfections.

On the other hand, an ecocentric would suggest that harming the environment for economic benefit is unethical; this finds its extreme manifestation in the extinction of species. Every extinction is an incremental decay in stopping life which in turn corrupts mankind. Extinction terminates the body and the soul of a species after which nothing of that kind ever again lives or dies. A shutdown of a unique life stream by mankind, the super killer, is the most destructive, the most unpleasant event.

> Several billion years worth of creative toil, several million species of teeming life, have been handed over to the care of this late-coming species in which mind has flowered and words have emerged. Life on earth is a many splendoured thing; extinction dims its lustre. If, in this world of uncertain moral convictions, it makes any sense to claim that one ought not to kill individuals without justification, it makes more sense to claim that one ought not to super-kill the species, without super-justification. That moves from what is to what ought to be. But this is no fallacy being committed by ethical naturalists, rather it is the humanists who cannot draw their ethical conclusions who are mistaken in their logic.
>
> (Rolston III 1992)

The importance of theology and philosophy in the development of economic ideas, especially during the classical period, is well known due to the works of Thomas Malthus, Adam Smith and John Stuart Mill. Growing environmental problems in our times have led to fresh interest in the religious and philosophical dimensions of man and his environment touching many subject areas including economics. In Western religions, such as Judaism, Christianity and Islam, humans are the focus of ethical concern, but Eastern religions such as Buddhism, Taoism, Hinduism, Zen, and even the pre-Christian faiths of Europe, have a much wider focus. Interpretation of religious positions varies quite considerably from person to person and also from one period to another. In this chapter, I shall start from the Judaeo–Christian viewpoint then move on to other areas that are now widely debated.

JUDAEO–CHRISTIAN THEOLOGY AND THE ENVIRONMENT

According to some, the roots of the resource and environmental crisis lie in the teaching of the Judaeo–Christian doctrine of creation. The Old Testament states, 'Then God said, let us make man in our image, after our likeness; and let them have dominion over the fish of the sea, and over the birds of the air, and over the cattle, and over the earth, and over every creeping thing that creeps upon the earth' (Genesis 1:26). It is worth noting that in the Old Testament the word creation is not actually used, instead expressions such as the heaven and earth, all that lives, are used. The word creation is used in the New Testament (Peacocke 1979).

A number of writers point out that our reckless attitude towards the environment is deeply conditioned by beliefs about our nature and destiny in which religious convictions play a profound role. The Judaeo–Christian faith separates God, and ultimately human beings, from nature as we are made in the image of God. This reduces nature to a mere object, a physical fact, and desecrates it. In contrast with Asian religions and the paganistic beliefs of pre-Christian Europe, Christianity has not only established a dualism of humans and nature, but insisted that man should exploit nature for his own ends. The Christian doctrine has therefore brought a despotic and utilitarian empire mentality to nature which has led to a growing ecological crisis.

This is one of a number of views on Christianity, various aspects of which have been debated extensively, as I shall explain later on. However, it is necessary to emphasise that if, in essence, religion is at the root of environmental troubles, then the solution requires a fundamental spiritual reorientation.

Entrusting man with the earth and other beings, giving him the status of an emperor, created a ruthless Christian mentality. McHarg (1977) refers to the Old Testament as a disturbing document, a text of compound horror which has cultivated a legitimised ruthlessly utilitarian and ultimately destructive attitude towards nature:

> If you want to find one text . . . which will guarantee that the relationship of man to nature can only be destructive . . . which can explain all the destruction and all the despoliation accomplished by Western man for at least 2000 years, then you do not have to look any further than this ghastly calamitous text.

In the traditional Jewish attitude, ecological questions are not the faithful's world-view: the earth is vast with endless resources; it is here to exploit and the only restriction to this process is the ability to subdue wilderness with other human groups. In the Pentateuch and the rabbinical texts, it is clear that nature exists for the use of mankind. According to a rabbinical interpretation of the Bible, in the early Middle Ages God shows the Garden of Eden to Adam and says to him: 'All I have created, I created for you' (Midrash Rabba, Kahelet 7:28). So God created man at the end of his work so that he may directly come to the banquet. It is a little like a king who starts to build a palace and when it is complete he then invites his most favoured and important guests to a feast (Babylonian Talmud, Sanhedrin 38a).

Stahl (1993) reports that the benediction that a Jew has to pronounce when he sees a tree in blossom is this: 'Blessed be thou God, Lord of the Universe, who has made the world so that it lacks nothing, and has brought into being godly creatures and godly trees so that man can enjoy them.' This blessing is printed in the prayer book to be recited on appropriate occasions.

Another point about the Jewish faith's attitude towards the environment is that nature is wild and in disorder, not readily available to meet mankind's needs. Nature, therefore, must be tamed to suit man's needs. For instance, Joshua orders Ephraim and the Manasseh tribes to go up to the woods on the mountain to fell them to make the area habitable with a view to settling there (Joshua 17:14–18). The wild beauty of nature would be a destructive influence on the faithful undermining their efforts of prayer. Nearly 2,000 years ago in Mishna, it was argued that whoever is walking along the road reciting and then stops in admiration of a tree, or a landscape, is committing a sin by indulging in idle thought (Mishna, Auoth 3:7). In the sixteenth century, a well-regarded rabbi emphasised that the faithful should not stop studying the Holy Law and indulge in idle thoughts as that would be the moment when God would withdraw his protection (Duran 1961).

Not all traditional Jews regarded nature as beautiful. For instance, Tuan (1970) and Thomas (1984) argue that as a rule traditional folk did not regard untamed nature as pretty, but rather something to be touched by human hands to be turned into, say, gardens or orchards, which would then be regarded as beautiful. In a study of Jewish folk tales in Morocco, Noy (1967) argues that the attitude of the community towards nature has been a negative one. In the study all references to nature were identified, such as mountains, forests, rivers, streams, birds, plants and animals. Then, by considering their context, these were divided into those having negative, positive or neutral connotations. The results show that 57 per cent supported a negative attitude, 15 per cent a positive one, with the remainder considered neutral. However, Stahl (1993) reports that traditional Jewish attitudes began to change over time, especially among European Jews under the influence of Western education.

Hebrew scriptures are also full of assertions that by looking at nature we can learn lessons from it. For instance, from the ant we can learn how to be diligent (Proverbs 6:6), from the ox and the ass Israel can learn how to behave (Isaiah 1:3), and from the fish and the fowl we can learn what the Lord has wrought. A fifteenth-century Jewish philosopher in Spain argued that from nature one should try to learn about some good trait, moral quality, or lesson of wisdom (Albs 3:1). In the seventeenth century, another Jewish moral philosopher, Modena, argued that we can learn about the wickedness of anger from the bear and of cruelty from the adder (Modena 1949).

The precise meaning of biblical and other doctrines has been debated. Barr (1972) contends that the biblical word 'domain' is not a strong one as it was used for ruling in general – even peaceful ruling as in the reference to Solomon (1 Kings 4:24). The word 'subdue' may be misunderstood to mean violence towards other species, but in fact it was used with reference to agricultural activities, such as tilling, to fulfil the basic needs of settlements (Genesis 2:5; 2:15).

It is explained by Ferguson and Roche (1993) that the Hebrew view with regard to man and nature was that man should look after nature on God's behalf and preserve it, not only as a source of food, but also for education and pleasure. Human mastery over nature is intended to resemble a protective goodness, not a predatory exploiter.

The notion of man as despot towards nature has been emphasised by Lynn White in a lecture, 'The historic roots of our ecological crisis', delivered at the American Association for the Advancement of Science in 1966. One year later his paper was published in *Science*, the organ of the American Association (White 1967). Although a committed Christian, White argued that the roots of our ecological crisis could be traced to Judaeo–Christian theology. This, first of all, established a position that separated man from nature and then guided the former to a position of supremacy over the latter. The scientific and technological revolutions which took place in the seventeenth and eighteenth centuries enabled man to pursue a ruthless and effective exploitation policy, ultimately leading to serious ecological problems.

Another factor which enhanced Western man's exploitative zeal was the triumph of Christianity over paganism, which had seen man as part of nature. In relation to the destruction of pre-Christian European faith, White described it as 'the greatest psychic revolution in the history of our culture'. Paganist ideas vanished almost completely as a result of the extermination campaigns carried out by the medieval Christians.

White does not deny the existence of different viewpoints in Christian faith. For example, St Francis of Assisi, whom he regards as the patron saint of environmentalists, was more reverential to creation. He was committed to a life of poverty and repentance. St Francis treated all living things as close kin, and emphasised the necessity of communion with nature. Of course, for some Christians, St Francis's beliefs were pretty close to heresy by giving human status to all species. They therefore turned to other sources such as sixth-century St Benedict who taught the wise use of natural resources. A number of scholars point out that St Benedict was much more relevant to the human condition than St Francis (see Livingstone 1994). However, St Francis was not unique in his approach to nature; for instance, the fourth-century St Chrysostom believed that all animals should be treated with great kindness as they are of the same origin as ourselves.

In contrast, Passmore (1975) notes that the predatory attitude is detectable in the writings of St Paul. To him, it was the Graeco–Christian arrogance which became Christianity's official position until recent times. Others, such as Thomas (1984), point out that White over-emphasises the extent to which human needs are motivated by religious teaching. Perhaps a bigger culprit is the establishment of private property-based market economics that leads to over-exploitation of nature. In other words, the abuse of the environment is much less theological and more economic. As evidence, Thomas points out that the Japanese worship of nature did not prevent widespread pollution. Tuan (1970), in his study of the non-Christian East, contends that, despite the prevalence of different religious traditions, the destruction of the environment there is just as bad. Despite the clear teaching of Taoism, the Chinese ill-treatment of nature such as deforestation, rice-terracing and urbanisation has always been a problem.

Another possible destructive factor towards the environment had been the democratisation following the French Revolution, which opened up new channels of social mobility, made wealth and privilege more accessible and, as a result, greater and greater participation took place in capital accumulation. In the United States, the frontier experience, which was supported by national policies, created private land ownership in the hands of wealth-seeking immigrants. Their drive to realise their dreams and to conquer the environment led to a reckless attitude, which was compounded by the absence of private and public environmental morality, the inability of social institutions to adjust to confront ecological crisis and faster technology.

White's paper drew fire from a variety of sources, but mostly from Christian scientists, all of whom argue that spiritual enlightenment could be very useful in solving our ecological crisis. Toynbee (1972) believes that the remedy to environmental problems lies in reverting from the *Weltanschauung* of monotheism to the *Weltanschauung* of pantheism, which is older and was once universal. Others pointed out that Christian doctrine actually taught stewardship and not recklessness. Ferguson and Roach (1993) believe that the biblical understanding of creation has been inadequately grasped by White and by those who hold similar views. In effect, the Judaeo–Christian tradition is well able to develop a contemporary ecological ethic. Destruction of the natural order is itself a sinful activity. Livingstone (1994) believes that God was a wise conservationist and economist: humans made in the image of God were to act as caretakers of creation. In John Calvin's order it is said, 'Let him who possesses a field, so partake of its yearly fruits, that he may not suffer the ground to be injured by his negligence; but let him endeavour to hand it down to posterity as he received it . . . let everyone regard himself as the steward of God in all things which he possesses.'

In the seventeenth century, Hale (1677) argued that man was created to be God's deputy and thus he should preserve the beauty and the productivity of the earth. Derham (1713), in a spirit of Christian stewardship, contended that God's infinite wisdom and care extends even to the service and well-being of the meanest, most weak and helpless insensitive parts of creation.

In later years the idea that everything was created for human use began to decline further, at least in parts of the Christian literature. Ill-treatment of animals and other creatures was frowned upon as many Christian scholars began to see that in the Old Testament animals were regarded as good in themselves, and not just for their potential service to humanity (Thomas 1984; Livingstone 1994).

According to these writers, if the faithful looks close enough there is sufficient wisdom in the Judaeo–Christian theology to encourage at least stewardship towards the environment. If this point is not emphasised it must be due to the failure of the established clergy. As Livingstone (1994) puts it:

> In so far as Christian theology has failed to take with sufficient seriousness a concern for the environment, and indeed in so far as the Church has been complicit in practices resulting in ecological destruction, it must accept its fair share of the blame for botching up the world. We must beware of substituting irritation at Christianity's critics for serious self-criticism. Equally, we should not rest content with the complacency of these pessimistic eschatologies that see environmental catastrophe as the fulfilment of biblical prophecy.

A few years later, Lynn White himself, after publication of his much debated paper, argued that there are indeed passages in the Old Testament that teach us to be respectful to all species. Unfortunately, in the past they had seldom been so interpreted and it is time to have a fresh look at the scriptures. If environmental problems, at least in part, have been the result of misinterpretation of the biblical doctrine, then there is a lot to be said in putting the matter right. However, Kay (1989) argues that the environmentalism that exists in the Bible must be understood in its own context, which may be different from current concerns. Still, this should not prevent us from the responsibility of reopening the meaning which has either been lost or suppressed over the years.

It is quite clear that the Bible implies that nature is not sacred in the sense that it should not be worshipped as this would be idolatry. This does not mean that man should be disrespectful towards nature. On the contrary, man, as the most favoured species of the creator should show a respect commensurate with the nature's source in God. According to Barr (1972), the biblical notion of dominion should be understood in terms of the notion of kingship in antiquity. Genesis conveys a picture of paradise in which man and other species live in peace and harmony. In this context, the notion of man's domain approximates to the well-known idea of the shepherd king. Dominion also involves the understanding of man as a co-creator with God, but unlike God, who creates from emptiness, man creates from the order and framework imposed upon nature. Therefore, when he toils to create he must honour the integrity of that order.

This is basically the viewpoint of scholars with mainly Christian convictions who look for greater meaning in words and assertions than are in the holy books. Furthermore, they believe in the necessity of addressing ecological crisis from a spiritual viewpoint. Unlike Passmore (1975), who contends that ecological problems are actually special types of social problems that can be solved by political action and with the helping hand of science and technology, Judaeo–Christian scholars, and indeed followers of other faiths, believe that there must be a spiritual dimension. Relying exclusively on politics, science and technology would be myopic (Livingstone 1994).

ISLAM

In Islam, just as in the Judaeo–Christian tradition, the orientation is that man is at the centre of creation, implying an anthropocentric ethic.

According to Islam, God (Allah) created man and woman – Adam and his wife – from a clod of clay or dust and breathed into this creation the breath of life. All humans, regardless of colour, race and social standing, are descended from Adam and Eve, and are thus equal members of the extended family. All are equal before God. This, however, does not mean that mankind should abuse what is created for him – nature.

In Islam, it is an explicitly expressed sin to defile or destroy creation, leading to punishment (Yildiran 1994). Islam requires human beings to look at themselves and all creation and learn about them and to understand that God is the creator of all things. Therefore, humans are an integral part of nature with the privilege of benefiting from it, and also with the responsibility of protecting the environment.

Islam's holy book, the Koran, contains statements intimating that God has created the world for humans as well as for others. One section states: 'Have you observed the fire which you strike out; was it you who made the trees thereof to grow, or were we the flower? We, even we, appointed it a memorial and a comfort for the dwellers in the wilderness' (Surah Waqish 56; 63–72). Elsewhere, it is stated: 'The beneficent has made known the Koran. He has created man. He has taught him utterance. The sun and the moon are punctual. The stars and trees adore. And the sky, He was uplifted; and He has set the measure' (Ar-Rashman 55:1–7).

EASTERN FAITHS

A wide gap exists between Eastern and Western philosophies. But an even wider discrepancy may exist between a tradition's ideals and its expression in the real world, and this is most marked in Eastern cultures with regard to attitudes towards the environment. Such gaps may be taken as one of the signs of maladjustment in society. As I tried to explain earlier on, in the main, Westerners see nature as subordinate, although the extent of this has been debated. Easterners (Chinese, Indian, Japanese and other non-Christian and non-Muslim Asians) see themselves as part of nature.

However, we ought to recognise that a culture's ethos about its environment seldom covers more than a fraction of the total range of philosophies and attitudes to life in general. In the flow of things that affect us, it could be argued, religious ideals rarely have a major role to play and this is most marked in the Christian European civilisation. Christianity teaches forgiveness and non-violence, which is vividly illustrated by the expression 'turn the other cheek', and yet the history of Christian Europe has demonstrated violence of the most extreme kind over and over again, right up to the present time. The situation with regard to the environment in the East is only a little better. Perhaps dysfunctions and contradictions are inevitable in complex cultures, East as well as West.

Eastern faiths reject the Western view of the relationship between humans and nature. In Taoism and Buddhism, also in similar faiths such as Hinduism and Zen, humans do not have dominion over the earth. According to these faiths, although humanity may be the most intelligent and creative species, they are not given any particular mission to alter the order of nature. Divine values are built into the environment and thus all living things are equally important. This is the way that things are and this is the way things should stay.

While the Western view is one of dominance to some and stewardship to others, Buddhism and Taoism offer a passive 'let it be' approach to our relationship with nature. Like Buddhism, Tao upholds the notion 'do nothing and from unforced order greater order results'. In such faiths, things free of domination are naturally self-governing and self-creating. Furthermore, nature is not a mere instrument for others' ends, i.e. a resource, but something of great value in itself. In other words, nature is something to be cherished, to be left alone to take its own course, and not to be interfered with or destroyed by policies created by mankind. In Eastern thought, the dominant view is reversed: value for humans is achieved above all by identification with nature (Sylvan and Bennett 1988). Human deeds that are likely to damage the natural order are, basically, immoral, irrespective of how useful they may be to individuals. It may also be quite necessary to rely on knowledgeable persons, such as priests and gurus, to find out how to behave. Such reliance does not seem to be generally accepted in the West today, but it is a highly respected code of behaviour in the East.

Tuan (1970) contends that Westerners have become interested in contrasting their aggressive and exploitative philosophies towards nature with the harmonious views of Eastern faiths. This position should be commended with generosity, but it lacks realism and fails to recognise inconsistencies and paradoxes that exist in human existence in the East, as well as in other parts of the world. Furthermore, it may be quite misleading to pin aggressive European attitudes on to Judaeo–Christian theology as such behaviour existed well before Christianity arrived. For example, in Ancient Greece the pre-Socratic philosopher Xenophanes, impressed by the engineering achievements of his time, believed in the material progress of mankind. Sophocles wrote in Antigone about the power of man to tear the soil with his plough. Aristotle, impressed by the technical ingenuity of the day, stated 'vanquished by nature we become masters by technique'

(*Metaphysics* 847a20). The Romans were even more robust in admiring mankind's power over nature. In *The Decline and Fall of the Roman Empire* (1776–88), Edward Gibbons wrote admiringly: 'public roads ran in a direct line from one city to another with very little respect for the obstacles either of nature or private property. Mountains were perforated, and bold arches thrown over the broadest and most rapid streams.'

An adoptive attitude towards the environment does indeed have ancient roots in China stemming from the animistic belief. Tuan (1970) reports that the concept of *feng-shui*, adapting the residences of the living and the dead so as to co-operate and harmonise with the local currents of the cosmic breath, encouraged architects to build structures that seem to fit into the landscape rather than to dominate it. Many important constructions, including the Walled City, were built to observe and placate the spirits of the earth, incorporating the need to contemplate terrestrial harmony and adapt man to the environment. There are records as early as the Eastern Chou period (eighth to third centuries BC) indicating the existence of conservation officers for forests and mountains to protect trees and animal species. These officers, in addition to having a spiritual understanding that nature should not be disturbed, warned common folk about the harmful consequences of deforestation, such as soil erosion and flooding. Furthermore, the cutting down of forests encouraged horse-riding barbarians to penetrate deep into China.

As human needs developed, conformity to the spiritual order began to decline. Deforestation on a vast scale was carried out as the Chinese population grew, which necessitated the expansion of agricultural land at the expense of the forests. At the same time, the timber required in the construction of cities and the need to make charcoal for industrial fuel also took their toll on the forests.

In addition, Buddhism introduced into China the idea of cremation of the deceased which created wood shortages, especially in the south. Similar problems occurred in Japan as Buddhists were blamed for using up seven-tenths of the nation's timber resources in the seventeenth century. In addition to cremation, timber was used in building huge Buddhist halls and temples. Even writing was responsible for deforestation as the soot needed to make black ink came from burnt pine. Buddhism and Taoism do not even favour green as a colour.

Eastern faiths have become a guiding philosophy for some environmental movements, especially in India where environmental problems are worsening as a result of the nation's efforts to industrialise rapidly, and which, since gaining independence, has used Western experience as a model. According to Gadgil and Guha (1994), some environmental movements contend that the resource and environmental illiteracy of development planning are directly responsible for the impoverishment of the nation's resource base and the quality of the environment in general. Crusading Gandhians reject the modern way of life and see environmental problems from the viewpoint of moral decay in which materialism and consumerism pull people away from nature. They maintain that India should abandon her pursuit of Western models of economic development and return to her traditional roots where nature and all life forms are treated with respect.

Another powerful environmental group in India is called the Ecological Marxists, who see environmental degradation as a political and economic problem. It is not the moral values, but rather unequal access to resources which are at the root of India's ecological crisis. The rich destroy the environment in search of profit, whereas the poor do so simply to survive. In contrast with Gandhians, environmental Marxists display a hostility towards the traditional values and, in part, blame the country's predicament on old cultural attitudes. Gandhian environmentalists have been successful in carrying their message of moral revival across the country, and even further afield, in lecture tours, conferences and publications.

SECULAR ETHICS

There are a number of different and often conflicting viewpoints amongst the secular writers with respect to ethical conduct towards the environment in general. The Kantian or formalistic moral stand is that the essence of good conduct is to follow a universal ethical principle irrespective of its practical consequences (Kant 1785). Kant was well aware that nature would be a means to human ends (Infield 1963). However, he considered that observing nature would quickly teach us that caring attitudes exist in the natural world, especially in the animal kingdom, by parents towards their offspring, and this would foster a similar caring attitude in people. However, Kant did not argue that the study of nature leads to greater caring for other species, (Frasz 1993). It is implicit in Kantian thought that just as one should treat human beings with care and respect, since each is an end in his or her self, this attitude could be extended to other spheres such as the environment in general. Kant believed that in a kingdom of ends everything has a dignity. Items that relate to human needs in general have a market value. But that which is the fundamental condition for all value must be an end in itself and its value in interest. Such is its dignity. In Kantian philosophy, humans are definitely ends in themselves and there is no equivalent value for people. There is nothing that can be substituted for harm to an individual. Since one's own well-being depends upon the respect of others, one is morally required to respect other individuals' well-being.

Booth (1994) contends that in the tradition of Kant we are not permitted to use the environment in a manner which would disrupt the well-being of any individual. For example, health damaging activities such as the emission of noxious gases to the air which will be inhaled by people would be contrary to Kantian ethical conduct. If human health, and even features of the natural environment, are so highly valued then nothing would be justified for their loss. The only condition which could warrant such deeds is that not undertaking them would result in even greater harm to human health and the natural environment.

Utilitarian ethics, on the other hand, define good conduct in terms of its consequences to other human beings and possibly to other species such as higher animals. As early as 1789, Jeremy Bentham, a utilitarian political economist, argued that the one question we have to ask ourselves with regard to the animal kingdom is not can they talk, or can they reason, but rather, can they suffer (Thomas 1984)? As the idea that the world existed only to benefit mankind began to decline during the eighteenth and nineteenth centuries, the utilitarian school's recognition of non-human species began to rise.

Welfare economics is supported by traditional utilitarian ethics aims to maximise social welfare. If there are some losers along the way they should be paid compensation. The Pareto criterion requires that an economic activity, say an investment, is permissible if it makes some people better off without making anybody worse off. However, in practice it is almost impossible to have any project that is likely to fulfil this requirement, and thus the Pareto criterion has been replaced by the so-called Kaldor–Hicks principle which requires compensation to be paid to the losers, at least in theory. After taking compensation into account, if there is a net gain to the community at large, then the economic activity will be acceptable.

Booth (1994) argues that, if an economic activity damages the environment, the losers from it should be compensated for their losses in some fashion that would permit them to obtain an equivalent level of happiness by other means. The possibility of substitution between instruments in the quest for human happiness makes economic activity permissible. However, if there is no substitute for the loss of happiness resulting from environmental damage, then traditional welfare economics fails in its ability to determine an ethical use of nature. This may appear to be a far-fetched view, but Booth quotes some actual case material in the recent history of American wilderness preservation which supports his position (see also Nash 1982). If features of the natural environment are so valuable to some individuals, who would accept nothing in compensation, then the traditional welfare economics which underpin cost-benefit analysis would no longer be sufficient.

Unlike calculation of net present value in cost-benefit analysis, the conflict between human efforts for material advancement and the preservation of the natural environment giving rise to ethical questions is not easily answered. One position which is advanced by Tylor (1986) is that destruction of the environment shall not be undertaken unless it is absolutely essential to maintain the real incomes for all individuals at a level required for the living of a *decent* human life.

In addition to Kantian ideas and various forms of utilitarian doctrines there are, of course, other ways of looking at environmental issues from a moral viewpoint within the secular school In this respect, Wanden (1995) distinguishes between two interconnected ethical issues: the moral object and the moral agent.

The moral object

In this we try to ascertain what has an ethical value. Should humans be the only objects that deserve moral consideration or should this be widened to other species and ultimately the whole of creation? As I discussed above, the early and narrow interpretation of Judaeo–Christian doctrine makes mankind the only moral object, but this view has now been challenged by many scholars.

In the past, it was common not to include all humans in the scope of ethical obligations. Unfortunately, even today certain groups still practise selection. Instead, moral obligations are extended only to certain groups, such as one's own tribe, extended family, religion, or colour.

The medieval European Christian attitude towards Moslems, which found its full expression in the crusades, aimed to eradicate them by all possible means from the Holy Lands and Europe. Nazi ideology towards Jews, Slavs and other 'dirty and weak races' paved the way to the construction of extermination camps. The Serbian attitude towards the indigenous Moslems and Catholics of former Yugoslavia has brought back the horrors of the Nazi era. Slavery imposed upon blacks in Europe and North America in the past, and institutional discrimination against them in South Africa, are still fresh in our memories. These are some dreadful examples of selective behaviour. Hooker (1992) contends that we are slowly waking up to the fact that moral care should be extended to all people, regardless of ethnic origin, religion, colour, gender, political opinion and so on.

The issue of moral object is central to debates in environmental ethics. One group, anthropocentrists, believe that human life is more valuable than all other forms of life, or perhaps even the only morally valuable form of life on this planet. Another group, biocentrists, contend that humans have no more ethical value than any other species.

The anthropocentric position has been defended on at least three counts. First is biological, in that mankind is biologically the most developed species. We occupy the last and the highest point in biological evolution which is millions of years old. The human brain is the largest and our neural system the most complex amongst all species. Second is psychological – namely, that only mankind possesses consciousness and the power of abstract reasoning. Only humans can make moral choices in complex situations. Only humans can consider and debate philosophical concepts such as ethics, justice, the possibility of life beyond biological existence and so on. Therefore, we are the only ones who can make moral judgements. Third is philosophical; that is, a human personality is largely formed by its relationship to others in a cultural environment. A person's life depends not only on how they themselves see it, but also on the judgement of others. That is, a person's ego is formed in the meeting with the other, which means that social relationships between individuals carry a fundamental moral significance. These views have been advanced by a number of philosophical schools such as hermeneutics and critical philosophers. According to Wanden (1995), it is not clear which one of the human qualities is morally decisive.

The biocentric position is that all life forms could, and should, have the same ethical value as humans and this consideration should include animal, plant and other species. Here, all living things have intrinsic ethical value; there is no distinction between humans and amoebae as both have the same moral status. Albert Schweitzer is the best known representative of this school. Furthermore, the ecosystem as a whole, with all its constituent parts, is ethically valuable and thus requires respect from the most advanced and dominant species – mankind. Here, it is implicit that it is not an individual identity that carries moral value, but the ecological system which expresses that identity. Of course, this does not necessarily mean that the dominant species could, without upsetting the ecological order, treat an individual cruelly. The ability to feel pain by some species ought to prevent ill-treatment of pain-feeling identities such as mammals, birds, frogs and lizards. As I mentioned earlier, Bentham, by his question 'Can a species feel pain?' made this issue part of an ethical conduct.

Another point which is linked to the anthropocentric position is that of consciousness. It is not only humans who possess consciousness; many higher animals such as apes and dogs are also in possession of this. If the ability to feel pain is sufficient, together with consciousness, for ethical value, certainly higher animals ought to be given ethical consideration. Singer (1975, 1981) and Reagan and Singer (1976) contend that the circle of ethical concern must be extended at least to higher animals who do feel pain and pleasure. From this view, the animal rights movement has grown.

The moral agent

In this, the focus is on the being that makes ethical decisions for the environment. Who should make the moral decisions about the environment? The answer to this question must be the most dominant species, humans, because we are the only ones who can conduct a moral debate. But which humans? Who exactly has the moral authority to decide about environmental protection or a certain level of environmental deterioration, as the case may be? Underneath these questions there lies the distinction between the ethics of freedom and the ethics of law. According to Wanden (1994, 1995), these concepts represent a fundamental moral dilemma of our times, although their roots stretch back to antiquity.

The ethics of freedom implies that every person is free to make decisions about their own well-being and has the moral right to perform necessary actions. Today, almost all democratic traditions uphold the ethical principle of individual rights and preferences within the framework of the existing law. A pluralist democracy provides a vehicle for registering individual preferences to obtain an expression about the will of the electorate.

In addition, the free market mechanism, which is a feature of all democracies, is a useful, and for some, the only reliable structure to register individual preferences. The forces of supply and demand measure the values of all desired commodities including environmental goods. Prices, by and large, inform the decision-makers about what people are prepared to pay for the preservation of environmental attributes. Sometimes market prices may be unreliable due to a variety of reasons, or may be absent. If the former is the case, then true prices (shadow prices) can be estimated, with some difficulty, by using established cost-benefit methods. If the latter is the case, then there is a host of survey methods and experimental techniques to ascertain the willingness of the agents to pay.

Defenders of the market system to protect the environment argue that there is no viable alternative to the forces of supply and demand. If, for example, pushing most kinds of biodiversity to the point of extinction would be too costly, then market forces will come to the rescue. The more scarce a resource gets, the more people will be willing to pay for it. Therefore, various measures will be taken to protect the endangered resources. For example, drug companies have realised that conservation of biodiversity makes good business. In this respect, a number of pharmaceutical companies have agreed to pay tropical countries to protect endangered species (Kula 1994). Profit-seeking companies are now screening organisms that are found in tropical rainforests with a view to producing effective drugs to fight heart disease and cancer. Here, the agents, by using market forces, are taking measures to protect their own interests, which might be more helpful for species' protection than, say, passing legislation.

Most agree that, currently, we have too much pollution which is damaging the environment and hence human health. If economic agents are compelled to pay by way of taxation for, say, their discharge of industrial as well as household smoke, then such damaging activities would decline. The polluters would reduce their emissions because by doing so they would save money.

There are well-known valuation methods for environmental protection if market prices do not exist, or are insufficient. In this the moral agent, by using market methods, may try to determine the value of the moral object. This ties in with anthropocentric ethics. At the other end of the spectrum, such as biocentric ethics, the preferences of individuals cannot be considered decisive for how much of the environment should be conserved. It may be unethical to allow the destruction of any part of the environment, in spite of the signal given by the market, but this does not mean that the market value of the attribute is useless. It could be important in putting together practical policies. But from the viewpoint of biocentric philosophy, the market values, no matter how they are obtained, lose much of their importance as they constitute a fundamentally inadequate criterion to value the environment. Furthermore, looking at the problems from such a perspective is unacceptable to the ethics of law in which our main duty is to conform to the laws of nature, not to change them.

The alternative to the market system is reliance on the political process for environmental ambition. According to some, a pluralist democratic structure is much more reliable than the forces of the market as it avoids an uneven distribution of income and wealth, which concentrates excessive power in the hands of a small, but powerful, group of economic interests. Political parties are free to accept any one of the different ethical positions mentioned above. Nowadays, Green parties exist in most democratic countries which adhere, in the main, to biocentric ethics. Conservatives, on the other hand, tend to be more anthropocentric. Almost all parties from all political shades of opinion run their election campaigns on environmental programmes in addition to other issues.

The idea of using the political process in determining the environmental ambition ties in with the ethics of freedom. The ethics of law, on the other hand, tend to undermine the representative democracy. In preserving the environment, there are economic consequences which could be very costly. If the market mechanism is side-stepped in favour of a political process, prices and costs involved in environmental preservation would need to be determined by experts. This means that the political system then has to pick up the expertly determined environmental bill, irrespective of budget constraints or the general economic conditions. In other words, in the ethics of law, the political system becomes subordinate to ecological considerations – in other words, democracy steps aside and ecology takes over.

At present, the ethics of freedom is the dominant paradigm in the West, especially in its utilitarian form. According to Wanden (1994) this concept with its emphasis on human interest is a principle of abstract economics rather than a principle of ethics, and thus should not be taken for granted in environmental ambition. In spite of its shortcomings, the ethics of law could be a respectable alternative to anthropocentric utilitarianism, which has dominated our way of thinking and living for so long and created very serious environmental problems; some of these, such as actual and potential nuclear contamination, endanger safety and the existence of many species, including humans.

It ought to be mentioned that the environment, which people are urged to treat with care, is a highly complicated construction. The old idea that nature functions like a predictable clock seems no longer to be widely accepted. On the contrary, the idea that nature often displays chaotic behaviour leading to unpredictable outcomes is on the rise. The complexity and unpredictability of nature is linked to the chaos theory which has been developed in the last few decades (see Prigogine and Stengers 1990; Jantsch 1980). The idea is that environmental and, indeed, other human structures change spontaneously from existing equilibrium and enter into more complex states in which each system constructs itself. This happens not gradually, in the long run, but in a burst of activity during a rather short space of time. The point of emphasis in this is that we do not know fully either the laws that govern the existing equilibrium or the breaking point which gives way to new structural formations. It has been suggested that primitive life first began and then developed as a result of spontaneous transformations of lifeless matter absorbing energy from the sun (Ho 1988).

Wanden (1994) contends that the chaos theory of the environment has important consequences for policy making. First, complexity of the environmental structures makes it difficult to predict the consequences of some economic activities, such as carbon or sulphur emissions. Ecosystems that absorb such substances may be much more or less resilient than we anticipate. Second, our economic systems may be equally unpredictable in view of the introduction of a new environmental policy or an existing one. For example, the introduction of carbon taxes may impact more heavily on certain economies than on global emission levels and alternative patterns of production and trade. Since we do not know the environmental or economic break-points and what would emerge afterwards, it is difficult to be certain about environmental policy based upon some ethical philosophy.

Furthermore, the very definition of the environment, let alone its complex laws, fragility and resilience, is in itself a cumbersome case to determine. Etymologically, an environment is what surrounds us. Geometrically, both Cyprus and Leicester are surrounded by sea, but only in the former case is the sea an environment. If the radius is long enough a person will be surrounded by everything there is. One crucial feature of an environment is the individual's immediate surroundings, but even this is ambiguous. A person would consider the street outside or a nearby park to be his or her environment, but will not give the same title to the rubble under the floorboards of the house, perhaps because the rubble has no effect on his or her life. But the sun and the moon, which are very distant objects, have an immense influence on all life, including the life of the individual in question and yet these are seldom considered as a crucial part of the person's environment.

In effect, the concept of the environment ought not to be restricted to geographical proximity. Friends or family, living thousands of miles away, are an important part of one's life, whereas a next-door neighbour for whom one does not care, is not. Today's typical academics are born in one location, may grow up in another, and are then employed at a university in yet another place. They are ready to move on for promotion and flit from one conference to another; by using the Internet, they can communicate with colleagues in all corners of the globe and tap into information which perhaps originates from the other side of the world. The academic is totally at home with all these situations. In other words, home for today's intellectual is nowhere in particular. The concept of the environment is, perhaps, or ought to be, the same for all, wherever they may live (Cooper 1992).

GAIA

In an attempt to explain the survival of life on earth for over 3 billion years, James Lovelock, an independent-minded scientist, published his influential book *Gaia: A New Look at Life on Earth* in 1979. Lovelock describes how, despite being a turbulent planet which has been hit many times by huge meteorites, its life forms have not only survived, but actually thrived, for a period of time stretching over 3.5 billion years. The name 'Gaia', which was carefully chosen by the author, was that given to the Mother Earth goddess by the ancient Greeks. In his analysis, Lovelock treats life and the global environment as two parts of a single system, Gaia, which regulates and repairs itself. The former means keeping the global environment conducive for life to continue and thrive, for which the temperature must be neither too cold nor too hot. The latter implies that if the system is knocked dangerously off balance it can repair itself. This all means that our planet is a living thing which is nearly immortal, able to survive major disasters, but it does not mean that any particular species, such as humans, is guaranteed survival.

The Gaia hypothesis is highly controversial, attracting vociferous supporters as well as opponents. The latter argue that the hypothesis is not based upon proper scientific investigation, but upon some vague philosophical or even religious convictions. Supporters believe that the Gaia theory, like many other theories dealing with the history of the world, is testable, but that such tests are not easy to carry out. Furthermore, it is argued that we may have to await advances in our understanding of the formation of the solar system before we can properly test Gaia or other theories of a similar kind (Watson 1991). For example, today, Mars is a cold and lifeless planet. But scientists know that Mars was once much warmer and there is evidence of surface erosion by running water. This means that temperatures were once above freezing, making some scientists speculate that once there was life on Mars, but it became extinct as the planet lost more of its atmosphere and cooled down considerably. As far as the Gaia theory is concerned, it assumes that once life is formed on a planet similar to earth it is likely to bring resilience and immortality; but this is highly unlikely. If, however, after the planet became alive, a truly catastrophic event had wiped out all life, this would not necessarily contradict the Gaia theory. This prediction could be tested by a properly manned mission to Mars to look for early evidence of life and also a possible catastrophic event.

With respect to the regulatory aspect of planet Earth, most scientists believe that the sun was once about 30 per cent less hot than it is now. If this happened now, it would turn the oceans into ice, terminating life for an overwhelming number of species. Almost everyone is certain that such cooling down did not happen on Earth after the formation of life as almost all species require temperatures above zero to thrive. One explanation of this is that when the sun was less hot, the Earth's atmosphere was thicker, with carbon dioxide creating a greenhouse effect strong enough to keep temperatures up. As the sun has become hotter, the greenhouse gases in the atmosphere have been reduced, making the surface temperature reasonably stable and comfortable for life.

On the idea of the Earth mending itself, the planet has the ability to sail through cosmic stormy waters. It has been estimated that once in every 100 million years the Earth is hit by giant meteors that wipe out most of its species, but new species quickly arise (on a geological timescale) to replace the old ones. For instance, it is believed that following the last collision, and the subsequent breakdown of the global environment, dinosaurs and other species were wiped out; as the turbulence subsided, however, recovery and regulation began to operate together, with new species soon emerging and life on Earth rapidly regaining control.

Followers of the Gaia theory tend to be critical about all anthropocentric environmental philosophies, including Boulding's concept of spaceship economy, which was explained in Chapter 9. According to Gaia supporters, humans must ultimately see themselves as an integral part of the greater reality and planet Earth's systems as part of a living whole. From this perspective, the destruction of the biodiversity should be a key ethical issue. Humans should be less greedy and not damage any part of the environment – this is a kind of stewardship on behalf of Mother Earth itself.

DEEP ECOLOGY

The deep ecology movement, which tries to promote a shift in values, perceptions and lifestyles from anthropocentrism to ecocentrism in mankind's relationship with the environment, emerged spontaneously and informally during the ecological movement of the 1960s. According to Sessions (1995), its roots go back to the teaching of Taoism, Zen Buddhism, St Francis of Assisi and, more recently, writers such as Aldous Huxley, George Orwell, Robin Jeffers, John Muir and many others. Its development has been almost parallel with the land ethics popularised by Leopold (1949) and, in particular, Carson (1962). The latter was concerned about the widespread use of pesticides in modern farming, which, in her view, inflicted serious damage on many species and even posed a threat to human health; nor did it coincide with Albert Schweitzer's reverence for life principle.

Another important development in the 1960s was the rejection of anthropocentrism, which had been expressed lucidly by Gifford Pinchot, Head of the US Forest Service at the turn of this century. He argued that there are just people and resources. Even animals and other species have no value for their own sake; they are merely resources for mankind to exploit, enjoy for recreation and for their aesthetic value. In addition, they should be saved for future generations for similar exploitation and enjoyment (see Fox (1981) and Sessions (1995) for a complete discussion of Pinchot versus Muir). In the 1960s, Norwegian philosopher Arne Naess and American poet Garry Synder began to promote the idea of deep ecology internationally, an effort which is still continuing (Naess 1989; Synder 1977, 1994).

Deep ecologists believe that the community of all living species is the greater reality and the greater value. Industrial and commercial development of the last couple of centuries aimed to create an economic and technological 'underworld' for consumers, but instead it created a 'waste world', leading to the physical and spiritual deprivation of mankind as well as the world as a whole. Industrial control of the media not only created an illusion of affluence and economic growth, but now is threatening the viability of humans. A good part of the education system, instead of educating young people, is now preparing them for jobs in the destructive commercial and industrial society on which we have become so needlessly dependent. The time is long overdue for us to ask searching questions about the values of our society and the direction in which we are heading.

Relentless materialism degrades the quality of human life as well as the environment. Simple and natural living maximises the quality of our life and enriches our experience as human beings on this planet. Our separation from nature has created a trauma by failing to satisfy the most basic human needs. The result is widespread addiction to consumerism and drug dependency. Recovery will first of all require a renewed sense of affinity with nature.

Capra (1995) argues that economic policies in pursuit of growth, measured in terms of gross national product, have nothing to do with human well-being. The assumption that more and more growth is better is fundamentally wrong. Unfortunately, economists are unwilling to recognise that the economy is only one aspect of the social fabric. The subject that they claim to study is torn and isolated from its very foundation. The simplistic and highly unrealistic models of economists are totally misleading. The movement towards deep ecology, in which a new vision of reality is emerging, is gathering momentum, and this will be the basis of our future economic systems and social institutions.

Naess (1995) draws a distinction between shallow and deep ecology. To him, the former is a fight against pollution and resource depletion for the purpose of maintaining the health and welfare of the rich. He characterises the deep ecology movement by seven points:

1 Rejection of the man-in-environment image. Instead, the 'man is a part of the environment' image is promoted as 'man is not himself without the environment'.

2 Biospheric egalitarianism. In this, man acquires a veneration for the ways and forms of life with an understanding from within. The quality of life depends upon the deep pleasure and satisfaction we receive from a partnership with nature in which other forms of life are also partners. The adoption of a master–slave attitude towards nature leads to alienation.

3 Principles of diversity. Concepts such as 'the survival of the fittest' and 'struggle for life' should be understood to mean ability to coexist with other forms of life. Diversity enhances the potential for coexistence with other species. 'Live and let live' is a better ecological principle than 'either you or me'.

4 Anti-class position. According to Naess, human diversity is in part due to exploitation and suppression by certain groups. The exploiter and the exploited live different lives and, by doing this, they basically deprive themselves by belonging to different classes. The principle of diversity does not extend to enforced differences. Likewise, deep ecology does not favour classes such as developed and under-developed nations, rich and poor.

5 Non-degradation and non-depletion postures. These objectives are in common with shallow ecologists, but deep ecologists should not serve them in that they should not take up jobs which involve activities that degrade the environment and needlessly deplete natural resources. When anti-pollution devices are installed in industry, prices go up, thereby widening the gap between the social classes. Fighting for anti-pollution objectives alone are not sufficient as these increase evils of other kinds. Non-polluting, non-depleting modes of production must be promoted.

6 Complexity. The natural environment is extremely varied and complex which makes the ecologist think about the vast system that he or she is a part of.

7 Decentralisation. Local autonomy must be strengthened in order to adopt an ecological life for which links in the hierarchical chain need to be weakened. Consider two houses, one built from local material and skill, the other from imported material which requires, say, exportation of foodstuffs. The former may require only 5 per cent of the energy used by the latter.

Naess argues that a deep ecologist should take into account all seven points simultaneously, otherwise success in one direction will lead to failure in other areas. He also points out that the seven-point survey is rather vague and will be tenable if made more precise in certain directions. These points are not derived by logic or induction, but rather by the experience and suggestions of field workers from all over the world. The deep ecology movement is clearly normative, but based in part upon the results of scientific research from all corners of the world. Finally, Naess emphasises that deep ecology, like other ecology movements, is ecophilosophical rather than ecological.

> Ecology is a limited science which makes use of scientific methods. Philosophy is the most general form of debate on fundamentals, descriptive as well as prescriptive, and political philosophy is one of its subsections. By an ecosophy I mean a philosophy of ecological harmony or equilibrium. A philosophy is a kind of sophia wisdom, is openly normative, it contains both norms, rules, postulates, value priority announcements and hypotheses concerning the state of affairs in our universe. Wisdom is policy wisdom, prescription, not only scientific description and prediction.
>
> (Naess 1995: 155)

Deep ecology, although an influential movement, has been criticised by a good many thinkers and sometimes by its own supporters. For example, Sessions, one of the leading exponents of the movement, points out that some of his colleagues underplay or even totally ignore the crucial role of human overpopulation in the present and future environmental crisis (Sessions 1995: 4). Others, such as Hooker (1992), charge the movement with having no serious fundamental theory and that, furthermore, deep ecology is too simplistic a conception of our ethical circumstances as it ignores tensions and conflicts. Cooper (1992:165) finds the movement's efforts to promote new environmental ethics monotonous and depressing:

> Why has it seemed important to promote a 'new' environmental ethic? The popular answer is that without one, we shall continue a plunge towards catastrophe. . . . Left by itself, this answer has a disingenuous ring, for it proposes a 'new' ethic, not as moral truth, but as a convenient myth, a holy lie, one of Nietzche's 'falsehoods without which man cannot live'. But as a term like 'ecophilosophy' might suggest, there is a further answer. A 'new' ethic is required not only on pragmatic grounds, but by a true appreciation of the place of human beings in the world 'elsewhere'.

Cooper adds that many of the concepts are vague and shallow. For one thing they do not even define properly what nature is supposed to be.

Gore (1992) charges deep ecology as being inherently misanthropic. Naess's ecophilosophy portrays humans as being an alien presence on the earth and as having free will. Sessions (1995) in defence of the movement, argues that Gore deliberately misinterprets deep ecology to promote his own human-dominant Christian stewardship position. Bookchin (1987) charges the deep ecology movement with an attack on humanity in general. In the view of deep ecologists, humanity is an ugly and malignant product of natural evaluation, destructive rather than constructive in its deeds as well as thoughts. Deep ecologists, on the other hand, deny such implications. If people criticise capitalism, they are then accused of communism and are labelled as enemies of the system. In effect, they may be equally critical of communism. Deep ecologists are certainly critical of human-based, 'centre of the world or universe' philosophies, but they are not anti-human.

LAND ETHICS

In 1949 Aldo Leopold published a book entitled *A Sand Country Almanac*, in which basic principles of the so-called Leopold's Land Ethics were established. In this he argued that, from a philosophical viewpoint, an ethic is the differentiation of social from anti-social conduct. An ethic, ecologically, is a limitation on freedom of action in the struggle for existence. In a historic context, the first ethic dealt with conduct between individuals, the second ethic with the relation between the individual and society. And yet there has been no ethic dealing with our relation with land, animals and plants. Unfortunately, land is still a property, a slave. Land is a factor of production, ownership entails privileges but not obligations. The extension of ethics to land and nature is not only an evolutionary process but an ecological necessity.

All forms of ethics so far have evolved on the basis that individuals are members of a community of independent parts. While their natural inclinations lead them to compete for a place in the community, their ethics guide them to co-operate. The land ethics simply enlarges the boundaries of the community to include all human environment.

Leopold issues a warning to the conqueror of nature, man:

> In human history, we have learned (I hope) that the conqueror role is eventually to conquer. Why? Because it is implicit in such a role that the conqueror knows *ex cathedra*, just what makes the community clock tick, and just what and who is valuable, and what and who is worthless in community life. It always turns out that he knows neither, and this is why his conquests eventually defeat themselves.
>
> (Leopold 1949)

Conservation is a state of harmony between humans and the land and the best way to achieve this is by education. Unfortunately, land use ethics are still governed by narrow and short-sighted economic interest, but no important change in ethical consideration can be achieved without a change in our intellectual emphasis and convictions. According to Leopold, the main reason why conservation has not become a reality is that philosophy and religion have not yet heard of it. Humans can be ethical about something that they can see, feel and understand.

> A land ethic, then reflects the existence of ecological conscience, and this in turn reflects a conviction of individual responsibility for the health of the land. Health is the capacity of the land for self-renewal. Conservation is our effort to understand and preserve this capacity.
>
> (Leopold 1949: 236)

It is almost impossible for an ethical consideration to land and nature to exist without love and high regard for its value, much broader than the limits set by economics. For city dwellers who are separated from the land by gadgets and middlemen think of it as a space between towns. They have 'outgrown' land. For modern farmers, on the other hand, the land is an adversary, something that keeps them in hard labour. The case for land ethics would therefore appear to be hopeless. But land ethics is an evolutionary process which needs pioneers.

FEMINISM AND THE ENVIRONMENT

According to some, the caring and nurturing female attitude towards nature which once existed in pre-Christian Europe was replaced in the course of history by an aggressive and domineering male attitude. The establishment of Christianity marked the sea change. Biblical texts such as, 'Then God said, let us make man in our image, after our likeness; and let them have dominion over the fish of the sea, and over the birds of the air, and over the cattle, and over all the earth, and over every creeping thing that creeps upon the earth' introduced the intrusive male vision towards the environment. Nevertheless, the female concept, although diminished, survived. The scientific revolution of the seventeenth and eighteenth centuries put the final nail in the coffin of the organic and feminine world (Merchant 1980).

Despite the onset of Christianity, the feminine image of the world, captured in expressions such as 'Mother Earth' and 'virgin territories' survived for a long time, imposing a cultural constraint and restricting reckless behaviour. For example, in the past, various ceremonies which included praying and fasting preceded the opening up of mines because it was regarded as a sexual violation of mother earth. In the sixteenth century, a number of documents were produced to aid mining enterprises which eliminated such rituals (ibid.).

With regard to agriculture, for a long time, family- or community-based farm enterprises maintained the health of the countryside. However, the shift towards market capitalism coupled with new technology marked the beginning of the end for the medieval agrarian economy and hence the ecosystem. Windmills and watermills began to appear almost everywhere in Northern Europe and forest clearance intensified. Manuals began to appear to assist farmers with the draining of wetlands, reduction of bogs, reclamation of territory from the sea, pest control, and the introduction of new crops. These promised an increase in productivity of up to tenfold, which was irresistible. There were efforts to maintain the holistic and feminine philosophy of nature but, in the face of the new economics and technology, the mission was impossible.

According to Merchant, it was Francis Bacon who legitimised the domination of nature which is umbilically connected with the domination and exploitation of women. In expressions such as 'interrogating nature', Bacon draws upon practices for investigating witches. In *The Works of Francis Bacon* it is written:

> Neither am I of opinion . . . that superstitious narratives of sorceries, witch crafts, charms, dreams, divinations, and the like where there is an assurance and clear evidence of the fact should be altogether excluded . . . [for] a useful light may be gained, not only for a true judgement of the offences of persons charged with such practices, but likewise for the further disclosing of the secrets of nature. Neither ought a man to make scruple of entering and penetrating into these holes and corners, when the inquisition of truth is his whole object.
>
> (Spedding and Ellis *et al.* 1870)

Turning nature into a slave to serve man was legitimised by Bacon, and this easily served the interests of the land and mine owners, emerging industrialists and the merchants. Capitalistic, mercantalistic and male theories began to exert their pressure on the female vision of nature. This also gave way to class and gender alienation in the emerging capitalist social structure.

Livingstone (1994) argues that Merchant's analysis of history from a female viewpoint is not altogether persuasive. The pre-Christian world's attitude was perhaps not as favourable to nature as Merchant makes it out to be.

Ecofeminists are also critical of a number of new environmental movements, especially the deep ecology. Their charge is that the deep ecology movement is highly critical of anthropocentricism as if it was a kind of gender neutral philosophy. In fact, it was not anthropocentricism but rather androcentricism (i.e. male centredness) which was the real root of the environmental problems (Zimmerman 1987). Some feminists, such as Warren

(1987), tie the liberation of women to the elimination of all systems of aggression, and thus they are, by and large, in favour of ecocentric egalitarianism. Deep ecologists, on the other hand, tend to agree that men have been far more implicated in the history of ecological destruction than women (Fox 1995). Furthermore, they assert that there are other social groups, such as capitalists, Westerners and whites, which have been far more implicated in the history of ecological destruction. According to them, it is too simplistic, on empirical grounds, to single out a single group, such as men, and blame them for past environmental or other mistakes. It implies that women have no power in the community and so should not be burdened with any responsibility for ecological destruction. Feminist ecologists imply that we should first get our social interactions right (especially those between men and women), then everything else will fall into place. But this may be a wishful thinking.

THE SELFISH GENE

In 1976 Richard Dawkins, an Oxford zoologist, published a book entitled *The Selfish Gene* for the purpose of explaining the evolutionary process. In this, he argues that all species, including humans, are survival machines as all try to preserve the selfish molecules known as genes. Thus, from an evolutionary point of view, the purpose of life for all creatures is survival. He states that numerous writers who have written on altruistic attitudes between humans and also our relationship with nature, have got it utterly wrong because they have misunderstood how evolution works. They have missed the point by wrongly assuming that the important thing in evolution is the good of the species (or the group) rather than the good of the individual (or the gene).

If we were told that a particular Chicago gangster had enjoyed a long and prosperous life in the Chicago underground world, we would have a pretty good idea about the character and quality of the person. Like that gangster, our genes have survived in an extremely hostile and competitive environment for millions of years. Thus, the most important characteristic of our genes is their ruthless selfishness, which gives rise to individual selfishness.

There are special circumstances in nature where survival may require extremely limited altruism at an individual level but, since altruistic behaviour is limited and confined to only special circumstances, concepts like universal love, brotherhood of man, do not make evolutionary sense.

Dawkins develops his theory of evolution by noting that nobody was around to observe and tell us what had happened at the beginning. The most plausible starting point is the so-called 'primeval soup' – the origin of all life on this planet – which probably contained water, methane, carbon dioxide and ammonia. With energy supplied by the sun, the 'soup' began to develop a large number of molecules and in particular amino acids, which are the building blocks of proteins and living organisms. Then, at some point, a molecule 'building block' began to replicate itself, probably by accident, marking the beginning of the copying process. This was probably not the biggest or the most complex molecule in the 'soup', but it had the remarkable property of being able to create copies of itself. In the early stages, copies and further copies were not perfect, giving rise to diversification and evolution in the 'soup'.

Since the 'soup' was not capable of supporting infinite numbers of replicator molecules, the evolutionary process was fiercely competitive and, as the replicators became numerous, they used up the building blocks in the 'soup' at a very fast rate, making them a scarce and precious resource. Many varieties became extinct because of the competition, and a new higher level of stability was achieved in which each struggled to maintain its own stability while trying to undermine that of its rivals. Some discovered ways and means of breaking up molecules of rival kinds and using the released building blocks to make their own copies. They were the first carnivores. But their victims also discovered methods of protecting themselves. A protective 'coat' was probably the first survival device and, as survival got tougher, the 'coat' began to develop more elaborate shapes.

Instead of floating loose in the 'primeval soup', those which survived swarmed in large colonies for safety and self-preservation. These were the genes that are in all living things – viruses, bacteria, plants, animals and humans. The fundamental chemistry of all species is rather uniform and the replicators, the genes, of all living things have, essentially, the same kind of construction. The genes are composed of molecules of DNA (deoxyribonucleic acids), and each of these molecules consists of a long chain of smaller molecules called nucleotides. In other words, we are survival machines programmed to preserve the 'selfish' genes. Although this may be an astonishing statement, it is a fact.

The selfishness of the genes gives way to the selfishness of individual behaviour. Evolution is not morality based at all; it is ruthlessly selfish.

> My own feeling is that a human society based simply on the gene's law of universal ruthless selfishness would be a very nasty society in which to live. But unfortunately, however much we may deplore something it does not stop it being true. . . . Be warned that if you wish, as I do, to build a society in which individuals co-operate generously and unselfishly towards a common good, you can expect little help from biological nature.
>
> (Dawkins 1976)

Dawkins makes it known that we should not stop in our efforts towards building a caring human society which may include nature with all its living entities. However, in doing so, we should not ignore or underestimate the forces that govern our behaviour, or the behaviour of all other things that exist in the natural environment. A lifestyle that is based upon human beings living and caring for each other as well as for their environment is an interesting but unrealistic goal – one which no other species has ever attempted. However, any efforts to achieve this would be greatly undermined by Mother Nature herself, who is programmed to guide, or even force, us towards a single selfish goal – survival. Every economic and environmental policy must therefore bear this in mind.

12

SUMMARY AND CONCLUSION

Environmental impoverishment by way of acute resource depletion and pollution is not new. As mentioned earlier, growing economic activities in biblical times led to large-scale deforestation, over-salinisation, land erosion and desertification in the Middle East and North Africa. During the height of the Roman Empire, land and water in and around the capital became highly contaminated by industrial, agricultural and human waste. In Ancient China, environmental problems created by intensive logging and rice terracing became noticeable as early as 800 BC. In 1388 the English parliament was sufficiently concerned at river pollution to impose a hefty penalty of £20 on those who cast dung, the remains of animals killed and other rubbish into ditches and rivers (Clapp 1994). Such problems, however, were highly localised affecting most of the population in the immediate surroundings. In contrast, present environmental concerns, which are growing in magnitude and complexity, affect on a global scale, and they will continue to affect vast numbers of people for many generations to come.

During the Middle Ages, there was not a great deal of growth in the level of economic activity in most parts of Europe, but this began to change with the arrival of the age of mercantilism. In spite of highly protective measures employed by governments, trade with Asia and America began to grow noticeably. During that time, mercantilist thinkers believed that the wealth and power of the nations would be enhanced by the accumulation of only a certain type of natural resources, namely precious deposits, especially gold. Population growth was taught to be a good thing for the strength and the well-being of the state.

French physiocrats were one of the earliest schools to challenge the mercantilist doctrine by arguing that it was not gold but the land and its food producing capacity that was the foundation of wealth. Quesnay, in his famous *Tableau* tried to prove that agriculture was the driving force behind economic growth and wealth accumulation. Another notable feature of the Physiocrats was their belief in the importance of the natural order which was established by God's infinite wisdom for the benefit of humanity. Therefore, the natural order should not be interfered with by the state or any other powerful group.

Adam Smith, the founder of modern economics, believed that in an atmosphere of free trade the pursuit of self-interest would achieve prosperity for mankind; that, in the progress of society, agriculture would lead the way, but as trade and industry developed the relative share of agriculture would decline. Smith did not express a great deal of concern about natural resource scarcity, pollution or population growth, and in this respect he was in a minority among the largely pessimistic classical economists. In contrast, Malthus contended that the pressure of a growing population on a fixed supply of land would result in starvation, the ultimate check on growing human numbers. Ricardo, thinking along similar lines, pointed to the diminishing quality of natural resources in the face of growing economic activity which would eventually terminate both the growth of population and economic progress.

J. S. Mill's approach to the stagnation debate was interesting in the sense that he questioned the desirability and necessity, as well as the feasibility of the doctrine of relentless economic growth. According to him, there was no need to struggle for growth in the developed world where the real problem was the distribution of wealth, not its growth. Furthermore, he asserted that, since continuous growth is against the natural order, mankind would eventually be compelled by the forces of nature to abandon the whole idea. Twenty-seven years after the publication of Mill's *Principles of Political Economy*, Jevons lent him some support after examining the issue of economic progress in the face of resource exhaustion by focusing on British coal, which at that time was the main source of energy.

However, there was some opposition to the stagnation doctrine and the law of diminishing returns single-mindedly defended by Malthus, Ricardo, Mill and Jevons. According to Henry Carey, in the progress of society, the direction of movement has been towards increasing returns, which have been most conspicuous in mining and agriculture. Even in relatively recent times, many communities established settlements on elevated but easily defended land where the quality of the soil was rather poor. That is, unlike the advocates of the law of diminishing returns, man, with some exceptions, has occupied and worked the poor land first and then moved to other areas, such as lowlands, with good soils. Therefore, most communities encountered increased returns aided, continuously, by the evolving agricultural technology. A similar situation took place in mining as communities worked out the deposits in their surrounding areas first and then moved to more lucrative but distant mines. This process was also aided by improved mining technology, capital accumulation and growing association and co-operation between communities. Carey also criticised the Ricardo theory of rent by stating that, in essence, there was no difference between crop and timber yields on land except that the latter took much longer to mature. Therefore, payment to landlords, either for extracting wood or growing corn, should be the same.

Population growth and resource limitation, which were dominant in the writings of most classical economists, did not impress the socialists. Sismondi did not have much regard for the Malthusian theory in which population growth overruns subsistence. When workers lived in a free and fair society, which in Sismondi's view did not exist at that time, they would be good judges of their circumstances and thus would not marry too early or multiply fast. Hodgkin believed that the value of a product can be attributed entirely to the amount of labour it embodies, but that the capitalist system, by instituting claims on land and capital, deprived, in a most appalling way, the true creators of value, the workers. In later years, Karl Marx tortuously developed this view as the labour theory of value. Unimpressed by the Malthusian theory, Marx argued that the predicament of the masses was not due to the pressure of population on fixed resources, but rather to the theft of surplus labour by the dominant classes. Engels intimated that, as advances in science and technology can be a much stronger geometric progression than population growth, the Malthusian theory was wrong.

Marx reasoned that increasing returns are more likely in the extractive sectors, such as fishing, mining and quarrying, due to improvements in the extraction and processing methods. But, it is in the nature of the capitalist system to exploit natural resources in a reckless manner, including the fertility of agricultural land, which will add to the crises hastening the end.

There is an important difference between Marxist thought and the Ricardo–Malthusian theory about how the crises develop. In the former, recklessness, together with falling profits and the limited purchasing power of the impoverished masses, will strangle capitalism. In the latter, the problem is one of the law of diminishing returns in the face of a growing population which will stagnate the system. In the views of Malthus and Ricardo, there is no alternative to stagnation but, according to Marxists, there are other solutions to the problems.

In the neo-classical age, issues such as population growth, resource scarcity and social engineering appeared to be subdued, although they did not disappear entirely from the literature. The main preoccupation of the economists was marginal utility and the value of goods, including natural resource-based commodities. In addition there was a fair amount of discussion by Bohm-Bawerk, Sorley and Marshall about rents from land and mines. From the viewpoint of environmental economics, developments in two areas were important: the economics of exhaustible resources and of externalities.

As early as the mid-nineteenth century, J. S. Mill realised that mining was a quite different operation to those of farming, the production of fabricated goods and the service sector, in the sense that it eventually involved total exhaustion. Today's extraction means a reduction in future profits and, conversely, extraction tomorrow involves a reduction in present profits.

Sorley expanded on this idea by emphasising that there is a definite antagonism between present and future production from mines. By presenting his analysis in the context of a review of the British iron and coal trade, Sorley gave this theory a practical dimension. Gray was the first economist who undertook a thorough analysis of the economics of mining, as distinct from any other sector. Although Hotelling is most often credited with the creation of the seminal work in the theory of exhaustible resources, it was Gray first who analysed the issue in depth. In a mathematical model, Hotelling considered mining operations as a kind of cake-eating activity and emphasised the concept of user cost and the choice of time horizon to depletion.

On the issue of the side effects of economic activities in the neo-classical age, Marshall made the first approach to the economic analysis of environmental externalities. In later years, Galbraith argued that Marshall's work did not prepare us for the extent and complexities of externalities and its colossal effect on the environment.

With regard to intertemporal externalities, however, interventionist Arthur Pigou did realise the far-reaching consequences of reckless operations resulting from focusing on the present and near feature. Furthermore, he also pointed out that to underestimate future necessities and solutions to even the most pressing problems was one of the most fundamental human weaknesses. Therefore, as the trustee for all generations, Pigou urged governments to defend present, as well as future, generations from reckless exploitation of natural assets. As a policy instrument, he recommended fiscal measures as well as outright legislation to protect destructible resources. Although, when Pigou argued his case, legislation to protect the environment – and, to a much more limited extent, fiscal measures – were already in place in Western countries, many believe that Pigou's writings gave an impetus to economists to study these issues more closely. Today, some fiscal measures such as environmental taxes, limited as they may be, are called Pigovian taxes.

J. K. Galbraith argues that, since growth under some profit constraint is the most important objective of modern corporations, it then becomes one of the main objectives of modern capitalist societies; thus, damage to the environment comes as no surprise, especially when its protection is way down the list of priorities. Galbraith believes that, although desirable, it may be that slowing down economic growth is not a practical solution. Our politicians, corporate managers and even workers will not have it. The idea of internalising environmental externalities by way of redefining or creating property rights on commonly used resources or by imposing taxation on external effects and then using this revenue to compensate victims is not only hopeless but ridiculous. According to Galbraith, the only workable solution to our environmental problems, therefore, is by tight legislation on harmful activities so that growth can then be allowed to continue only in certain directions which must be clearly defined.

E. J. Mishan believes that the conventional aspiration of faster and greater development is not only harmful but unsustainable. True, our environmental problems have been created by unrestricted growth, but it may be possible to correct past errors by instituting entitlements on democratically determined environmental rights. Individuals living in a civilised society should not be compelled to absorb harmful substances unless they agree to tolerate these.

Baumol and Oates contend that, instead of finding a perfect solution to environmental problems, a satisficing approach, which may include direct legislation as well as fiscal measures when and where appropriate, seems to be more realistic. With the fiscal approach, Baumol and Oates prefer taxation to subsidy because it is a more effective instrument in reducing the scale of undesirable activity.

On the other hand, free-market environmentalists reject fiscal measures as well as legislation as they draw attention to the 'Coase theorem', which suggests that given certain assumptions a desirable level of environmental degradation can be worked out by negotiations between the polluter and the polluted. The crucial factor is the assignment of property rights on previously common property resources. In this, there is no requirement or restriction on the nature of the deal made; it could be a bribe as well as a compensation. The feasibility of the property rights approach to environmental problems such as pollution has been criticised on a number of grounds. In a modern industrial society, there can be a very large number of victims and culprits involved in environmental matters, making the identification problem insurmountable. Even if the victims and culprits were identified, it could be extremely difficult to establish a bargaining strategy, and various diverse groups each trying to fight their own corner would complicate the 'solution' immensely. Furthermore, the transaction cost could be enormous during a bargaining process. On moral grounds, it is hard to defend Coase's solution if, as is often the case, the hardest hit are the poorest members of society, who should not be forced to pay bribes to powerful interest groups.

Among the three policy instruments – legislation, fiscal measures and bargaining solution – the last appears to be the least convincing, theoretically as well as practically. Furthermore, it has been completely overtaken by some urgent environmental problems. For instance, let us take the depletion of the ozone layer, which may affect the health of millions of people for many years to come. How is any government going to establish property rights on the protective ozone? In many other environmental problems, it is the future generations, especially distant ones, who are going to be hardest hit. In Coase's scheme of things, who would be bargaining with whom on behalf of future generations?

Despite its shortcomings, the property rights approach is not entirely useless, as it may have a purpose in a limited number of cases, such as the management of fisheries. Indeed, there is a good deal of evidence that the property rights approach which underpins the current New Zealand fishery policy is yielding satisfactory results.

As environmental policies are evolving, policy makers as well as economists are trying to understand the implications of regulatory legislation, outright abolition, fiscal measures and instituting property rights on the environment as well as on society. Pezzey (1989) and Hanley *et al.* (1990) argue that, so far, environmental taxes have been the exception rather than the rule, as the environmental protection package of most countries is dominated by the regulatory legislation. In my opinion, this may change slightly in the future, not because governments are interested in internalising external effects, but rather because they are in need of revenue to balance their budgets and environmental protection appears to be a good excuse to impose more taxes.

The development of policy-related literature on the environment has been greatly influenced by a good number of studies that have taken place in the second half of this century. Some of these studies had a pessimistic tone that things were getting out of hand. Chapters 8 to 10 discussed various aspects of these studies, starting from the 1952 US Presidential Material Commission. The theme of this report was that since natural resources are vital to the US economy, this alone justifies a substantial role for the government. Increasing natural resource scarcity make the welfare of future generations dependent on the will and the ability of current generations to manage the environment.

In the early 1960s, the issue of resource scarcity was tested by Potter and Christy and Barnett and Morse, who analysed the long-term price trends for important natural resource-based commodities. Their major assumption was that if prices were rising this would mean that scarcity was biting. On the contrary, their findings revealed that, with one or two exceptions such as timber, prices had a downward trend implying that, on the whole, resources were becoming less scarce. On the other hand, these researchers expressed concern that despite the uninterrupted increase in the production of natural resource-based commodities, living standards of the future may not be higher than today's because of the deteriorating effect of increasing output on the environment. In other words, the key issue in future welfare is not resource scarcity but the quality of the environment. However, this view was not shared by the US Bureau of Mines who, on the basis of known stocks and depletion rates, calculated 'stock life' for most critical commodities with alarming results, some of which indicated that within a few decades the world will run out of a number of critical commodities. On the other hand, other research has pointed out some serious problems in the work of the US Bureau of Mines and argues that there are no signs of total exhaustion.

Against this background, a short chapter by Kenneth Boulding entitled 'The economics of the coming Spaceship Earth', which was included in a book edited by Jarrett in 1966, became a landmark in the history of economic thought. In this chapter, Boulding argued that anyone who believes that exponential growth can go on forever in a finite world is either mad or an economist. Like many others, Boulding had been inspired by the photographs of the earth taken from space, which make it very clear that our world is really a small spaceship where all economic activities take place with ultimately exhaustible resources. He urged the economics profession to help shift the current thinking away from the endless plain psychology to a sustainable state psychology. As the levels of population and economic activity continue to increase, the scarcity and waste problems upon the spaceship will worsen. Our long-term survival depends on a shift from the cowboy economy to a spaceship economy. Man must first have sufficient information about a problem and then, before any improvements can be achieved, visualise a solution in his mind. If we fail to make the necessary psychological shift now, while we still have room for manoeuvre, we shall soon be forced to make the changes under much tougher conditions.

A few years after Boulding's article, a couple of reports were published in which the effects of growing population and economic activity on the world as a whole were explored by using mathematical modelling in a spaceship context. The first of these models, systems dynamics, was produced by Jay Forrester and employed forty-three variables linked together. His conclusion was that, as growth continues, the quality of life will progressively decline. At the moment, we are probably living in a golden age in which the standard of living is higher than at any time in the past or is likely to be in the future. However, his model, systems dynamics, was criticised for having only assumptions with no empirical basis.

The other study was made by the Club of Rome who, by employing different sets of assumptions, produced fourteen world models with eight variables. Like Boulding, the Club argued that, because the world has finite arable land, energy resources, mineral deposits and pollution carrying capacity, there must be limits to increasing economic activity, population and pollution. They concluded that, if there is no change in the established patterns of social and economic behaviour, economic progress will certainly cease within the twenty-first century at the latest, with tragic consequences. Their recommendation was that a dramatic change in lifestyle is necessary now to prevent impending chaos.

In the works of Forrester and the Club of Rome, population pressure on land, water, air and the extractive sector has been considered from a global viewpoint. Although, ultimately, the global perspective is useful, such models conceal immense diversity and uneven distributions of population and natural resources arising from natural, economic, social and political factors. These models suppress human and natural diversity and division and thus are over-simplistic, being only relevant in terms of a big, powerful and competent world government which would design policies and persuade its subjects to co-operate. Clarke (1973) argues that viewpoints and attitudes to the global population versus scarce resource debate vary enormously from the panic-stricken alarmists to the sublime optimists and, from these, value judgements arise on the desirability of environmental conservation, population and economic growth.

As outlined in Chapter 10, I have reluctantly concluded that some debates on sustainable economic growth are muddled. Is the idea of continued and relentless economic growth, but with improved conduct, merely wishful thinking? I do not deny the human urge to improve its material well-being, but perhaps we should not take this as inevitable. Despite its extremely gloomy report, the Club of Rome note that there is ample evidence of mankind's ingenuity and social flexibility for the necessary adjustment to a zero growth state. Equally, there is ample evidence of mankind's fallibility and thus human strength must be seen side by side with human weakness. Or are we like other species in the sense that we continue to expand as long as the resource base and our natural enemies allow? If so, until the environment strikes back, economic growth can be regarded as an expression of this natural instinct. The views of the classical economists such as Malthus, Ricardo and Mill fit into this category.

Is society a machinery that can be manipulated so that an agreeable balance with nature can be reached? Some believe or hope that we are able to change our ways to avoid catastrophe. By and large, the sustainable development school imply that we are capable of making the necessary adjustment and mending our ways to grow indefinitely in a sustainable fashion. If so, how can human societies be manipulated? Some economists rely on market-based solutions, including taxation and subsidies. Others feel these are not enough and that legislation and regulatory structures, which may have to be supplemented by fiscal measures, must be in place, and that education and leadership are not emphasised sufficiently in the economic literature.

A number of writers within the sustainable development school, including economists, are now in search of an ethical foundation for their views. Pearce and his colleagues emphasise that, as a concept, sustainable development has or should have a strong ethical dimension. They believe that, since humans are the only species which really matters, this concept should be anthropocentric (man-based). It is true that the anthropocentric outlook is an ethical one, but it is not necessarily an environmentally friendly one. As discussed in Chapter 11, there is now a growing literature on the moral aspects of environmental conduct which includes religious, as well as secular, viewpoints. Christians, and others of similar faiths, have always recognised that because people must eat, clothe and house themselves, the normal functions of production and distribution are necessary to meet those needs; but for salvation, which is the Christian's ultimate purpose in life, these functions must be placed in a proper perspective. In all human deeds and thoughts, including economic activities, the Law of God, which includes mankind's relationship to the environment, must be borne in mind. It seems unfair to blame Christianity for our environmental ills – the reckless use of resources predates Christianity, and currently exists in excessive forms in areas influenced by 'environmentally friendly' faiths such as Taoism.

Alternatives to religious ethics exist. However, the proponents of secular ethics such as Gaia, Land Ethics, Deep Ecology, and so on, would do well to be more specific about what kind of 'Nature' they want to defend. This is particularly relevant when Nature is evolving constantly and sometimes unpredictably.

PAST EXPERIENCE OF FLOATING EARTH

The only certain feature of the sustainability issue is its inherent uncertainty. Lecomber (1979) contends that no examination of past experience can yield much insight into the future state of affairs. Arguably there is some truth in this. However, some past events can help our thinking about the possibility of everlasting growth. Bass (1993), in a thought-provoking article on ecology and economic growth in small islands, argues that in the past the islanders' efforts to make their economies grow led not only to environmental destruction, but to the termination of economic growth as well. By copying the Western-style frontier culture, their development struggle failed with the liquidation of their natural capital.

A small island, with its sensitive and interdependent physical, ecological, social and economic structures, is in effect a floating earth, which is not far removed from the concept of Spaceship Earth. In the past, some islands developed natural resource-based 'progress' models which relied on the exportation of primary commodities – and eventual failure was inevitable. For example, in the nineteenth century, the islands of Kiribati and Nauru exported their phosphate, and New Caledonia its nickel, while, after colonisation, Mauritius, Hawaii, Barbados and Honduras exhausted their most valuable timber deposits. Due to interdependence and the agility of island ecology and social systems, the removal of such resources led to substantial environmental and social impoverishment as the removal of forests led to soil erosion and displacement of people. The alternative monoculture which was introduced after depletion was not long-lasting as cash crops turned out to be pest and disease prone and the land eventually became exhausted as diversity, biological productivity and resilience diminished. Populations, unable to survive on derelict soils, were forced to emigrate.

When the Caribbean islands were depleted of their forests, the introduction of a cash crop export economy led to major physical and social changes. Road networks were introduced, many hills were flattened, population growth accelerated, energy consumption increased and, with immigration and emigration, the social and cultural fabrics were altered. The islands were not able to develop any sustainable economic activity as boom and bust became an established pattern.

Perhaps the history of some other islands provides a more agreeable subsistence equilibrium. For example, the Polynesian and Melanesian islands relied upon subsistence affluence before they came into contact with European civilisation. Exploitation of natural resources was restricted to meet the needs which were collectively determined and their labour surplus was used to support elaborate religious and political systems. Even on islands with poor soil there was an established and agreeable steady state of equilibrium with no growth (Hamnett 1986). There were a lot of cultural restrictions on resource use incorporating a holistic view of their environment with the result that the islanders upheld the view that available resources are for future as well as present generations and cherished their environment. Grove (1990), in an article entitled 'The origins of environmentalism', argues that following the colonisation of tropical islands, doctors, botanists and other scientists who were sent there on various missions provided inspiration for Western conservationists. These islands are places where the concept of resource limitation, ecological and cultural interdependence are inescapable. There may even be lessons to be learned by development economists.

THE LATEST 'EVIDENCE'

A lot of water has passed under the bridges of history since Malthus wrote his *Essay on the Principle of Population as it Affects the Future Improvement of Society* in 1798. At the threshold of the twenty-first century, we are still concerned about the same questions that troubled Malthus and other classical economists. Are we going to be trapped in a dismal state of existence eventually? An economist's instinct appears to be the identification of recent trends about the key variables and to try to visualise the future by using them. In this section, I discuss the views of the Worldwatch Institute, a group of rather pessimistic but serious researchers who study world trends with a view to helping policy makers and others create a better future.

The Malthusian proposition that population growth would outstrip the growth of food supply has been reversed during the past four decades, largely due to the existence of farm support policies, especially in the developed world, and improved agricultural technology. Between 1950 and the middle of the 1980s, the total world grain output increased by 2.6, exceeding population growth by a wide margin. In the world fisheries, the total output increased even more dramatically – between 1950 and the end of the 1980s catches went up by 4.6. There were isolated incidences of famine, mainly in Africa, which were largely the result of wars, but the spectacular increase in food output in most areas of the world produced an overall improvement in human nutrition and raised hopes that the Malthusian theory and Huxley's prophecies were perhaps an exaggeration.

The Worldwatch Institute (1994) suggests that in the race between population growth and the increase of food supplies the tide has recently turned.

Between 1984 and 1993, grain output per person fell by 11 per cent globally. Grain availability per person is a good approximation of improving agricultural performance and growing affluence, as the latter is connected with livestock products, the demands for which are income elastic. The Worldwatch Institute contends that 1984 was a watershed year, when growth in farm output peaked, and from then on an era of much slower growth in agricultural yield began.

The situation in fishing has also changed. In the four decades to 1990, the fish harvest increased from 22 million tons to 100 million tons, improving the per capita fish harvest from 9 kilograms to 19 kilograms. The United Nations Food and Agricultural Organisation (FAO 1993) believes that fish stocks around the world are at their limits and it may not be possible to obtain harvests higher than those of recent years. Furthermore, increasing contamination of seas, stemming from industrial as well as agricultural activities, together with growing coastal tourism are bound to have an adverse effect on fish stocks. Figure 12.1 shows the FAO's estimate of maximum sustainable yields in world fisheries which peaked in 1989.

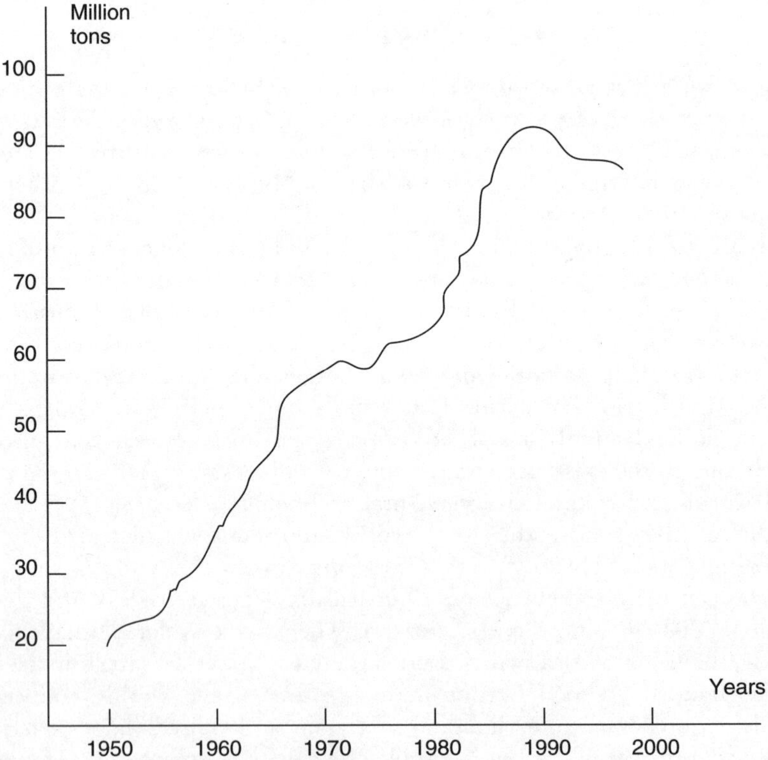

Figure 12.1 World fish harvest, 1950–92
Source: FAO (1993)

As for livestock, in the four decades to 1990, the beef and mutton output increased by 260 per cent. But, as with the overfishing of oceans, grasslands are at their maximum carrying capacity due to overgrazing (Brown 1994). With the saturation, and even decline in some regions, of carrying capacity growth of livestock, populations must increasingly rely on grain output. However, as reported earlier, the world grain harvest has already been slowing down noticeably. Therefore, experts predict that per capita meat availability will decline indefinitely as human numbers grow (FAO 1987, 1988–91; US Department of Agriculture 1992, 1993).

Despite the substantial slowdown in the growth of food supplies, there has been no relenting in the explosion of human numbers. Worldwatch Institute reports that during the four decades to 1990 the world added 2.8 billion heads, an average of 70 million per year. But during the next four decades to 2030 the net addition to human population will be 3.6 billion, an average of 90 million per year. Figure 12.2 shows the annual addition to the world population between 1950 and 1993.

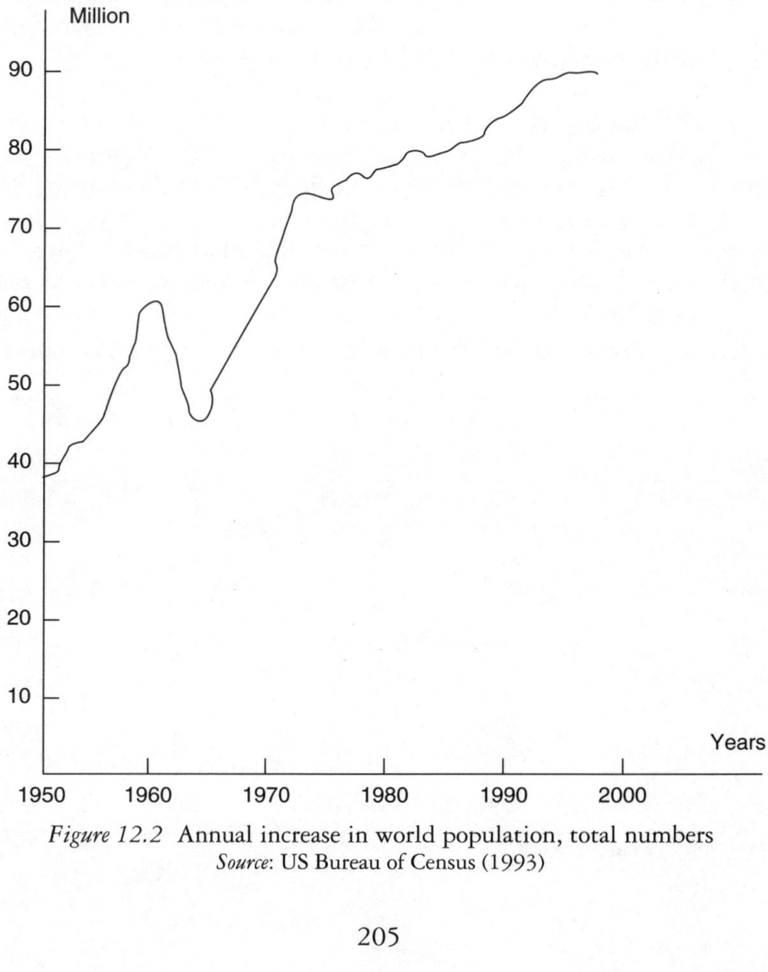

Figure 12.2 Annual increase in world population, total numbers
Source: US Bureau of Census (1993)

The dip in numbers in the early 1960s was due to the famine caused by the 'Great Leap Forward' in China, discussed in Chapter 2. In the 1970s, the introduction of family planning in a number of countries appeared to be working as the net addition of heads began to decline slightly. In the 1980s, however, family planning failed in some countries which initiated record-breaking additions to global population.

With the current trends, Worldwatch Institute (1994) and the US Bureau of Census (1993) drew up the estimates of the most populous countries for the year 2030. Table 12.1 reveals some amazing figures. For example, in Iran, the population is expected to increase by more than elevenfold over an eighty-year period between 1950 and 2030. This is far in excess of the prediction made by Malthus, who suggested that if unchecked the population would double every twenty-five years. Nigeria confirms almost exactly the Malthusian growth estimate; other countries such as Pakistan and Ethiopia/Eritrea come pretty close. One notable characteristic of Iran and Nigeria is that they both experienced an oil bonanza in the 1970s and the early part of the 1980s which allowed them to import foodstuffs. On the other hand, both countries suffered wars: Iran with Iraq, whereas Nigeria had civil war in Biafra which took large casualties among the reproductive population.

Many countries shown in the table are likely to overshoot their food carrying capacity even before the year 2030 is reached. Collectively, their demand will probably exceed the world's exportable supplies (Brown 1994). Take, for example, China. Due to the implementation of a one child per family policy, she has one of the slowest population growth rates in the developing world. Even with this, China is expected to add 490 million heads to its population between 1990 and 2030. The country is undergoing

Table 12.1 Population estimates of the world's twelve most populous countries for the year 2030

	Estimated populations (millions)		*Increase 1950–2030*	
Country	*2030*	*1950*	*-fold*	*million*
China	1,624	563	2.9	1,061
India	1,443	369	3.9	1,074
United States	345	152	2.3	193
Indonesia	307	83	3.7	224
Nigeria	278	32	8.7	246
Pakistan	260	40	6.5	220
Brazil	252	53	4.8	199
Bangladesh	243	46	5.3	197
Iran	183	16	11.4	167
Russia	161	114	1.4	47
Ethiopia and Eritrea	157	21	7.5	136
Mexico	150	28	5.4	122

Source: Worldwatch Institute (1994)

a rapid industrialisation which is transferring vast amounts of land from agriculture to industry and infrastructure. Rapidly rising incomes are also increasing demand for animal produce which is using up grain previously used for direct human consumption. Furthermore, industrialisation has created many environmental problems such as air, water and land pollution which are bound to have an adverse effect on agricultural productivity, especially in the immediate areas.

Garnaut and Ma (1992) estimate that, with current trends in China, grain imports could go up from 12 million tons in 1993 to between 50 and 100 million tons by the year 2000. If her economy continues to expand rapidly, her demand for imported grain could exceed the world's entire exportable surplus by the year 2015. This is assuming no adverse weather conditions or flood disasters occur in China.

India, which is the second most populous country in the world, will add another 590 million heads to her population by 2030. With soil erosion, which is a serious problem, and falling water tables it is highly unlikely that she will be able to feed her estimated 1.44 billion population. The situation in Nigeria and Pakistan will be no better. It is quite possible that soon these countries may find themselves as international charity cases, but with populations so large one wonders how the world's community will be able to help them on a sustained basis. Current charity cases such as Haiti, Sudan, Burundi and Rwanda have already entered the Malthusian age with dictatorial regimes which are unlikely to change, as predicted by Huxley. The latter country is about the same size as Wales, but has a population of about eight million, mostly engaged in agricultural pursuits. There are numerous land disputes within, as well as between, tribes. Population growth is one of the highest in the world which is adding to the problems; many experts believe that the recent civil war was primarily the result of population pressure on land, which led to tribal warfare.

It would be rather optimistic to imagine that India will be able to retain her democracy with an ever-growing population and widening inequalities. As the gap between the rich and poor deepens, and land disputes intensify, especially between different ethnic groups, law and order could quickly break down, leading the government to impose an authoritarian regime to maintain social order and keep the country together. India could, in fact, become the first established democracy to fall victim to a Huxlian-type dictatorship. In other vulnerable countries such as China, Iran and Nigeria, where no real democratic tradition has ever existed, authoritarian regimes are likely to maintain and intensify their power.

At a global level, the latest predictions are that food availability per capita will fall rapidly as the population grows. Between 1984 and 1993, the world grain yield rose an average of 1 per cent per head, well below the rate of population growth. Agricultural experts contend that even with modern farming methods, which require abundant fertilisers and maintenance of soil moisture, the plant's photosynthetic efficiency will eventually halt the rise in output (USDA 1992). For example, rice yields in Japan stopped increasing in 1984 and have been falling ever since. In China, the world's largest rice grower, the yield has stabilised since 1990. A similar situation has been observed in other major rice-producing countries such as India, Pakistan, Indonesia and the Philippines (Worldwatch Institute 1994). Figure 12.3 shows the prediction of the per capita grain output. If current trends continue, per capita grain output will fall from the historic high of 346 kilograms in 1984 to 248 kilograms in 2030.

As for seafood supplies, the situation is very similar and the Worldwatch Institute contend that oceanic and inland fisheries cannot sustain a catch greater than the record harvest in 1989. Increasing fish output would require a very substantial increase in fish farming which would use vast amounts of grain, water and land. This does not seem to be likely due to the anticipated shortages in all these resources. Figure 12.4 gives a prediction of per capita fish output between 1980 and 2030.

In the next few decades the grain yield is expected to improve very little and population growth is expected to continue unabated; modern farming methods are not only reaching their limits, but creating substantial environmental problems, and industrial pollution is causing global concern. With

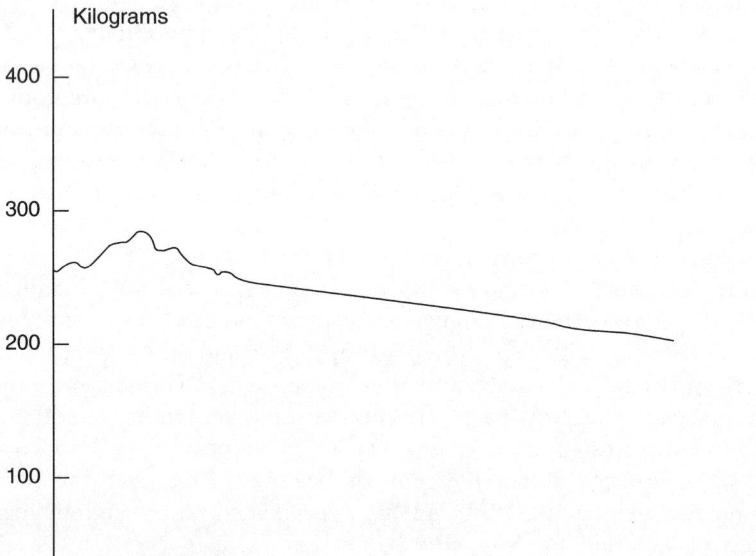

Figure 12.3 Projection of per capita world grain output
Source: Worldwatch Institute 1994

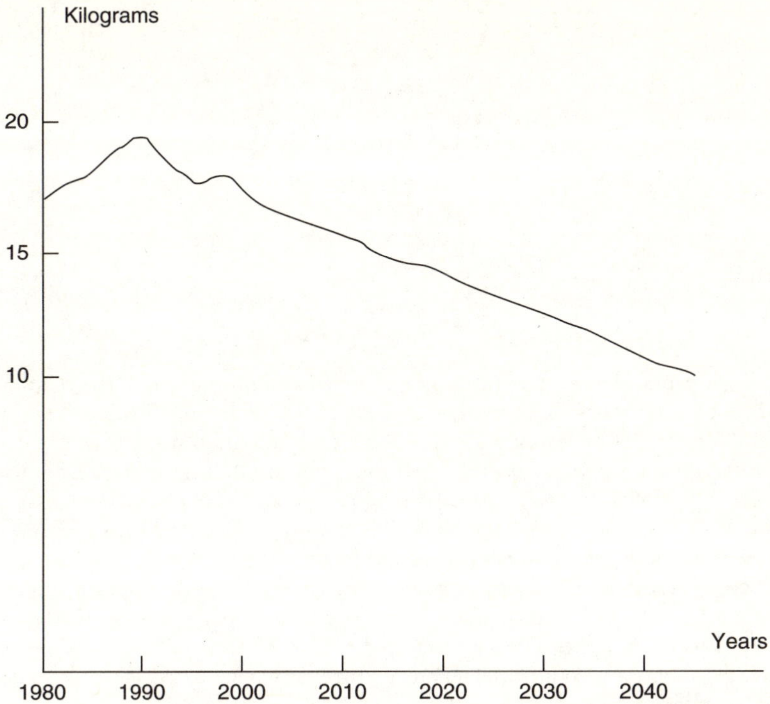

Figure 12.4 Projection of per capita world fish output

these already happening, the future looks less than rosy. Many are beginning to believe that we are at the threshold of a Malthusian age, covering most of the world.

It is quite conceivable that even in a Huxlian-type dictatorship there are likely to be some areas of relative comfort which would act as a magnet for the rich and powerful and the skilled. If one must speculate about which countries are likely to be in a better shape than the rest of the world, the USA, Canada, Australia, New Zealand and a few European countries would probably prove to be the most likely cases. But no doubt these countries would tighten their already strict immigration policies to keep out the unwanted masses.

GLOSSARY

Ad valorem tax An indirect tax which is levied as a proportion of the retail price.

Balance of payments A statement of a country's trade and financial transactions with foreign countries over a particular period of time, usually one year. These transactions are divided up into two main parts: (a) current account – which is made up of visible trade, and (b) investment and other capital transactions – which is made up of such items as the inward and outward flow of money for investment and international grants and loans.

Balance of trade A statement of a country's trade in visible imports and exports. As a result of international trade, when the flow of payments is not the same in both directions, the difference is referred to as the balance of trade. When exports exceed imports, a country has a trade surplus; when imports exceed exports, it has a trade deficit.

Birth rate A ratio which gives the average number of live births born into a population in a year for every 100 or 1,000 population.

Business cycle Fluctuations in the level of national income (GNP) alternating between periods of depression and boom conditions.

Capital The contribution to productive activity made by investment in physical capital (e.g. factories, offices, machinery, tools) and in human capital (e.g. general education, vocational training).

Capital accumulation An increase in man-made equipment such as machinery, tools, buildings and other structures, and stocks of goods, used for or capable of being used for the production of goods and services.

Capital-intensive A firm or industry which produces its output of goods or services using a ratio of capital input to laboured input which is higher than the average ratio for industry as a whole.

Capitalism A method of organising the economy to produce goods and services, whereby the means of production are privately held by individuals and firms. Economic decision-making is highly decentralised with resources being allocated through a large number of goods and services markets. The market synchronises the decisions of buyers and sellers and by establishing an equilibrium price determines how much of a good will be produced and sold.

Capital stock The net accumulation of a physical stock of capital goods (buildings, plant, machinery, etc.) by a firm, industry or economy at any one point in time.

Coase's theorem This theorem is based upon the argument that externalities do not give rise to a misallocation of resources provided there are no transaction costs and given property rights that are well-defined and enforceable. Here the parties – the producer and consumer of the externality – would have a market incentive to negotiate a mutually beneficial deal; that is, to internalise the externality. The neutrality theorem states that the outcome of this trading process would be the same irrespective of whether it was the producer or consumer of the externality who held the property right of veto over the use of the resource.

Communism A political and economic doctrine which advocates that the state should own all property and organise all the functions of production and exchange, including labour. Communism involves a centrally planned economy where strategic decisions concerning production and distribution are taken by government as opposed to being determined by the price system in a market-based private enterprise economy.

Constant returns to scale The case where a proportionate change in all inputs changes output by the same proportion.

Consumer sovereignty The influence of consumers exercising freedom of choice in a free market over the activities of producers of goods and services. In general terms, if consumers demand more of a good then more of it will be supplied.

Cost-benefit analysis A technique for enumerating and evaluating the total social costs and total social benefits associated with an economic project. It is of particular value and relevance where public services are concerned, involving both cost and benefit to the general public; thus a public service may be justified in circumstances which a private organisation would regard as 'uneconomic'.

Death rates A ratio showing the number of people in a population who die per 100 or 1,000 population per year.

Decentralisation The diffusion of economic decision-making to many different decision-makers rather than concentrating such decision-making centrally. In an economy, this is achieved by the adoption of the price system which devolves decisions to individual consumers and suppliers. In a firm, decentralisation involves delegating authority to make decisions 'down the line' to particular divisions and departments.

Decreasing returns to scale The case where a proportionate increase in all inputs causes output to increase by a smaller proportion.

Discounting The process by which future costs and revenues are converted into a present net worth. Future money is considered to be worth less than present money, a rate of interest being used for discounting.

Diversification This is used with reference to either the variety of industry within a region, or the range of products sold by a firm. In its former context, diversification of a region's industrial structure increases the variety of industry from which employment opportunities arise. With regard to firms, diversification refers to a policy of spreading the range of products marketed and has the analogous motive of reducing reliance upon the vagaries of the markets of a small number of products.

Division of labour The process whereby labour is allocated to the activity in which it is most productive – i.e. in which it can make best use of its skills. Thus, each worker specialises in a single process, or group of processes, and no one person carries out all the tasks in the production of a good. Division of labour is generally synonymous therefore with the specialisation of labour.

Economic growth This refers to the increased output for a nation over the long term, i.e. the increasing capacity to produce. This value is expressed in percentage terms, as a rate. W. W. Rostow sees economic growth as passing through five stages: the traditional economy; pre-take-off, in which there are the beginnings of economic progress; take-off itself; the push to maturity in which technological advance is utilised in the economy; and the time of large-scale production and 'mass consumption'.

Efficient production Production is efficient where there is most output for given inputs, using resources to their best. It can only be defined with reference to the state of technology.

Endogenous variable A variable which is explained within the model.

Excise duty A duty imposed on home-produced goods and domestically provided services.

Externalities Direct effect of the actions of individuals, groups or firms on the welfare of other individuals, groups or firms in ways that are not transmitted by market prices.

Factor endowments The relative availability of different production factors in a country or region.

Factors of production The inputs used in the process of production. Traditionally, the three main factors used for analysis are land, labour and capital, with entrepreneurship often included as a fourth.

Fiscal measures This is the policy pursued by a government for raising the revenue necessary to meet its expenditure. It embraces the scope and degree of taxation, national debt and government borrowing.

Free goods Goods that have no price tag because of their natural abundance – such as fresh air and sunshine – and do not require the use of scarce factors of production to create them.

Free-market economy See **Capitalism.**

Full employment A situation in which everyone who is willing to work at the market rate for his type of labour has a job, except for those who are changing from one job to another – that is, it excludes frictional unemployment. Under full employment there is no lasting unemployment nor any unemployment arising from a deficiency in aggregate demand.

Gross national product (GNP) A measure reflecting the value of goods and services produced and sold by a country in a specific period – usually a year. GNP is measured as Gross Domestic Product (GDP) plus income accruing to domestic residents arising from investment abroad less income earned in the domestic market accruing to foreigners abroad.

Human capital Know-how and expertise embodied within the workforce. Investment in human capital should increase productivity in the same way as investment in machinery.

Increasing returns to scale The case where a proportionate increase in all inputs causes output to increase by a larger proportion.

Industrial revolution The transition from the domestic to the factory system is generally known as the 'industrial revolution'. The essential changes in industrial methods began to take place in earnest in the second half of the eighteenth century when the first great mechanical innovations were made and the working place was, in the main, transferred from the home to the factory.

Inflation A rise in the average level of prices, as measured by indices such as the Retail Price Index or Gross Domestic Product deflator. Both these indices measure inflation by comparing the current level of prices to the price level in some base year, chosen periodically.

International trade The exchange of goods and services between countries which results from variations in quality and production costs; such trading also increases the economic welfare of the countries involved by extending the range of goods and services available for consumption.

Investment Any addition to the nation's capital stock: goods, machinery, technology, etc. Investment will produce a stream of goods and services for future consumption, and thus entails the sacrifice of current consumption and the production of investment goods which are used to produce commodities.

Invisible hand Adam Smith believed that the greatest benefit to society as a whole was derived from the freedom of its individuals to pursue their own advantage and that, as a result of such freedom, each individual was 'led by an invisible hand to promote an end which was no part of his intention'.

Kaldor–Hicks principle Given the unlikelihood of any project fulfilling the Pareto criterion requirement, this has been replaced by the Kaldor-Hicks principle which requires compensation to be paid to losers. After taking compensation into account, if there is a net gain to the community at large, then the economic activity will be acceptable.

Keynesianism Economists who align themselves with Keynesian theories tend to support the following ideas:

a that aggregate demand plays a crucial role in determining the level of real output;
b that economies can settle at positions with high unemployment and display no natural tendency for unemployment to fall;
c that, through fiscal policy, governments can influence aggregate demand to reduce unemployment.

Labour theory of value This theory states that the value of an economic good derives solely from the amount of labour embodied in it. Labour is, therefore, considered as the source and measure of value.

Laissez-faire '*Laissez-faire, laissez-passer*' ('let things continue without interference') was the term originally taken up by the physiocrats. Adam Smith later developed this thought as a rule of practical economic conduct. In applying it to foreign trade, he advocated the abolition of the restrictions imposed by mercantilism. Domestically, the principle meant non-interference in the employment of people or the determination of prices in order that the individual might follow his own self-interest, untrammelled by restrictions.

Law of diminishing returns This law holds that if additional units of one factor of production are employed, with all other factors being held constant, the output generated by each additional unit will eventually diminish – thus, the marginal product of factors declines when they are employed in increasing quantities.

Malthusianism Malthus argued that land is finite and that its productivity can, at best, increase only arithmetically (1, 2, 3, 4, . . .), while population increases geometrically (1, 2, 4, 8, . . .), thus the increase in population will outrun the increase in food supply. Consequently, most people will be condemned to live in misery and poverty with wars, epidemics and famines serving to slow the growth of population. Malthus's gloomy view of population growth contrasted sharply with the optimistic views about long-term economic development held by his contemporaries and contributed to the belief that economics was the 'dismal science'. Although Malthus did not foresee the dramatic improvements which have taken place in agricultural techniques, nor the tendency of population growth to slow in industrialised countries, his ideas still cause concern, especially in developing countries.

Marginal utility The increase in total utility resulting from a one-unit increase in the consumption of a particular commodity; holding the quantities of other commodities constant.

Market failure The provision by a competitive market of an output level that is not the socially optimal output.

Marxism The ideology of Karl Marx, a German philosopher, argued that in each stage in history one particular class in society would become powerful because of its ownership of the means of production; meanwhile, another class would be developing whose interests clashed with those of the dominant class. The new class would eventually overturn the old and set itself up as the new dominant group. Marx predicted that the capitalist system could not by its very nature survive, that it would in the course of time be replaced by socialism, and that the class which would effect the revolution would be the new industrial working class or 'property-less proletariat', who would overthrow the dominant capitalist class and take over the means of production. Initially, under socialism, the nation's productive assets would be acquired and controlled by the state, but eventually under Communism the workers themselves would collectively own the means of production, with goods and services being distributed according to people's needs.

Mercantilism A school of thought which emerged from the expansion of international trade in the sixteenth century. The subsequent establishment of merchant power led to the realisation within the developing nation-states that national wealth – and hence, national strength – was greatly dependent upon the balance of foreign trade. Mercantilists, in recognising the growing power of national economy, were in favour of state intervention in economic activity in order to maximise national wealth and, since they valued gold and silver as an index of national pcwer, they were preoccupied with the accumulation of precious metals. A favourable balance of trade could be obtained by selling more merchandise to foreigners than was bought and then insisting on any deficit payments being made in gold or silver – and such wealth could be used to finance wars. However, despite these limitations in their thinking, they did make important contributions to the development of economic policies and the analysis of international trade problems.

Money supply The stock of liquid assets within an economy which can be freely exchanged for goods or services.

Nationalisation The process of taking private industry into public ownership and control.

Natural resources This term is identified with land – that is, the natural endowment provided by nature. The term also refers to commodities or assets with some economic value which do not exist as a result of any effort of mankind.

Neo-classical A broad, catch-all term used to describe economists and economic theories that are based on the notion of supply and demand, Say's Law, and marginal utility and marginal productivity theories. In general, neo-classical economists are in favour of free-markets, arguing that the economy will correct itself in the long run if government and other obstacles are removed.

Net present value This is the present value of all the future net cash flows from a project less the capital outlay, the initial cost of the project. It is the addition which the project brings to the owner's or shareholder's wealth.

Normal good The demand for this good will increase as a result of an increase in income. The entire demand function will shift to the right. Income elasticity is positive.

Optimum allocation This is achieved when the most favourable economic conditions apply.

Pareto criterion A change in the allocation of resources that renders at least one person better off and nobody worse off.

Perfect competition The 'ideal type' market structure where many buyers and sellers, both actual and potential, trade a homogenous good. Perfect information rules and no single small buyer or seller can possibly affect the market price. There is freedom of entry and exit.

Physiocrats A group of eighteenth-century French economists led by François Quesnay, who were reacting against the narrow and restrictive policies of mercantilism. In their view, agriculture was the only source of wealth and they advocated free trade and laissez-faire, seeing the state's role as simply one of preserving property and upholding the natural order. They maintained that state revenue should be raised by a single direct tax levied on the land.

Production function This shows the functional relationship between inputs and outputs, the maximum amount of output for every level of input. It is typically assumed that as the volume of employment rises, the level of output rises also, but at a diminishing rate – the law of diminishing returns.

Profit maximisation The straightforward goal of introductory neo-classical theory – to acquire the biggest surplus of total revenues over total costs.

Progressive tax A tax on income which increases proportionately as income rises.

Property rights These institutional rules specify what people are entitled to do with resources and goods. Formal and informal rules which give rights over use, ownership and disposal may be more or less clearly defined. There are different property right structures – private, communal and collective.

Public ownership See **Nationalisation**.

Rent The return paid to an input such as land that is fixed in quantity.

Resource substitution The producer has to choose between the factors of production, judging by productivity.

Returns to scale This is the effect upon output when the scale of production is increased, in the sense that all the factors are increased proportionately.

Ricardian rent Ricardo said that rent was 'that portion of the produce of the earth which is paid to the landlord for the use of the original and indestructible powers of the soil'.

Scarcity A situation where the needs and wants of individuals exceed the supply of resources available to satisfy them. Hence, choices must be made between those wants that can be satisfied and those that cannot, and available resources rationed, either through price control or by a distribution system.

Self-sufficiency The extent to which an individual (or household) restricts his consumption to products produced by himself. Developing countries with a large agricultural sector show a higher degree of self-sufficiency than industrial countries where specialisation of labour is the norm.

Shadow price The true scarcity price of a resource which may or may not coincide with the market price.

Social welfare The general well-being of a society and its individual members, the provision of which has become a central issue in most modern societies – i.e. the extent to which it is the responsibility of the state or the individual. One aspect of the debate is the argument that, since the needs of individuals and communities vary and change with time and place, social welfare is not quantifiable.

Socialism A political ideology which emerged in the nineteenth century in opposition to the capitalist systems then prevailing throughout Europe. Within the social and economic systems of socialism, the equality of individuals is of paramount importance and means of production are collectively owned. Several variants of socialism have evolved during the twentieth century – from Marxism to the social-democratic systems of western Europe – but all agree on the need for some degree of collective intervention in the economic affairs of the state.

Socially optimal output The quantity of output for which marginal social benefit equals marginal social cost.

Standard of living A concept denoting the amount of material well-being to which an individual or social group is accustomed.

Subsidies Grants made by the state to suppliers of goods and services which may be intended to keep prices down, supplement the incomes of producers or maintain a service or employment.

Sustainable development This is a development strategy that manages all assets, natural resources, and human resources, as well as financial and physical assets, for increasing long-term wealth and well-being. Sustainable development as a goal rejects policies and practices that support current living standards by depleting the productive base, including natural resources and leaves future generations with poorer prospects and greater risk than our own. As mentioned in the text, there are many other definitions of this term.

Technological progress A change in the state of the art available for combining and transforming resources into goods and services which leads to a reduction in the average cost of production.

Welfare economics A branch of economics which studies the social desirability of alternative arrangements of economic activities and allocations of resources. Thus, it is the analysis of the optimal behaviour of individual consumers at the level of society as a whole.

Welfare state A welfare state is established when government activity extends from the provision of the essential services of external defence, relief of dire poverty, law, order and justice, to the provision of social services in order to increase the economic and social welfare of the community.

BIBLIOGRAPHY

Adelman, M. A. (1993) 'Modelling world oil supply', *Energy Journal* 14: 1–32.

Anderson, T. L. and Leal, D. (1991) *Free Market Environmentalism*, Westview Press, Boulder CO.

Ashley, W. (1920) *Introduction to English Economic History and Theory*, 4th edn, Longman, London.

Baan, P. J. A. and Hopstaken, C. F. A. M. (1989) *Schade Vermetsting: Schade Als Gevola Van Emissie Van Stikstaf en Foster en Batten Van Emissie Beperking*, Delft.

Barnett, H. (1979) 'Scarcity and growth revisited', in V. K. Smith (ed.) *Scarcity and Growth Reconsidered*, Johns Hopkins University Press, Baltimore MD.

Barnett, H. and Morse, C. (1963) *Scarcity and Growth: the Economics of Natural Resource Availability*, Johns Hopkins University Press, Baltimore MD.

Barney, Gerald O. (study director) (1982) 'The Global 2000 Report to the President', a report prepared by The Council on Environmental Quality and the Department of State, Penguin, Harmondsworth.

Barr, J. (1972) 'Man and Nature – the ecological controversy and the Old Testament', *Bulletin of John Rylands Library* 55: 19–20.

Barrett, S. (1990) 'Memorandum to House of Commons Select Committee on Energy', published as briefing paper 'Pricing the environment: the economic and environmental consequences of a carbon tax', *Economic Outlook, 1988–1993*, February, London Business School, London.

Bass, M. J. (1993) 'Ecology and economics in small islands: constructing a framework for sustainable development', in E. B. Barbier (ed.) *Economics and Ecology*, Chapman and Hall, London.

Bator, M. F. (1958) 'The anatomy of market failure', *Quarterly Journal of Economics*, 7: 351–79.

Baumol, W. J. and Oates, W. (1971) 'The use of standards and prices for protection of the environment', *Swedish Journal of Economy* 73: 45–54.

— (1975) *The Theory of Environmental Policy*, Prentice-Hall, Englewood Cliffs NJ.

Beckermann, M. (1974) *In Defence of Economic Growth*, Jonathan Cape, London.

Benjamin, B., Cox, P. R. and Peel, J. (1973) *Resources and Population*, Academic Press, London.

Böhm-Bawerk, E. von (1894) *The Positive Theory of Capital*, G. E. Stedard, New York.

Boltjes, T. Y K. (1959) 'Stuurlaas Varen', *Water Bodem Lucht* 44 (3/4): 114.

Bookchin, M. (1987) 'Social ecology versus Deep Ecology: Green perspectives', *Newsletter of the Green Programme*, Summer.

Booth, D. E (1994) 'Ethics and the limits of environmental economics', *Ecological Economics* 9, 241–52.

Boulding, K. E. (1945) 'The consumption concept of economic theory', *American Economic Review* 35: 1–14.

— (1950) 'Income or welfare', *Review of Economic Studies* 17: 77–86.

— (1966) 'The economics of the coming Spaceship Earth', in H. Jarrett (ed.) *Environmental Quality in a Growing Economy*, Johns Hopkins University Press, Baltimore MD.

— (1978) *Ecodynamics: A New Theory of Societal Evolution*, Sage, Beverly Hills CA.

Bromley, D. W. (1978) 'Property rules, liability rules and environmental economics', *Journal of Economic Issues* 12: 43–60.

— (1989) *Economic Interests and Institutions: The Conceptual Foundations of Public Policy*, Basil Blackwell, Oxford.

Brown, B. J. *et al.* (1987) 'Global sustainability: toward definition', *Environmental Management* 11: 713–19.

Brown, L. (1990) *State of the World, 1990*, Earthscan, London.

— (1994) *The State of the World, 1994*, Earthscan, London.

Brundtland Report (1987) *Our Common Future*, Oxford University Press, Oxford.

Bubbert, M. K. (1968) *Resources and Man*, Preston Cloud (ed.), National Research Council, W. H. Freeman, San Francisco.

Buchanan, J. M. (1967) 'Cooperation and conflict in public goods interactions', *Western Economic Journal*, 109–21.

— (1969) 'External diseconomies, corrective taxes and market structure', *American Economic Review*, March.

Buchanan, J. M. and Stubblebine, W. (1962) 'Externality', *Econometrica* 29: 371–84.

Campbell, M. (1993) 'Moscow in danger of acute nuclear peril', *Sunday Times*, 9 May.

Cannan, E. (1917) *Theories of Production and Distribution*, King, London.

— (1964) *A Review of Economic Theory*, Cass, London.

Cantillon, Richard (1931) [1755] *Essai sur la nature du commerce en général*, H. Higgs (ed.), Macmillan, London.

Capra, F. (1995) 'Deep Ecology – a new paradigm', in G. Sessions (ed.) *Deep Ecology for the 21st Century*, Shambhala, Boston MA.

Carey, H. (1837) *Principles of Political Economy*, Kelly, New York.

— (1858) *The Principles of Social Science*, Kelly, New York.

Carson, R. (1962) *Silent Spring*, Houghton Mifflin, Boston.

Cassel, G. (1918) *The Theory of Social Economy*, McCarty (trs), Unwin, London.

Catton, W. R. and Dunlop, R. E. (1980) 'A new ecological paradigm for post-exuberant sociology', *American Behavioural Scientist* 24: 15–47.

Church, R. (1986) *The History of the British Coal Industry. Vol. 3, 1830–1913, Victorian Pre-Eminence*, Clarendon Press, Oxford.

Clapp, B. W. (1994) *An Environmental History of Britain since the Industrial Revolution*, Longman, London.

Clark, C. W. (1976) *Mathematical Bioeconomics*, Wiley, New York.

Clark, C. W. and Munro, G. R. (1975) 'The economics of fishing and modern capital theory; a simplified approach', *Journal of Environmental Economics and Management* 2: 92–106.

Clark, C. W., Clark, F. H. and Munro, G. L. (1979) 'The optimal exploitation of renewable resource stock: problems of irreversible investment', *Econometrica* 47: 25–47.

Clark, J. B. (1927) *The Distribution of Wealth*, Macmillan, New York.

Clark, J. M. (1939) *The Social Control of Business*, McGraw-Hill, New York.

Clarke, J. I. (1973) 'Population pressure on resources; the problem of evaluation', in B. Benjamin, P. R. Cox and J. Peel (eds) *Resources and Population*, Academic Press, London.

Clough, S. B. and Cole, C. W. (1946) *Economic History of Europe*, D. C. Heath, Boston.

Coase, R. (1960) 'The problem of social cost', *Journal of Law and Economics* 3: 1–44.

Cole, H. S. (1973) 'The structure of the world models', *Thinking about the Future – A. Critique of the Limits to Growth*, Chatto and Windus, London.

Cole, H. S. and Curnow, R. C. (1973) 'An evaluation of the world models', *Thinking About the Future: A Critique of the Limits to Growth*, Chatto and Windus, London.

Cole, H. S. D., Freeman, C., Johado, M. and Pavit, K. L. R. (1973) *Thinking About the Future: A Critique of the Limits to Growth*, Chatto and Windus, London.

Cooper, D. E. (1992) 'The idea of environment', in D. E. Cooper (ed.) *Economics in Question, Ethics and Global Issues*, Routledge, London.

Copes, P. (1972) 'Factory rents, sale ownership and the optimum level of fisheries exploitation', *Manchester School of Social and Economic Studies* 40: 145–63.

Dales, J. H. (1968) *Pollution, Property and Prices*, Toronto University Press, Toronto.

Daly, H. E. (1990) 'Towards some operational principles of sustainable development', *Ecology and Economics* 2: 1–6.

Daly, H. E. and Cobb J. B. (1989) *For the Common Good*, Green Print, London.

Darwin, C. (1859) *The Origin of Species*, John Murray, London.

— (1983) *Autobiographies*, G. D. Beer (ed.), Oxford University Press, Oxford.

Davey, E. S. (1960) 'The human population', *Scientific American* 203: 195–204.

Dawkins, R. (1976) *The Selfish Gene*, Oxford University Press, Oxford.

Deleyne, J. (1973) *The Chinese Economy*, Harper and Row, London.

Demsetz, H. (1969) 'Information and inefficiency: another viewpoint', *Journal of Law and Economics* 12: 1–12.

Derham, W. (1713) *Physico-Theology or a Demonstration of the Being and Attributes of God from His Work of Creation*, 8th edn, London.

Deverajan, S. and Fisher, D. C. (1981) 'Hotelling's economics of exhaustible resources, fifty years later', *Journal of Economic Literature* 19: 65–73.

Diggle, G. A. (1961) *A History of Wildness*, Widnes, New York.

Douthwaite, R. (1992) *The Growth Illusion: How Economic Growth has Enriched the Few, Impoverished the Many and Endangered the Planet*, Lilliput Press, Dublin.

Duran, S. (1961) 'Shield of the Fathers', (Hebrew) Private Publications, Jerusalem.

Durand, J. D. (1967) 'The modern expansion of world population', *Proceedings of American Philosophical Society* 111: 136–59.

Edel, M. (1973) *Economics and the Environment*, Prentice-Hall, Englewood Cliffs NJ.

Engels, F. (1844) *The Condition of the Working Class in England in 1844*, Otto Wigand, Leipzig.

Ezekiel, M. (1938) 'The Cobweb Theorem', *Quarterly Journal of Economics*, February.

FAO (1987) *World Crop and Livestock Statistics*, FAO Publications, Rome.

— (1988–91) *Production Yearbooks*, FAO Publications, Rome.

— (1993) 'Marine fisheries and the law of the sea; a decade of change', Fishery Circular No. 853, FAO, Rome.

Farrell, J. (1987) 'Information and Coase's theorem', *Journal of Economic Perspectives*, vol. 1: 113–129.

Faustmann, M. (1849) 'Gerechnung des Wertes Welchen Waldbaden Sowie Noch Nicht Haubare Holzbestänce für die Waldwirtschaft Besitzen', *Allgemeine Forst und Vagd-Zeitung* 25: 441–5.

Ferguson, B. and Roche, P. J. (1993) 'Christian attitudes to nature and the ecological crisis', *Irish Biblical Studies* Vol. 15, June.

Fisher, I. (1892) *Mathematical Investigations into the Theory of Value and Price*, Yale University Press, Princeton NJ.

— (1927) 'A statistical method for measuring utility and justice of progressive income tax', in W. Fellner (ed.) *Ten Economic Essays Contributed in Honour of J. Bates Clark*, Macmillan, New York.

Forrester, J. W. (1971) *World Dynamics*, Wright-Allen Press, Cambridge MA.

Fox, S. (1981) *John Muir and his Legacy: The American Conservation Movement*, Little, Brown, Boston MA.

Fox, W. (1995) 'The deep ecology–ecofeminism debate and its parallels', in G. Sessions (ed.) *Deep Ecology for the 21st Century*, Shambala, Boston MA.

Frasz, G. B. (1993) 'Environmental virtue ethics: a new direction for environmental ethics', *Environmental Ethics* 15: 259–74.

Freeman, C. (1974) 'Malthus with computer', in H. S. D. Cole, C. Freeman, M. Jahoda and K. L. R. Pavit (eds) *Thinking About the Future: A Critique of the Limits to Growth*, Chatto and Windus, London.

Fusfeld, D. R. (1977) *The Age of the Economist*, Scot Foresman, Illinois.

Gadgil, M. and Guha, R. (1994) 'Ecological conflicts and the environmental movement in India', *Institute of Social Studies* 101–34.

Galbraith, J. K. (1958) *The Affluent Society*, André Deutsch, London.

— (1967) *The New Industrial State*, André Deutsch, London.

— (1972) *American Capitalism,* André Deutsch, London.

— (1974) *Economics and the Public Purpose*, André Deutsch, London.

— (1977) *The Age of Uncertainty*, BBC, London.

— (1993) *The Culture of Contentment*, Penguin, London

Garnaut, R. and Ma, G. (1992) *World Grain Situation and Outlook*, USDA, August, Washington DC.

Gass, I. G. (1976) 'The earth's physical resources', *Energy Resources*, Open University Press, Milton Keynes.

Georgescu-Roegen, N. (1974) *The Entropy Law and the Economic Progress*, Harvard University Press, Cambridge MA.

Gerasimov, I. P. and Gindin, A. M. (1977) 'The problem of transferring run-off from Northern Siberian rivers to the arid regions of the European USSR, the

Soviet Central Asia and Kazakistan', in G. K White (ed.) *Environmental Effects of Complex River Development*, Westview Press, Boulder CO.

Gordon, H. S. (1954) 'The economic theory of common property resource: the fishery', *Journal of Political Economy* 62: 142.

Gore, A. (1992) *Earth in the Balance: Forging a New Common Purpose*, Earthscan Publications, London.

Gray, L. C. (1913) 'The economic possibilities of conservation', *Quarterly Journal of Economics* 27: 497–519.

— (1914) 'Rent under assumption of exhaustibility', *Quarterly Journal of Economics* 28: 466–89.

Griffin, J. M. and Steele, H. B. (1980) *Energy Economics and Policy*, Academic Press, New York.

Griffin, J. M. and Teece, O. J. (1982) *OPEC Behaviour and World Oil Prices*, Allen and Unwin, London.

Grove, R. (1990) 'The origins of environmentalism', *Nature* 345: 11–14.

Hale, M. (1667) *The Primitive Origination of Mankind*, Cambridge University Press, Cambridge.

Hamnett, M. P. (1986) 'Pacific island resource development and environmental management', paper to Interoceanic Workshop on Sustainable Development and Environmental Management of Small Islands, Puerto Rico, 3–7 November.

Hanley, N., Moffatt, J. and Hallet, S. (1990) 'Why is more notice taken of economists' perceptions for control of pollution?', *Environment and Planning* 22: 142–9.

Harrod, R. F. (1952) *Economic Essays*, Macmillan, London.

Hartwick, J. M. (1978) 'Investing returns from depleting renewable resource stocks and intergenerational equity', *Economic Letters* 88: 141–9.

Hartwick, J. M. and Olewiler, N. D. (1986) *The Economics of Natural Resource Use*, Harper and Row, New York.

Hayek, F. A. (1972) *A Tiger by the Tail*, Institute of Economic Affairs, London.

Hays, S. P. (1959) *Conservation and the Gospel of Efficiency: The Progressive Conservation Movement 1890–1920*, Harvard University Press, Cambridge.

Herfindahl, O. C. (1967) 'Depletion and economic theory', in Masson Gaffney (ed.) *Extractive Resources and Taxation*, University of Wisconsin Press, Madison.

Hiley, W. E. (1967) *Woodland Management*, Faber and Faber, London.

Ho, M. W. (1988) 'On not holding nature still: evolution by process not by consequence', in Ho, H. M. and Fox, E. (eds) *Evolutionary Process and Metaphors*, Wiley, New York.

Hollander, S. (1973) *The Economics of Adam Smith*, Heinemann, London.

Holzman, F. D. (1958) 'Consumer sovereignty and the role of economic development', *Economia Internazionale* 11.

Hooker, C. A. (1992) 'Responsibility, ethics and nature', in D. E. Cooper and J. A. Palmer (eds) *The Environment in Question*, Routledge, London.

Hotelling, H. (1925) 'A general mathematical theory of depreciation', *Journal of the American Statistical Association* 20: 340–53.

— (1931) 'The economics of exhaustible resources', *Journal of Political Economy* 39: 137–75.

— (1947) Unpublished letter to Director of National Parks Service.

Hueting, F. (1980) *New Scarcity and Economic Growth: More Welfare Through Less Production*, North Holland, Amsterdam.

Hull, C. H. (1954) *The Economic Writings of Sir William Petty*, Augustus M. Kelly, New York.

Hutchinson, T. W. (1953) *A Review of Economic Doctrines 1870–1923*, Clarendon Press, Oxford.

Huxley, A. (1959) *Brave New World Revisited*, Chatto and Windus, London.

Infield, L. (1963) 'Immanuel Kant: duties to animals and spirits', in *Lectures on Ethics*, Harper and Row, New York.

Ise, J. (1926) *The United States Oil Policy*, Yale University Press, New Haven.

Jantsch, E. (1980) *Self-Organising Universe*, Pergamon, London.

Jarrett, H. (1966) *Environmental Quality in a Growing Economy*, Johns Hopkins University Press, Baltimore MD.

Jevons, W. S. (1865) *The Coal Question: An Inquiry Concerning the Progress of the Nation and the Probable Exhaustion of our Coal Mines*, Macmillan, London.

Jorgensen, D. and Griliches, Z. (1967) 'The explanation of productivity change', *Review of Economics and Statistics* 34: 250–82.

Kahn, H. (1976) *The Next 200 Years*, Marrow, New York.

Kant, E. (1785) *Grundlegung der Metophysik der Sitten*, Rectam, Stuttgart.

Kapp, K. W. (1950) *The Social Cost of Private Enterprise*, Cambridge University Press, Cambridge.

Kay, J. A. (1989) 'Human domination over nature in the Hebrew Bible', *Annals of the Association of American Geographers* 79: 214–32.

Kendrick, J. W. (1961) *Production Trends in the US Economy*, Princeton University Press for National Bureau of Economic Research, Princeton.

Keynes, J. M. (1931) *Essays in Persuasion*, Rupert Hart-Davis, London.

Kneese, A. V. (1971) 'Environmental pollution economics and policy, *American Economic Review* 61: 153–6.

Kraus, J. B. (1930) *Scholastic, Puritanismus, und Kapitalismus*, Duncker und Humblot, Leipzig.

Krupnick, A., Oates, W. and Van de Verg, E. (1983) 'On marketable air pollution permits: the case for a system of pollution offsets', *Journal of Environmental Economics and Management* 10: 233–47.

Kula, E. (1989) 'Politics, economics, agriculture and famines: the Chinese case', *Food Policy* 14: 13–17.

— (1994) *Economics of Natural Resources, the Environment and Policies*, 2nd edn, Chapman and Hall, London.

— (1996) 'Social project appraisal and historic development of ideas on discounting a legacy for the 1990s and beyond', in K. Kirkpatrick and W. Wise (eds) *Development Projects: Issues for the 1990s*, Edward Elgar, London.

— (1997) *Time Discounting and Future Generations: Harmful Effects of Untrue Economic Theory,* Quorum Press Greenwood Publishing Group, Newport RI.

Lange, O. and Tylor, F. M. (1938) *On the Economic Theory of Socialism*, Augustus M. Kelley, New York.

Lecomber, R. (1979) *The Economics of Natural Resources*, Macmillan, London.

Leopold, A. (1949) *A Sand County Almanac*, Oxford University Press, Oxford.

Lerner, A. P. (1971) 'Priorities and efficiency', *American Economic Review* 61: 517–30.

Livingstone, D. N. (1994) 'The historical roots of our ecological crisis: a reassessment, *Fides et Historia* 26: 38–55.

Lovelock, J. E. (1979) *Gaia: A New Look at Life on Earth*, Oxford University Press, Oxford.

L'Vovich, M. I. (1978) 'Turning the Siberian waters to south', *New Scientist* 79: 834–6.

McHarg, I. (1977) 'The place of nature in the city of man', *Annuals of American Academy of Political Sciences* 352: 2–12.

McKelvey, V. (1972) 'Mineral Resource Estimates and Public Policy', *American Scientist* 60.

Maddox, J. (1972) *The Doomsday Syndrome*, Macmillan, London.

Magnus, A. (1894) 'Commentarii in IV Sententiarum, Petri Lombardi, Dist. 16', *Opera Omnia* 29 (article 46), Paris.

Malthus, R. T. (1890) [1798] *An Essay on the Principle of Population as it Affects the Future Improvement of Society,* 3rd edn, Ward Lock, London.

— (1815) *On the Nature and Progress of Rent*, Baltimore Press, Baltimore MD.

Marsh, G. P. (1865) *Man and Nature: or Physical Geography is Modified by Human Action*, Charles Scribner, New York.

Marshall, A. (1890) *Principles of Economics*, Macmillan, London.

Marstrand, P. K. and Sinclair, T. C. (1973) 'The pollution subsystem', in S. D. Cole, C. Freeman, M. Johodo and K. L. R. Pavit (eds) *Thinking About the Future: A Critique of the Limits to Growth*, Chatto and Windus, London.

Marx, K. (1859) *Contribution to the Critique of Political Economy*, translated by S. W. Ryazonskaya, Lawrence and Wishart, 1971, London.

— (1867) *Das Kapital, First Volume,* translated by S. Moore. Lawrence and Wishart, 1977, London.

— (1885) *Das Kapital, Second Volume*, translated by S. Moore, Lawrence and Wishart, 1974, London.

— (1894) *Das Kapital, Third Volume,* translated by S.Moore, Lawrence and Wishart, 1977, London.

— (1951) *Theories of Surplus Value: Part 1*, Lawrence and Wishart, London.

— (1969) *Theories of Surplus Value, Part II*, Lawrence and Wishart, London.

Marx, K. and Engels, F. (1948) *The Communist Manifesto*, Norton, London.

Meadows, D. H., Randers, D. L. and Behrens, W., III (1972) *The Limits to Growth*, Pan Books, London.

Merchant, C. (1980) *The Death of Nature, Women, Ecology and Scientific Revolution*, Harper and Row, London.

Mesarovic, M. D. and Pestel, E. C. (1974) *Mankind at the Turning Point*, Dutton, New York.

Mill, J. S. (1848) *Principles of Political Economy*, Appleton, New York.

Mishan, E. J. (1967) *The Cost of Economic Growth*, Penguin, London.

— (1977b) *The Economic Growth Debate*, Allen and Unwin, London.

Modena, L. (1949) 'Plant of Righteousness' (in Hebrew), Makhbirat Lesifruth, Tel Aviv.

Montgomery, W. (1972) 'Markets in licences and efficient pollution control programmes', *Journal of Economic Theory* 5: 395–418.

Naess, A. (1989) *Ecology, Community and Lifestyle*, Cambridge University Press, Cambridge.

— (1995) 'The shallow and the deep long range ecology movements: a summary', in G. Sessions (ed.) *Deep Ecology for the 21st Century*, Shambala, Boston MA.

Nash, R. (1982) *Wilderness and American Mind*, 3rd edn, Yale University Press, New Haven CT.

Nordhaus, W. D. (1973) 'World dynamics: measurement without data', *Economic Journal* 83: 1156–83.

Nordhaus, W. D and Tobin, J. (1972) *Is Growth Obsolete?*, National Bureau of Economic Research to the Anniversary Colloquium, Columbia University Press, New York.

Nove, A. (1992) *Alec Nove: A Biographical Dictionary of Dissenting Economists*, Edward Elgar, London.

Noy, D. (1967) *Jewish Folktales from Morocco* (Hebrew), Bitfutsoth Hagala, Jerusalem.

Olson, M. and Zeckhauser, R. (1970) 'The efficient production of external economies, *American Economic Review* 60: 512–17.

Ormerod, P. (1994) *Death of Economics*, Faber and Faber, London.

O'Riordan, T. (1988) 'The politics of sustainability', in R. T. Turner (ed.) *Sustainable Development Management*, Belhaven Press, London.

Page, R. W. (1973) 'Non-renewable resources sub-system', in D. S. D. Cole, C. Freeman, M. Jahoda and K. L. R. Pavit (eds) *Thinking About the Future: A Critique of the Limits to Growth*, Chatto and Windus, London.

— (1974) 'Population sub-system', in D. S. D. Cole *et al.* (eds) *Thinking About the Future – A Critique of the Limits to Growth,* Chatto and Windus, London.

Page, T. (1977) 'Equitable use of resource base', *Environment and Planning* 9: 15–22.

Palmer, J. A. (1992) 'Towards a sustainable future', in D. E. Cooper and J. A. Palmer (eds) *The Environment in Question: Ethics and Global Issues*, Routledge, London.

Passmore, J. (1975) 'Attitudes to nature', in R. S. Peters (ed.) *Nature and Conduct: Royal Institute of Philosophy Lectures* 8: 251–64.

— (1980) *Man's Responsibility for Nature*, Duckworth, London.

Pavit, K. L. R. (1973) 'Malthus and other economics', in H. S. D. Cole (ed.) *Thinking About the Future: A Critique of the Limits to Growth*, Chatto and Windus, London.

Peacocke, A. R. (1979) *Creation and the World of Science*, Oxford University Press, Oxford.

Pearce, D. W. (1983) *Cost-Benefit Analysis*, 2nd edn, Macmillan, London.

— (1991) *Blueprint 2: Greening the World Economy*, Earthscan, London.

— (1993) *Blueprint 3: Measuring Sustainable Development*, Earthscan, London.

Pearce, D. W. Markyanda, A. and Barbier, E. (1989) *Blueprint for a Green Economy*, Earthscan, London.

Pearce, D. W. Markyanda, A. and Barbier, E. (1990) *Sustainable Development: Economics and the Environment in the Third World*, Edgar, Aldershot.

Pearce, D. W. and Turner, R. K. (1990) *Economics of Natural Resources and the Environment*, Harvester Wheatsheaf, London.

Pezzey, J. (1989) *Economic Analysis of Sustainable Growth and Sustainable Development*, Environment Department Working Paper No. 15, World Bank, Washington DC.

Pigou, A. (1912) *Wealth and Welfare*, Macmillan, London.

— (1920) *Income*, Macmillan, London.

— (1929) *Economics of Welfare*, Macmillan, London.

— (1935) *Economics in Practice*, Macmillan, London.

Pinchot, G. (1910) *The Fight for Conservation*, Doubleday, New York.

Potter, N. and Christy, F. T. (1962) *Trends in Natural Resource Commodities – Statistics of Prices, Output, Consumption, Foreign Trade and Employment in the United States, 1870–1957*, Johns Hopkins University Press, Baltimore MD.

Prigogine, J. and Stengers, J. (1990) *Order out of Chaos*, Flamingo Fontana, Glasgow.

Rajaraman, I. (1976) 'Non-renewable resources: a review of long-term projects', *Futures* 8.

Rappaport, R. A. (1967) *Pigs for the Ancestors*, Yale University Press, New Haven CT.

Reagan, T. and Singer, P. (1976) *Animal Rights and Human Obligations*, Prentice-Hall, Englewood Cliffs NJ.

Repetto, R. (1986) *World Enough and Time*, Yale University Press, New Haven CT.

Respail, F. V. (1857) *Historie Naturelle de la Sante et de la Maldie*, Paris.

Retting, R. B. (1989) 'Is fishery management at a turning point? Reflections on the evolution of rights', in P. A. Neher, P. Arnason and N. Mollett (eds) *Rights Based Fishing*, Academic Press, London.

Ricardo, D. (1971) [1817] *Principles of Political Economy and Taxation*, Pelican Books, London.

Roach, P. and Robinson, J. T. C. (1989) *Economic Theories of Exhaustible Resources*, Routledge, London.

Robinson, J. T. C. (1989) *Economic Theory of Exhaustible Resources*, Routledge, London.

Roll, C. (1953) *A History of Economic Thought*, Faber and Faber, London.

Rolston, H. III (1992) 'Changes in environmental ethics', in D. E. Cooper and J. A. Palmer (eds) *The Environment in Question: Ethics and Global Issues*, Routledge, London.

Roover, R. R. (1970) 'The concept of just price; theory and economic policy', I. H. Rima (ed.) *Readings in the History of Economic Theory*, Rinehart and Winston, New York.

Rothbard, M. (1982) 'Law, property rights and free market environmentalism, *Cato Journal* 2: 55–100.

Russell, B. and Whitehead A. N. (1926) *Principia Mathematica*, 2nd edn, Cambridge University Press, Cambridge.

Russell, J. (1991) *Environmental Issues in Eastern Europe: Setting an Agenda*, Royal Institute of International Affairs, London.

Russell, N. P. (1990) 'Efficiency of farm conservation and output reduction policies', *Manchester Working Papers in Agricultural Economics*,WP/900–02, University of Manchester, Manchester.

Samuelson, P. A. (1976) 'Economics of forestry in an evolving society', *Economic Inquiry* 14: 466–92.

Schaefer, M. D. (1957) 'Some consideration of population dynamics and economics in relation to the management of marine fisheries', *Journal of Fisheries Research Board of Canada* 14: 669–81.

Schumpeter, J. A. (1954) *History of Economic Analysis*, Allen and Unwin, London.

Scitowsky, T. (1954) 'Two concepts of external economics', *Journal of Political Economy*, 62.

Scott, A. D. (1955) 'The fishery: the objectives of sole ownership', *Journal of Political Economy* 63: 116–24.

Scott. A. T. (1967) 'The theory of mine under conditions of uncertainty', in M. Gaffney (ed.) *Extractive Resources and Taxation*, University of Wisconsin Press, Madison.

Scotus, J. D. (1894) 'Quaestiona in librum quartum sentenarum', *Opera Omnia* (dist. 15, QU2, No. 23) 18, Paris.

Sessions, G. (1995) 'Ecocentrism and the anthropocentric detour', in G. Sessions (ed.) *Deep Ecology for the 21st Century*, Shambala, Boston MA.

Sherman, F. (1990) 'The meaning and ethics of sustainability', *Environmental Management* 14: 1–8.

Shiva, V. (1992) 'Recovering the real meaning of sustainability', in D. E. Cooper and J. A. Palmer (eds) *The Environment in Question: Ethics and Global Issues*, Routledge, London.

Simon, J. L. (1984) *The Resourceful Earth: A Response to Global 2000*, Blackwell, London.

Sinclair, T. C. (1973) 'Environmentalism', in D. S. D. Cole, C. Freeman, M. Jahoda and K. L. R. Pavit (eds) *Thinking About the Future: A Critique of the Limits to Growth*, Chatto and Windus, London.

Singer, P. (1975) 'Animal liberation', *New York Review*, New York.

— (1981) *The Expanding Circle, Ethics and Sociology*, Farrer, Strauss and Girou, New York.

Sismondi, J. C. L. S. (1951) [1827] *New Principles of Political Economy*, G. Sotiroff (ed.) Geneva.

Slade, M. C. (1982) 'Trends in natural resource commodity prices: an analysis of the time domain', *Journal of Environmental Economics and Management* 9: 122–37.

Smith, A. (1852) *The Theory of Moral Sentiments*, ed D. D. Raphael and A. L. Mecfie, 1976, Clarendon Press, Oxford.

— (1869) [1776] *An Inquiry into the Nature and Causes of the Wealth of Nations*, Routledge, London.

Smith, L. G. (1993) *Impact Assessment and Sustainable Resource Management*, Longmans Scientific and Technical, Harlow.

Smith, V. L. (1977) 'Economics of wilderness resources', in V. L. Smith (ed.) *Economics of Natural and Environmental Resources*, Gordon and Breach, New York.

Solow, R. M. (1974) 'Intergenerational equity and exhaustible resources', *Review of Economic Studies Symposium 29–46.*

— (1986) 'On the intergenerational allocation of natural resources', *Scandinavian Journal of Economics* 88: 141–9.

Sorley, W. R (1889) 'Mining royalties and their effect on the iron and coal trades', *Royal Statistical Society Journal* 52.

Soussian, J. G. (1992) 'Sustainable development', in A. M. Mannion and L. S. Bowby (eds) *Environmental Issues of the 1990s*, Wiley, London.

Spedding, J. and Ellis, R. L. (1870) *The Works of Francis Bacon*, Longman Green, London.

Spiegel, H. W. (1952) *The Development of Economic Thought*, Wiley, New York.

Sraffa, I. and Dobb, M. (1951–5) *The Works and Correspondence of David Ricardo*, Cambridge University Press, Cambridge.

Stahl, A. (1993) 'Educating for change in attitudes towards nature and environment among oriental Jews in Israel', *Environment and Behaviour* 25: 3–21.

Stalwick, H. H. J. (1989) *Economiste gevolgen voor de veehouderiz van drietel milieuscenorio's*, CPB, Den Haag.

Stark, T. (1992) *Income and Wealth in the 1980s*, 3rd edn, Fabian Society, London.

Stigler, G. J. (1946) *Production and Distribution Theories*, Macmillan, London.

Stone, N. (1996) 'New light on a reign of darkness', *Sunday Times*, 31 March.

Surrey, A. J. and Bromley A. J. (1973) 'Energy resources', in S. D. Cole, C. Freeman, M. Johodo and K. L. R. Pavit (eds) *Thinking About the Future: A Critique of the Limits to Growth*, Chatto and Windus, London.

Swaney, J. (1987) 'Elements of a neo-institutional environmental economists', *Journal of Environmental Issues* 21: 1739–79.

Sylvan, R. and Bennett, D. (1988) 'Taoism and Deep Ecology', *Ecologist* 18: 148–59.

Synder, G. (1977) *The Old Ways*, City Lights Books, San Francisco.

— (1994) *Coming into the Watershed*, Pantheon Books, New York.

Tamminga, G. and Wijnands, J. (1991) 'Animal waste problems in the Netherlands', in N. Hanley (ed.) *Farming and the Countryside*, AB International, Wallingford.

Taussig, F. W. (1915) *Principles of Economics*, Macmillan, London.

Thomas, K. (1984) *Man and the Natural World: Changing Attitudes in England, 1500–1800*, Penguin, London.

Thompson, A. E. (1971) 'The Forestry Commission: a re-appraisal of its functions', *Three Banks Review*, September: 30–44.

Thoreau, H. (1854) *Walden*, Walter Scott, London.

Tietenberg, T. (1992) *Environmental and Natural Resource Economics*, 3rd edn, Harper Collins, New York.

Townshend, J. (1986) [1786] 'A dissertation on the Poor Laws', in G. Hardin (ed.) *Population, Evolution and Birth Control*, W. W. Freeman, San Francisco.

Toynbee, A. (1972) 'The religious background of the present environmental crisis', *International Journal of Environmental Studies* 3: 141–6.

Trial Smelter Arbitral Tribunal (1939) 'Decision', *American Journal of International Law* 33: 182–212.

Tuan, Y. F. (1968) 'Discrepancies between environmental attitude and behaviour: examples from Europe and China', *Canadian Geographer* 12: 176–91.

— (1970) 'Our treatment of the environment in ideal and actuality', *American Scientist* May–June 1970: 246–9.

Turner, F. (1985) *Rediscovering America: John Muir, in His Time and Ours*, Sierra Club Books, San Francisco.

Turner, R. K. (1991) 'Environment, economics and ethics', in D. Pearce (ed.) *Blueprint 2*, Earthscan, London.

Turner, R. K. and Pearce, D. W. (1993) 'Sustainable economic development: economic and ethical principles', in E. Barbier (ed.) *Economics and Ecology from Frontiers and Sustainable Development*, Chapman and Hall, London.

Tylor, F. M. (1928) 'Presidential Address to the American Economic Association', American Economic Review, 1928.

Tylor, P. (1986) *Respect for Nature*, Princeton University Press, Princeton NJ.

US Bureau of Census (1993) *Department of Commerce, International Database*, November, Washington DC.

US Bureau of Mines (1970) *Mineral Facts and Problems*, US Government Printing Office, Washington DC.

US Department of Agriculture (1992) *USDA, World Grain Database*, Washington DC.

— (1993) *World Agriculture Production, August 1992–March 1993*, Washington DC.

US Department of Energy (1987a) *International Energy Annual 1986*, Washington DC.

— (1987b) *Monthly Energy Review* May 1987, Washington DC.

US President's Material Policy Commission (1952) *Resources for Freedom* (5 volumes), US Government Printing Office, Washington DC.

Von Thunen, J.H. (1826) Isolated State, English edn ed. P. Hall, Pergamon Press, London; German edn 1822.

Van Dobben, W. H. (1966) 'Het Vegetatieded Van De Aarde en de Invloed Van de Mens Daarop, in *De Groene Aarde*, Utrecht, Holland.

Wan, T. (1962) 'A compendium of documents on Communist China's great Cultural Revolution', *Ming-Pao Monthly*, Hong Kong.

Wanden, S. (1994) 'Environment, ethics and government', *European Environmental Law Review*, November, 296–301.

— (1995) 'Ethics, prices and biodiversity', paper presented at 1995 IUFRO Congress, Tampere, Finland.

Warren, K. J. (1987) 'Feminism and ecology-making connections', *Environmental Ethics* 9.

Watson, A. (1991) 'Gaia', *New Scientist,* 6 July.

White, L. Jr (1967) 'The historical roots of ecological crisis', *Science* 155: 1203–7.

Whitehead, A. N. and Russell, B. (1910–13) *Principia Mathematica*, Cambridge University Press, Cambridge.

Winpenny, J. T. (1991) *Values for the Environment*, HMSO, London.

World Economic and Financial Surveys (1990) IMF, Washington DC.

Worldwatch Institute (1994) *State of the World 1994*, L. Brown, A. T. Durning, C. Flavin *et al.*, Earthscan, London.

Yildiran, G. (1994) 'Environmental ethics: the need for a paradigmatic shift', in K. Curi *et al.* (eds) *Proceedings of the International Symposium on Environmental Ethics*, Bosphorus University Press, Istanbul.

Young, A. (1804) *General View of Agriculture of Hertfordshire*, G. and W. Nicol, London.

Young, A. A. (1928) 'Increasing returns and economic progress', *Economic Journal* 38: 538.

Young, D. R. (1981) *National Resources and the State*, University of California Press, Berkeley CA.

Zimmermann, E. (1987) 'Feminism, Deep Ecology and environmental ethics', *Environmental Ethics* 9: 21–4.

Zwartendyke, J. (1972) 'What is mineral endowment and how should we measure it?', *Mineral Bulletin* M. R 126, Canadian Government Department of Energy, Mines and Resources, Ottawa.

INDEX